ANT-MAN & WASP
SMALL WORLD

ANT-MAN & WASP
SMALL WORLD

WRITER & PENCILER **TIM SEELEY**

INKER **VICTOR OLAZABA**

COLORIST **VAL STAPLES**

LETTERER **SIMON BOWLAND**

COVER ARTISTS **SALVA ESPIN & GURU EFX**

EDITOR **JORDAN D. WHITE**

SUPERVISING EDITOR **MARK PANICCIA**

SPECIAL THANKS TO DONNY CATES

TALES TO ASTONISH #44-48 (1963)

PLOTS **STAN LEE**

SCRIPTS **ERNIE HART** (AS H.E. HUNTLEY)

PENCILERS **JACK KIRBY** (ISSUE #44) **& DON HECK** (ISSUES #45-48)

INKER **DON HECK**

LETTERERS **ART SIMEK** (ISSUES #44-45) **& SAM ROSEN** (ISSUES #46-48)

ART & COLOR RECONSTRUCTION **MICHAEL KELLEHER**

COLLECTION EDITOR **CORY LEVINE**

EDITORIAL ASSISTANTS **JAMES EMMETT & JOE HOCHSTEIN**

ASSISTANT EDITORS **MATT MASDEU, ALEX STARBUCK & NELSON RIBEIRO**

EDITORS, SPECIAL PROJECTS **JENNIFER GRÜNWALD & MARK D. BEAZLEY**

MASTERWORKS EDITOR **CORY SEDLMEIER**

SENIOR EDITOR, SPECIAL PROJECTS **JEFF YOUNGQUIST**

SENIOR VICE PRESIDENT OF SALES **DAVID GABRIEL**

SVP OF BRAND PLANNING & COMMUNICATIONS **MICHAEL PASCIULLO**

BOOK DESIGN **SEAN BELLOWS**

EDITOR IN CHIEF **AXEL ALONSO**

CHIEF CREATIVE OFFICER **JOE QUESADA**

PUBLISHER **DAN BUCKLEY**

EXECUTIVE PRODUCER **ALAN FINE**

ANT-MAN & WASP: SMALL WORLD. Contains material originally published in magazine form as ANT-MAN & WASP #1-3 and TALES TO ASTONISH #44-48. First printing 2011. ISBN# 978-0-7851-5567-6. Published by MARVEL WORLDWIDE, INC., a subsidiary of MARVEL ENTERTAINMENT, LLC. OFFICE OF PUBLICATION: 135 West 50th Street, New York, NY 10020. Copyright © 1963 and 2011 Marvel Characters, Inc. All rights reserved. $14.99 per copy in the U.S. and $16.50 in Canada (GST #R127032852); Canadian Agreement #40668537. All characters featured in this issue and the distinctive names and likenesses thereof, and all related indicia are trademarks of Marvel Characters, Inc. No similarity between any of the names, characters, persons, and/or institutions in this magazine with those of any living or dead person or institution is intended, and any such similarity which may exist is purely coincidental. **Printed in the U.S.A.** ALAN FINE, EVP - Office of the President, Marvel Worldwide, Inc. and EVP & CMO Marvel Characters B.V.; DAN BUCKLEY, Publisher & President - Print, Animation & Digital Divisions; JOE QUESADA, Chief Creative Officer; JIM SOKOLOWSKI, Chief Operating Officer; DAVID BOGART, SVP of Business Affairs & Talent Management; TOM BREVOORT, SVP of Publishing; C.B. CEBULSKI, SVP of Creator & Content Development; DAVID GABRIEL, SVP of Publishing Sales & Circulation; MICHAEL PASCIULLO, SVP of Brand Planning & Communications; JIM O'KEEFE, VP of Operations & Logistics; DAN CARR, Executive Director of Publishing Technology; JUSTIN F. GABRIE, Director of Publishing & Editorial Operations; SUSAN CRESPI, Editorial Operations Manager; ALEX MORALES, Publishing Operations Manager; STAN LEE, Chairman Emeritus. For information regarding advertising in Marvel Comics or on Marvel.com, please contact John Dokes, SVP Integrated Sales and Marketing, at jdokes@marvel.com. For Marvel subscription inquiries, please call 800-217-9158. **Manufactured between 5/5/2011 and 5/24/2011 by QUAD/GRAPHICS, DUBUQUE, IA, USA.**

10 9 8 7 6 5 4 3 2 1

#1

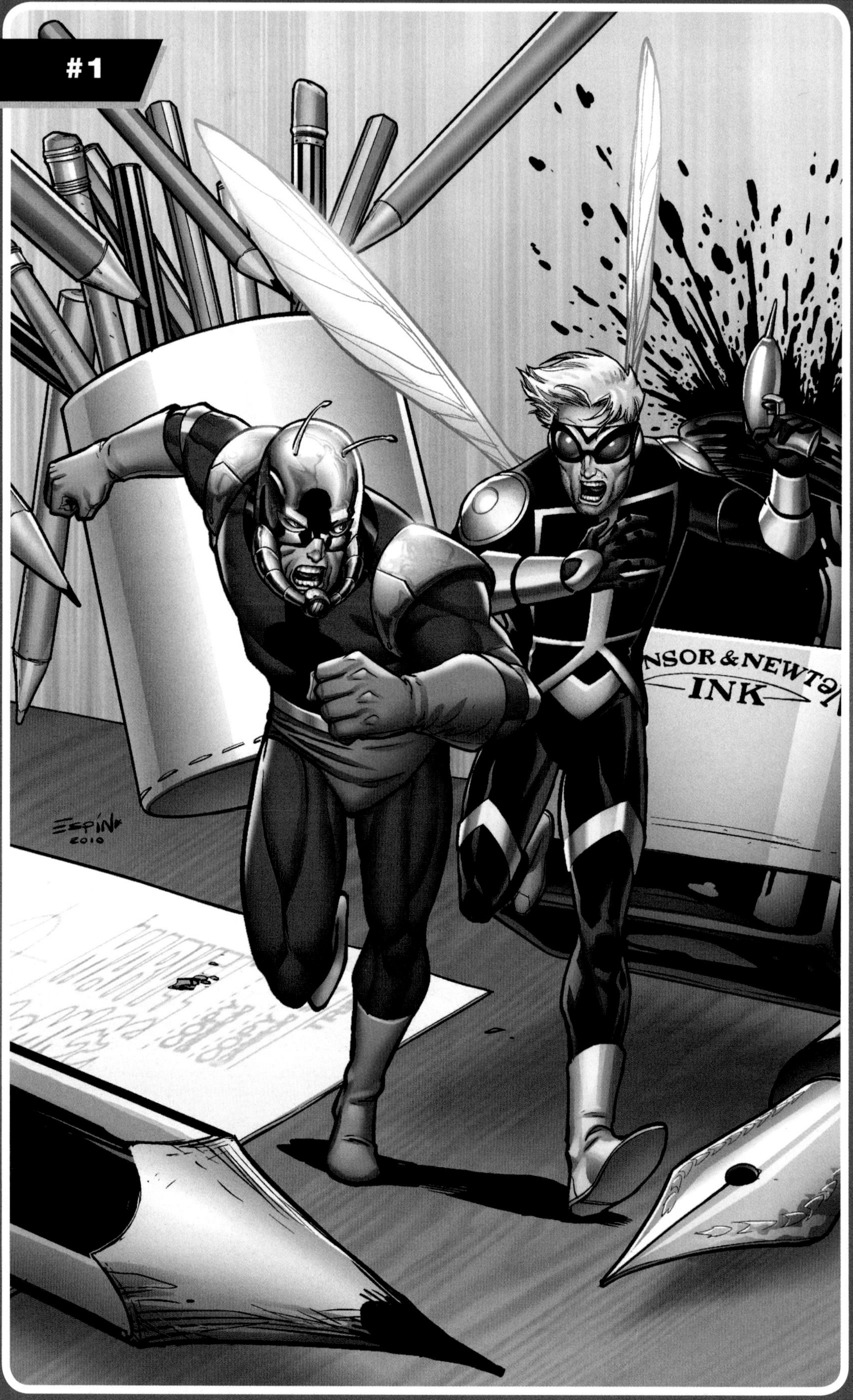
INK

INFINITE AVENGERS MANSION. HANK PYM'S LAB.

HELLO. MY NAME IS *HANK PYM.*

YOU MAY KNOW ME FROM MY VARIOUS COSTUMED SUPER HERO IDENTITIES: *ANT-MAN. GIANT-MAN. GOLIATH. YELLOWJACKET.* I AM A FOUNDING MEMBER OF *THE AVENGERS*, AND AM CURRENTLY A PROFESSOR AT THE *AVENGERS ACADEMY*, GUIDING THE HEROES OF TOMORROW.

TODAY, I OPERATE AS *THE WASP*, AN HOMAGE TO MY LATE WIFE, *JANET VAN DYNE.*

JAN *DIED* A HERO, TRYING TO SAVE THE WORLD.

SHE WAS A WONDERFUL WOMAN: INTELLIGENT, SINCERE, SELFLESS...JAN DIED AS SHE LIVED: *WITHOUT REGRETS.*

I CAN'T SAY THAT I LIVE WITHOUT REGRETS.

I'VE MADE MISTAKES. I'VE MISTREATED AND BETRAYED THOSE CLOSE TO ME. MY TEAMMATES. MY FRIENDS. EVEN JAN.

I INTEND TO MAKE UP FOR THOSE MISTAKES.

THAT'S WHY I'M OPENING THE *JANET VAN DYNE CENTERS FOR WOMEN.*

SIX CENTERS WILL OPEN THIS YEAR, PROVIDING FREE AND CONFIDENTIAL SERVICES, SHELTER, LEGAL ADVOCACY AND SUPPORT GROUPS TO WOMEN AND CHILDREN WHO ARE VICTIMS OF *DOMESTIC ABUSE.*

AND I WANT YOU TO JOIN ME IN PRESERVING JAN'S MEMORY.

GIVE FINANCIAL SUPPORT.

GET INVOLVED.

VOLUNTEER.

PLEASE, HELP SAVE SOMEONE IN NEED.

LIVE WITHOUT REGRETS.

AND THAT'S A WRAP.

THANKS GUYS. GET ME A FIRST CUT BY MONDAY IF YOU COULD.

TIGRA. HOW WAS I?

THAT WAS... WELL, I JUST WANTED TO TELL YOU, I'M REALLY IMPRESSED BY WHAT YOU'RE DOING, HANK.

THANKS, GREER.

WORKING WITH YOU AND THE OTHERS, TEACHING THE NEXT GENERATION OF HEROES, HAS MADE ME REALLY THINK ABOUT WHAT KIND OF LEGACY I'LL LEAVE BEHIND.

UP TIL NOW, MY "MARK ON TOMORROW" HAS BEEN A HUMAN-HATING ROBOTIC "SON" AND A NEW ANT-MAN WHO USES HIS SHRINKING POWERS TO SPY ON GIRLS IN THE SHOWER.

JAN - PROTECT WOMEN IN HER NAME.
BILL FOSTER - BUILD HIM HEAVEN.

I'D LIKE TO THINK I CAN DO BETTER.

BILL FOSTER - BUILD HIM HEAVEN.

OH MY GOD! YOU HAVE TO GO! WE'RE *UNDER ATTACK!*

DOCTOR DOOM IS ON A REVENGE-FUELED *RAMPAGE,* AND THERE'S NO TELLING WHAT HE'LL DO TO AN INNOCENT BYSTANDER LIKE YOU!

OH GOD, I KNEW I SHOULDN'T HAVE GONE HOME WITH AN *AVENGER!*

HERE! THE *FIRE ESCAPE!* I'LL HOLD HIM OFF AS THE *ALL-NEW ANT-MAN!* GO!

I'LL CALL YOU WHEN I'VE DEFEATED HIM AND THE COAST IS CLEAR!

REMEMBER, *DON'T* CALL ME!

OH GOD OH GOD OH GOD!

MY WORD, ERIC. WHAT WAS ALL THAT RACKET ABOUT?

Y'KNOW, I THOUGHT BEING AN AVENGER WOULD MEAN BETTER QUALITY ONE-NIGHT STANDS, BUT I STILL HAVE TO SEND A FEW DOWN THE FIRE ESCAPE SO THE NEIGHBORS DON'T SEE THEM. WOOF.

YOU HAVEN'T CHANGED A BIT, OLD BEAN. MIGHT I COME IN?

YOU'RE THE *BLACK FOX,* A WORLD-RENOWNED MASTER THIEF.

HOW WOULD IT LOOK IF I WAS SEEN WITH YOU?

I'M AN *AVENGER* NOW. A *SECRET* ONE, SURE, BUT I SHOULD RUN YOU IN JUST ON *PRINCIPLE.*

ARE YOU... SERIOUS?

NAH. MESSIN' WITH YOU. COME ON IN, YA OLD COOT.

SO WHAT'S NEW IN THE WORLD OF *GERIATRIC VILLAINY?*

WELL, I WAS ABLE TO ESCAPE FROM THE CLUTCHES OF THE GENDARME.

WITH A LITTLE HELP FROM ME.

PRECISELY.

YOU AND I HAVE HAD OUR SHARE OF, LET'S SAY *"UPS AND DOWNS"* IN OUR FRIENDSHIP, BUT I DO SAY WE'VE BEEN QUITE GOOD AT RETURNING ANY FAVOR, FNORD, AS FRIENDS DO.

≷GHUK≷ AHEM.

TO THAT END, I FELT IT WAS MY *DUTY* TO SHARE WITH YOU A BIT OF INFORMATION THAT MIGHT FURTHER *ENDEAR* YOU TO YOUR NEW TEAMMATES IN THE AVENGERS, FNORD.

C'MON, THE AVENGERS *LOVE* ME. I GOT MY RECOMMENDATIONS FROM *TONY STARK* AND *STEVE ROGERS!*

WHY DO YOU THINK THEY PUT ME ON THE SAME TEAM AS KNOCK-OFF IRON-MAN, ALBINO MOON-MAN, AND FUZZY SMURF? TO STAND OUT. I'M THE FEATURED STAR, MAN.

AH, BUT THERE IS ONE AVENGER WHO HAS BEEN WARY OF GIVING YOU HIS FULL SUPPORT. THE MAN WHOSE *MANTLE* YOU'VE CARRIED ON, FNORD, HANK PYM.

HMM. YEAH, I SUPPOSE HE DOES HAVE A TENDENCY TO GIVE ME *THE STINK EYE.*

I DID HIT HIM IN THE FACE WITH A RIFLE AND STEAL HIS ANT-MAN COSTUME...OR WAS THAT THE SKRULL? I DUNNO. I WON'T BRING IT UP.

YESTERDAY I RECEIVED THIS MESSAGE FROM THE ORGANIZATION KNOWN AS *A.I.M.*, ALSO KNOWN AS...

ADVANCED IDEA MECHANICS. EVIL NERDS IN YELLOW BEEKEEPER COSTUMES. I USED TO BE A *S.H.I.E.L.D.* AGENT, REMEMBER? I SKIMMED THE FILE.

IT IS A JOB OFFER INTENDED TO RECRUIT A MASTER THIEF TO STEAL AN *UNKNOWN,* BUT APPARENTLY *VERY SPECIAL* ITEM. THE JOB IS QUITE RISKY, BUT THE PAYMENT IS SIGNIFICANT, FNORD.

SO YOU'RE LETTING ME GIVE OL' HANK THE HEADS UP THAT *A.I.M.* WANTS ONE OF HIS TOYS, INSTEAD OF TAKING THE JOB YOURSELF? NICE. BUT HOW DO I KNOW I CAN TRUST YOU?

YOU DON'T, OF COURSE. BUT I DID BRING SOMETHING THAT I TOOK FROM YOU. I BELIEVE IT WILL SUFFICIENTLY, FNORD, DISPLAY MY *SINCERITY.*

MY *WII.*

YOU'VE GOT A DEAL. I HAVE AN APPOINTMENT TO SEE HANK ANYWAY. I COULD GO RIGHT NOW.

TIME FOR ONE ROUND OF CRICKET?

HM. MAKE IT *"JUST DANCE"* AND YOU'RE ON.

LATER...

NOK NOK

HEY, ERIC. IT'S ME... *ABIGAIL.*

CAN I COME IN?

HEY, ABIGAIL!

WOW. SO IT'S TRUE. I WANTED TO STOP BY AND SEE FOR MYSELF.

REMEMBER WHEN I SAID THAT I'D BE READY FOR A RELATIONSHIP WHEN I'D MADE MYSELF A BETTER PERSON?

IT RINGS A BELL.

WELL I'M ONE OF *"EARTH'S MIGHTIEST HEROES"* NOW. I'M AS GOOD AS A GUY CAN GET.

OH. BUT IT LOOKS LIKE I CAME AT A BAD TIME...

WAS JUST GONNA HEAD OVER TO AVENGERS MANSION. THE WASP WANTED TO LOOK OVER MY NEW ARMOR. I'M GOING TO HAND HIM SOME SUPER-SECRET-SUPER HERO INFO THAT OUGHT TO SCRATCH MY NAME OFF HIS STINK-LIST.

AND THE INFO CAME FROM--?

MY OLD BUDDY, BLACK FOX.

A SUPER HERO WHO HANGS OUT WITH SUPER VILLAINS.

I CAN'T BE *ALL* GOOD.

NO. AND OBVIOUSLY NOT GOOD ENOUGH TO WAIT FOR ME.

THAT'S--UH-- BLACK FOX'S?

SAVE IT, ERIC.

YOU'RE GETTING BETTER AT BEING A *SUPER HERO.*

BUT YOUR TRACK RECORD AS A *HUMAN BEING* STILL SUCKS.

--WHATEVER THE CAUSE OF THE ANOMALY, I HAVE DISCERNED THAT WE HAVE APPROXIMATELY *FORTY-THREE MINUTES AND TWENTY-SEVEN SECONDS* BEFORE OUR REALITY IS OVERWRITTEN BY THAT OF EARTH-9939.

UNLESS WE CAN COME UP WITH A WAY TO HALT THE *TIME-QUAKE.*

YES. NO PRESSURE.

RIGHT. OH, AND I WON'T LET THE FACT THAT EARTH-9939 IS A REALITY RULED BY A NECROMANTIC SORCERER VERSION OF BARON VON--

WHAT THE--?

HOW'S IT HANGIN', HANKY?!

I'M HERE FOR MY PHYSICAL, DOC. GOT A BIG *COUGH* READY JUST FOR YOU.

O'GRADY.

HANK! I TOLD O'GRADY YOU WERE BUSY, BUT HE MUST HAVE SHRUNK DOWN WHEN I WASN'T LOOKING--

IT'S FINE. I'LL TAKE CARE OF IT.

ERIC, I KNOW I TOLD YOU TO COME IN FOR THE ARMOR UPGRADE, BUT I'M IN THE MIDDLE OF--

I'M NOT JUST HERE FOR THE CHECK-UP.

HAVE *THE FURRY* BRING IN MY BAG. I BROUGHT US A FEW ADULT BEVERAGES, SO WE CAN SIT BACK AND HAVE A NICE MANLY CHAT.

SEE, I WAS KEEPING MY EAR TO THE *CRIMINAL UNDERGROUND,* Y'KNOW, USING ANTS AS SPIES LIKE YOU USED TO DO...

...AND I HEARD *A.I.M.* IS GUNNIN' FOR YOU. WELL, NOT *YOU,* ONE OF YOUR INVENTIONS. TURNS OUT THEY'VE GOT SOME SPIES IN THE *U.S. PATENT OFFICE* AND THEY---

ERIC.

RIGHT NOW, *REED* AND I ARE IN THE MIDDLE OF TRYING TO SOLVE A COMPLEX *CHRONAL ABERRATION...*

...WHICH, IF LEFT UNCHECKED, COULD MEAN EVERY MAN, WOMAN AND CHILD IN THIS WORLD IS SLAVE TO THE *HOUSE OF CHARNEL* BEFORE DINNER.

OH, YEAH? LET ME GIVE YOU A HAND. DID I MENTION I COME HIGHLY RECOMMENDED BY IRON MAN?

I *APPRECIATE* YOU TRYING TO HELP, BUT WORKING ON A PROBLEM OF THIS COMPLEXITY REQUIRES A CLASS EIGHT OR BETTER INTELLIGENCE.

I'VE BEEN WORKING HARD TO CONTROL MY TEMPER THESE PAST FEW MONTHS, BUT IF YOU DON'T WAIT, I MIGHT HAVE TO WASTE SOME OF MY CONSIDERABLE INTELLECT INSULTING YOU. CAPICHE?

UH... RIGHT. HEY, MR. F.

SOOO... I'LL COME BACK.

THANK YOU.

REED, HAVE YOU CONSIDERED CHECKING FOR TEMPORAL INTERFERENCE LOBES FROM AN OUTSIDE SOURCE?

WHATEVER. ENJOY YOUR *"DR. WHO CONVENTION,"* WEENIES.

LATER...

ROGERS MUST NOT BE PAYING YOU GUYS VERY WELL, BECAUSE THAT IS SOME CHEAP BOOZE.

I WAS WAITING FOR HANK, AND ALL OF A SUDDEN I GOT THIS *NASTY HEADACHE.*

THOUGHT MAYBE *DOCTOR.45* HERE COULD HELP ME OUT.

JARVIS D-
WORK H:
CLEAN
AFTER
YOURSE
—.MCA

YOU KNOW, IF THIS DOESN'T WORK, I CAN THINK OF SOMETHING THAT *MIGHT.*

GOOD LUCK WITH THAT.

I GUESS WHAT I'VE HEARD ABOUT YOU IS TRUE.

DON'T GET ANY IDEAS ABOUT PULLING YOUR *PEEPING-TOM* TRICK WITH ME. NO MATTER HOW SMALL YOU GET, I CAN STILL *SMELL* YOU.

AND YOU WOULDN'T WANT ME TO MISTAKE YOU FOR *A MOUSE.*

DID *BEE-BOY* FINISH SAVING THE WORLD YET?

O'GRADY, JUST RELAX AND STAY OUT OF TROUBLE.

TROUBLE? ME? WHAT KIND OF TROUBLE--?

--NO WAY, MY COSTUME IS WAY COOLER.

OOOH. *SCHOOLGIRLS.*

WELL, HELLO HELLO. IT'S FRIDAY NIGHT, AND SCHOOL IS *OUT.* WHERE ARE YOU KIDS HEADING?

TO THE GYM, OF COURSE.

WHY? YOUR ARROGANT AIR SUGGESTS YOU BELIEVE YOU HAVE A BETTER IDEA.

I'VE GOT *TWO* BETTER IDEAS.

HELL YEAH! SIGN ME UP, BRO!

I WAS ONLY TALKING TO THE GIRLS, *FRAT BOY.*

SOON.

≤SNRRRRK≤

FIRST, HE TRIED TO PUT THE MOVES ON US, AND THEN HE DRANK ALL THE LIQUOR HIMSELF. NOW HE'S PASSED OUT. CAN YOU *BELIEVE* THIS DORK?

I BELIEVE IT, VEIL.

HIS ATTITUDE SUGGESTED INSECURITY ABOUT HIS AGE AND STATION IN LIFE FOR WHICH HE ATTEMPTED TO COVER BY SELF-MEDICATING.

WHEN YOU PUT IT THAT WAY, I FEEL KIND OF BAD FOR HIM.

"FEELING BAD" IS A WASTE OF BRAIN POWER.

SHOULD WE GO FIND STRIKER AND TELL HIM WHAT WE DID?

NO. BEING USURPED AS ALPHA MALE IS MAKING HIM *SQUIRM.*

LET'S NOT END THAT TOO SOON.

FINESSE, YOU *RULE.*

I THINK WE CAN CALL THIS PARTICULAR CRISIS IN TIME AVERTED.

A PLEASURE WORKING WITH YOU, BIG BRAIN. GIVE MY LOVE TO SUE.

NOW...

WARNING

UNKNOWN BIOLOGICAL ENTITY IN HALL 4.

HALT! YOU ARE AN UNREGISTERED-- ZRRRKSH!

AVENGERS! BE ON ALERT! I REPEAT, BE ON---

WHAT THE HELL?!

WE HAVE A BREACH! I REPEAT, WE HAVE A BREACH!

SHRINK AND GROW AS YOU LIKE, DR. PYM. THE METAL IS NOW IN A STATE OF MOLECULAR FLUX.

MY MOTHER COULD WARP ANY MATERIAL TO HER WILL WITH JUST A GLANCE.

AND I HAVE MY MOTHER'S EYES.

♪ HMMM HMM... THE SANDMAN'S COMING IN HIS TRAIN OF CARS WITH MOONBEAM WINDOWS AND WITH WHEELS OF STARS... HMM HMM. ♪

DON'T MOVE!

♪ HMM. O HUSH YOU LITTLE ONES AND HAVE NO FEAR-- ♪

REPTIL! METTLE! SPREAD OUT!

--THERE IT IS.

♪ HMM.. RIDE WITH MR. SANDMAN TIL DAYLIGHT COMES AGAIN. ♪

A GREEN BETTIE PAGE WHO SINGS LULLABIES AND GOES WHEREVER THE HELL SHE WANTS.

ANYONE?

SECURITY BREACH, HUH?

I BET THIS HAS EVERYTHING TO DO WITH THAT *MUTTON-CHOPPED* ANT-JERK.

VEIL! FINESSE! YOU OKAY?

IS *SHRINKY DINK* IN THERE WITH YOU?

FZAK

ELECTRONIC SECURITY AIN'T GOT NOTHIN' ON MY VOLTAGE--

WHU--?

DON'T LET THE BEDBUGS BITE.

UH... HOLD IT, LADY! OR...*UH...*

AHHH! CRAP! MY HEAD!

SHAVING CREAM? WHAT'D YOU DO, YOU LITTLE PUNK?

WHAT'D *I* DO?!

WHO WAS THAT CHICK THAT JUST...JUMPED *INTO YOUR HEAD?!*

YOU KNOW WHAT I THINK? I THINK YOU LITTLE PUNKS *ROOFIED* ME!

IS THAT IT? YOU GUYS LIKE PLAYING *ETHER BUNNY?*

LAY OFF, GEEK...

...OR SO HELP ME I WILL GO *FULL* ELECTRIC BOOGALOO ON YOU!

STRIKER! POWER DOWN! *NOW!*

DR. PYM IS READY TO SEE YOU.

ARE YOU OKAY, O'GRADY?

IF THIS IS HOW YOU PLAY *CAT AND MOUSE,* JUST CALL ME *MICKEY.*

ALLLMOST.

GOT IT!

THANK YOU, *METTLE.* ACCORDING TO MY *POCKET TOOL'S* BESTIARY OF KNOWN ALIEN SPECIES, MY ATTACKER WAS A DENIZEN OF THE *MINDSCAPE* CALLED A *SLEEPWALKER.*

ONE OF THESE ENTITIES WAS ENROLLED IN *THE INITIATIVE,* UNDER MS. MARVEL, BUT APPARENTLY NOT ALL OF HIS KIND ARE AS MOTIVATED TOWARDS LAW ENFORCEMENT AS HE WAS.

HANK, YOU SHOULD REST A SECOND--

OBVIOUSLY SHE WASN'T HERE TO KILL ME. SO SHE MUST HAVE BEEN LOOKING FOR SOMETHING.

I CAN FIGURE OUT WHAT'S MISSING IN JUST A SECOND WITH AN INVENTORY CHECK...

DAMN IT. SHE CERTAINLY TOOK SOMETHING...SOMETHING EXTREMELY IMPORTANT. THIS IS WHAT YOU CAME TO WARN ME ABOUT, ERIC?

YEAH, MAN. IF ONLY YOU COULD HAVE TAKEN SOME TIME OUT OF THAT BUSY SCHEDULE FOR LITTLE OL' ANT-MAN.

TELL ME, ERIC, IF YOU WERE SO INTENT ON WARNING ME OF AN ATTACK...

WHY DID *YOU* BRING THE THIEF INTO THE INFINITE MANSION?

MARKEN, THE NETHERLANDS.

A.I.M. FRONT.

CADENC FISHING SUPPLY CO.

WE HAVE DELIVERY IN THREE...TWO...

AND WE HAVE DELIVERY. *AGENT ANESTHESIA* HAS COMPLETED THE ASSIGNMENT.

PYM TRACER LOCATED AAAAND... DEACTIVATED.

ADEQUATE WORK, AGENT ANESTHESIA.

REPORT TO SQUAD LEADER FOR DEBRIEFING.

SWEET DREAMS, DADDY.

SAND DOLLARS SENIOR RESORT.

KEY WEST, FLORIDA.

♪ HIS NAME WAS RICO, HE WORE A DIAMOND. ♪

BARTENDER. SEND THREE "BAHAMA MAMAS" TO THAT TABLE OF CHEEKY HENS THERE.

AND TELL THEM MR. FOX IS ON THE HUNT.

BEEP BEEP BEEP

EXCUSE ME, I MUST TAKE THIS.

MS. RAPPACCINI.

THANKS IN NO SMALL PART TO YOU.

YOUR GOOD WORK HAS ASSURED YOU A SPECIAL PLACE IN HEAVEN.

A.I.M. HEAVEN, THAT IS. WE'RE ABOUT TO BECOME THE PREMIER REAL ESTATE BROKER TO THE AFTERLIFE.

THE DELIVERY HAS BEEN MADE, MR. FOX.

NO WAY I'M LETTING YOU PIN THIS ON ME, PYM!

I'M ON THE *UP AND UP*, MAN! I CAME TO *WARN* YOU, NOT HELP SOMEONE STEAL FROM YOU!

ON THE UP AND UP? HOW DID YOU *REALLY* DISCOVER THE *A.I.M.* PLOT?

ALRIGHT, LOOK...I GOT A TIP FROM A FRIEND OF MINE. A GUY NAMED BLACK FOX. HE...HE OWED ME ONE.

BLACK FOX. INTERNATIONAL JEWEL THIEF. A MAN WHO RECENTLY ESCAPED FROM CUSTODY. YOU HELPED HIM ESCAPE, AND THAT'S WHY HE OWED YOU ONE. CORRECT?

AHH, MAAAN...

DID FOX ACT *UNUSUAL* IN ANY WAY?

YEAH, ACTUALLY. HE KEPT USING SOME CRAZY WORD. "FURD"...? NO, *"FNORD."* THAT'S IT.

I KINDA THOUGHT MAYBE IT WAS A *BRITISH* THING. OR MAYBE THAT HE WAS GOING *SENILE.* DUDE'S LIKE *BETTY WHITE* OLD.

"FNORD" IS A NONSENSICAL TERM FIRST COINED IN THE *PRINCIPIA DISCORDIA.* IT'S AN INTERJECTION WITH HYPNOTIC EFFECT THAT SETTLES INTO THE *SUBCONSCIOUS.*

SIMPLY PUT, FOX *MARKED* YOUR MIND. ONCE THE SLEEPWALKER GIRL FOUND IT, SHE COULD EASE YOU INTO A DEEP SLEEP AND USE YOUR DREAM STATE AS A *DOORWAY* TO THE MANSION.

FOX *"RICKROLLED"* MY BRAIN? ARE YOU *SERIOUS?*

YES. AND NOW *A.I.M.* IS IN POSSESSION OF ONE OF MY MOST IMPORTANT INVENTIONS.

DAMN! I CAN'T BELIEVE I TRUSTED THAT GUY FOR A SECOND!

TOTALLY DISTRACTED ME WITH THAT MEAN POP N' LOCK.

WHAT, HANK? WHAT'D THEY TAKE?

SEVERAL YEARS AGO, I BEGAN AN EVOLVING VIRTUAL CONSCIOUSNESS PROJECT WITH MY FORMER LAB ASSISTANT BILL FOSTER··"LIFELOG" SOFTWARE THAT WOULD ALLOW THE MIND TO LIVE BEYOND THE BODY.

BILL IMPLANTED A BETA OF THE SOFTWARE INTO HIS OWN BRAIN.

AS YOU KNOW, BILL, AS GOLIATH, WAS KILLED DURING THE SUPER HERO CIVIL WAR.

FEELING AT LEAST, IN PART, RESPONSIBLE FOR HIS DEATH, I REMOVED THE SOFTWARE, AND UPLOADED BILL'S CONSCIOUSNESS INTO AN IMMERSIVE SECONDARY REALITY INTENDED TO BESTOW THE USER WITH AN ETERNAL, UTOPIAN EXPERIENCE.

YOU CREATED... HEAVEN?

"IF A.I.M. IS FOLLOWING ITS USUAL M.O., IT INTENDS TO REVERSE ENGINEER MY INVENTION AND USE IT FOR THEIR OWN AGENDA.

"THAT MEANS TAKING IT APART.

"IN DOING SO, THEY WILL STRIP BILL'S WORLD, LAYER BY LAYER, TURNING UTOPIA INTO HELL..."

"AND DESTROYING BILL'S 'SOUL.' FOREVER."

THIS DEVICE WILL ALLOW ME AND ONE OTHER PERSON TO ENTER THE MINDSCAPE.

THERE WE'LL FOLLOW A TRAIL MADE BY PYM PARTICLES, SINCE MY TRACKING DEVICE HAS BEEN DEACTIVATED. THAT'LL LEAD US TO THE SLEEPWALKER WOMAN, AND HOPEFULLY TO *A.I.M.* TIGRA, YOU COME WITH ME.

ERIC, I'LL CALL SOMEONE TO ESCORT YOU HOME.

WHAT?!

NO WAY. *I'M* GOING WITH YOU, PYM.

ERIC, I THINK IT WOULD BE *BEST* IF YOU LEFT THIS TO--

LOOK. I'M DOING EVERYTHING I CAN TO BE A BETTER PERSON. AND IT'S...IT'S *REALLY* HARD FOR ME.

I'VE GOT RESPONSIBILITIES I HAVEN'T MANNED UP TO. I DRIVE EVERYONE AWAY, EVEN THE PEOPLE I CARE ABOUT. MY PERSONAL LIFE IS A MESS. BUT THIS, *THIS* I CAN FIX. I DON'T WANT ANOTHER MISTAKE TO BE *MY LEGACY,* MAN.

FINE. THEN I GUESS THIS IS A JOB...

FOR *ANT-MAN AND THE WASP.*

TeaM UP STYLE, BaBY!

#2

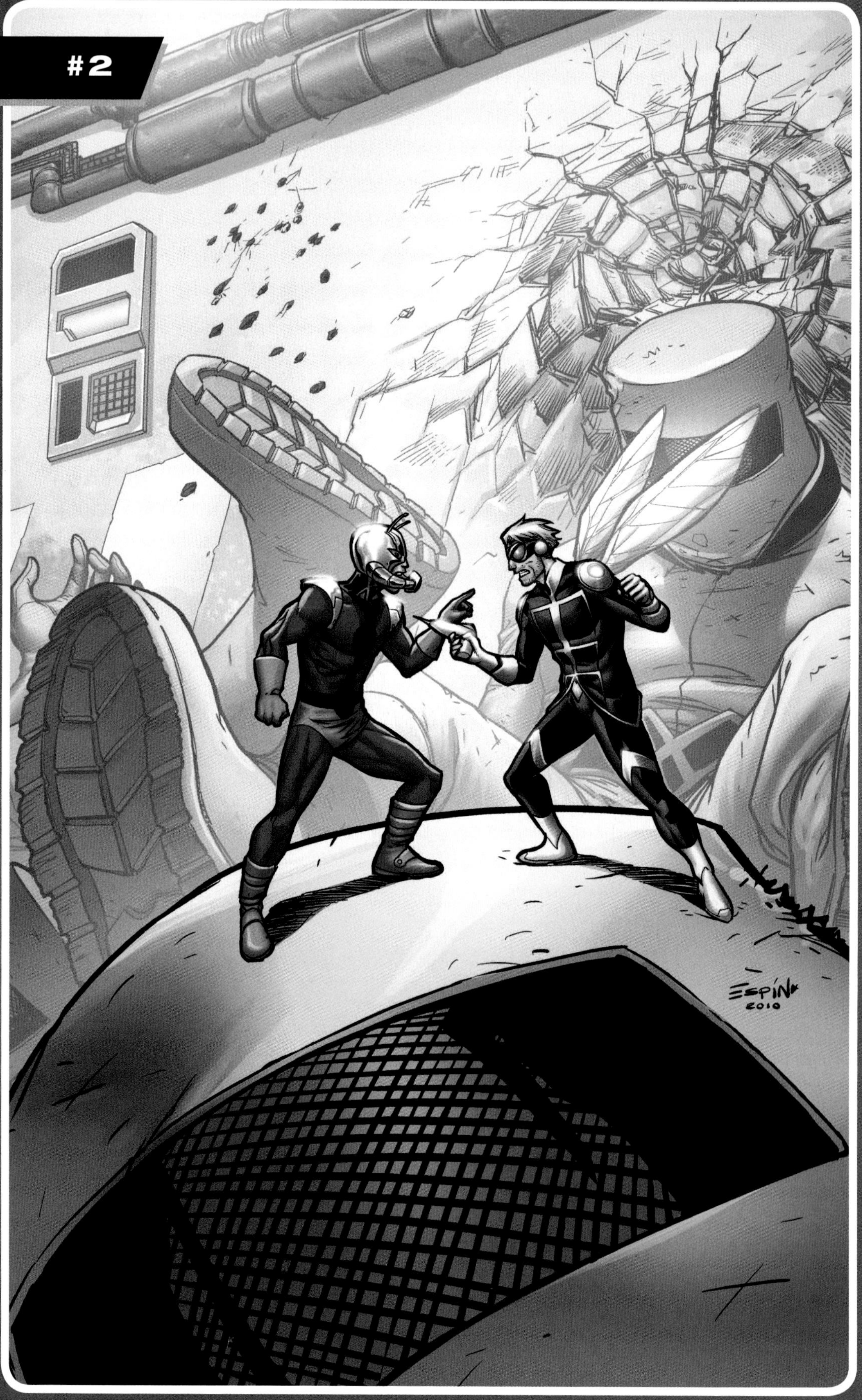
ESPIN
2010

I THINK.

I THINK MY LIFE IS FLASHING IN FRONT OF MY EYES.

EVERYTHING I'VE EVER THOUGHT. EVERYTHING I'VE EVER DONE.

OOH, ALLISON LAKELY. SHE WAS HOT. WONDER WHATEVER HAPPENED TO HER.

EVERYTHING THAT LED ME TO WHERE I AM TODAY. GROWING UP IN BOSTON. JUNIOR HIGH. HIGH SCHOOL. JOINING S.H.I.E.L.D. BECAUSE IT SEEMED EASIER THAN COLLEGE.

"FINDING" THE ANT-MAN COSTUME. BECOMING AN AVENGER. VISITING HANK PYM, AKA THE WASP AKA THE ORIGINAL ANT-MAN.

AND THEN FINDING OUT I'D BEEN PLAYED...USED TO STEAL AN ARTIFICIAL HEAVEN CONTAINING THE VIRTUAL "SOUL" OF BILL FOSTER, THE DEAD SUPER HERO ONCE KNOWN AS GOLIATH.

NOW I'M DROPPING EVERYTHING AND JOINING HANK ON A TRIP TO...TO...

...A *YES* ALBUM COVER?

THE MINDSCAPE. A POCKET UNIVERSE BORDERING THE MINDS OF SENTIENTS.

GHAH! I'M COVERED IN DIRTY THOUGHTS!

THE MINDSCAPE IS NOT A TRULY CORPOREAL PLACE. INSTEAD IT MIMICS MATTER USING NEUROLOGICAL IMPULSES AS THE BASIS OF ITS SUBSTANCE.

THE ONLY WAY FOR OUR PHYSICAL FORMS TO ENTER IS TO BE SHEATHED IN THE CONTENTS OF OUR SUBCONSCIOUS.

I COULDN'T BE PROUDER THAT THE HEIR TO MY *ANT-MAN* IDENTITY IS A MAN OF SUCH *VARIED* INTERESTS.

HEY, BLOW OFF, DOC. AT LEAST I'M NOT WEARING MY *GUILT* AS A *CUMMERBUND.*

HM. I'LL ADJUST THE SHELL TO BE INVISIBLE TO THE NAKED EYE...

HEH, SPEAKING OF THE *"NAKED"* EYE...

MARKEN, THE NETHERLANDS.

HELLO, *PREMIER INVESTORS.* WELCOME TO THE *A.I.M.CAST.*

I'M YOUR HOST, *SUPREME SCIENTIST MONICA RAPPACINI.*

THANKS TO ALL OF YOU WHO'VE LOGGED ON IN ANTICIPATION OF TODAY'S SALE.

AS PROMISED, WE AT *ADVANCED IDEA MECHANICS* BRING YOU THE FUTURE, TODAY.

WITH YOUR CONTINUED SUPPORT, *A.I.M.* IS ABLE TO PREVENT THE FINEST *YOUNG MINDS* FROM BEING TAKEN FOR GRANTED, AND CULTIVATE THEIR IDEAS FOR A MORE PERFECT WORLD.

TODAY, A.I.M. IS PUTTING THE FINISHING TOUCHES ON A NEW PRODUCT THAT CAN GIVE SOMETHING ONCE OFFERED ONLY BY SACRED TOMES AND PONTIFICATING CLERICS. SOMETHING ONLY *FAITH* COULD BUY...

WE HAVE FOR YOU AN *IMMORTALITY* NOT EVEN THE MOST REVERED PLACE IN HISTORY COULD MATCH.

A ZEST FOR LIFE HAS CAUSED MANY TO GO TO EXTREME LENGTHS TO PRESERVE IT.

BUT WHAT IF YOU COULD CONQUER THE FEAR OF DEATH? THE ANXIETY OF NOT KNOWING WHAT HAPPENS WHEN WE CLOSE OUR EYES FOR THE LAST TIME?

WHAT IF IT DIDN'T MATTER WHAT KIND OF PERSON YOU WERE ON THIS EARTH?

WHAT IF THERE WAS NO *ARCHANGEL* STANDING IN JUDGMENT... NO *FEATHER OF OSIRIS* TO WEIGH YOUR SOUL AGAINST?

FOR THE RIGHT PRICE, HEAVEN *IS* ASSURED. BECAUSE A.I.M. HAS MADE IT FOR YOU.

YOUR *"HOME AWAY FROM LIFE."* BID EARLY, AND BID OFTEN.

SPACE IS LIMITED.

AHH! CAN WE LEAVE?! THIS PLACE HAS...I DUNNO, WHATEVER THE HELL *THESE* ARE!

HOLD ON! MY *PYM PARTICLE TRACKER* HASN'T PICKED UP THE SLEEPWALKER'S TRAIL JUST YET.

STAY SMALL AND IN A TIGHT FORMATION.

WE CAN HANDLE THE SMALLER CREATURES AND AVOID DETECTION BY BIGGER AND MORE DANGEROUS ANIMALS.

FZAK

ALWAYS WITH THE ANSWERS. SO, TELL ME THIS, *GREAT ALL KNOWING HENRY.*

YOU CREATED A SYNTHETIC HEAVEN FOR YOUR BUDDY.

YOU EVER STOP TO ASK YOURSELF *"WHAT IF THERE'S A REAL HEAVEN?"*

YOU'RE KIDDING, I HOPE.

THE PARTICLE TRAIL LEADS THIS WAY.

KIDDING? I GREW UP IRISH CATHOLIC. HOW DO YOU THINK I RECOGNIZED GUILT SO QUICKLY?

I'M SERIOUS...WHAT IF YOU'RE PLAYING *GOD* FOR NO REASON?

I'VE SEEN A LOT OF THINGS IN MY LIFE. ALIENS, ALTERNATE REALITIES, THE BIRTH OF UNIVERSES...WONDERFUL, AMAZING THINGS.

ALL THOSE THINGS, ERIC, HAVE A FIRM BASIS IN SCIENCE. *SCIENCE* IS MY GOD. I SHALL HAVE NO OTHER GODS BEFORE IT.

BUT YOU WORK WITH THOR*!* AND HERCULES!

EXTRADIMENSIONAL ALIEN HEROES, LIKELY. *"GODS,"* MAYBE.

THEY DON'T PROVE THE EXISTENCE OF *THE* GOD. NOR OF AN ETERNAL RESTING PLACE FOR THE *"SOUL."*

BUT YOU DON'T KNOW, IS WHAT I'M SAYING.

I *KNOW,* FOR ME.

YOU ARE *SO* FRUSTRATING. THIS IS WHY YOU HAVE FEWER ACTION FIGURES THAN ALL THE OTHER AVENGERS.

THERE.

WHAT IS IT?

THE PARTICLES LEAD TO THIS. A MINDSCAPE SINGULARITY.

A *GATEWAY* TO A SINGLE SENTIENT MIND.

I KNOW YOU'VE *"SEEN IT ALL"* OR WHATEVER, BUT YOU HAVE TO ADMIT THAT'S PRETTY COOL.

YEAH. PRETTY COOL.

DID YOU SEE THAT?! WE CAME OUT OF THIS GUY'S FRICKIN' HEAD!

WHAT DID YOU EXPECT? WE EXITED A HUMAN MIND.

I SUPPOSE... I GUESS I'VE EXITED THROUGH WORSE. ASK LUKE CAGE.

WHAT'S WRONG WITH THIS GUY?

BRAIN DEAD. KEPT ALIVE BY THESE MACHINES.

A.I.M. MUST BE USING HIM AS A DOORWAY FOR THE SLEEPWALKER GIRL.

ANY IDEA WHERE WE ARE?

SOME KIND OF A.I.M. LAB, I'M SURE.

I'M TRYING TO DETERMINE A LOCATION, BUT I'M NOT GETTING ANYTHING.

IN FACT, IT APPEARS WE'RE NOWHERE. AND NO-WHEN.

SOOOOO, NOT MUCH CHANCE OF CALLING IN ANY BACKUP, THEN?

HALT, IN THE NAME OF SCIENCE!

A.I.M. ENTERED MY LAB AND TOOK ONE OF MY INVENTIONS.

WE'RE NOT GOING TO NEED BACKUP.

HOLD IT!

OBVIOUSLY THIS GUY IS IMPORTANT TO *A.I.M.*, RIGHT? OTHERWISE HE WOULDN'T STILL BE PLUGGED IN WHEN HE'S CLEARLY OLD AND BUSTED.

IN FACT, I'M WILLING TO BET THAT IF HE *DID* GET HURT SOME CRAP AND A FAN WOULD BE INVOLVED.

NOW, I DON'T KNOW WHO YOU GUYS THINK YOU'RE DEALING WITH HERE, BUT YOU SHOULD KNOW THAT I'M NOT YOUR DADDY'S SUPER HERO. I PLAY PRETTY DIRTY.

MAYBE YOU DIDN'T HEAR THAT I WAS ON OSBORN'S ALL-BAD GUY THUNDERBOLTS TEAM. OR THAT I'M BUDDIES WITH TASKMASTER.

SO, WHAT ARE YOU SAYING?

I'M SAYING I WANT YOU BOYS TO PUT DOWN THE HEAVY ARTILLERY AND WALK OUT THE DOOR.

OR WHAT? YOU'LL HURT THE OLD MAN? YOU'RE BLUFFING.

YOU SURE ABOUT THAT?

AH, PYM...SO PREDICTABLE.

THOUGH THIS NEW ANT-MAN ADDS AN INTERESTING ELEMENT...

SUPREME SCIENTIST.

PLEASE, ANESTHESIA, I TOLD YOU TO CALL ME MONICA.

IT'S MY FATHER. I THINK HE'S GETTING WORSE. I KNOW *A.I.M.* IS DOING EVERYTHING THEY CAN FOR HIM, BUT--

ANA, MY DEAR...YOUR FATHER'S CONDITION IS UNUSUAL, TO SAY THE LEAST.

WE STILL HAVE YET TO UNDERSTAND HOW HIS VEGETATIVE STATE AFFECTS YOUR ABILITY TO REMAIN IN THIS WORLD. WE DON'T WANT TO ENDANGER YOU, ESPECIALLY SINCE I'VE COME TO CONSIDER YOU TO BE LIKE THE DAUGHTER I NEVER HAD--

WOOT WOOT

BACKUP REQUEST IN SECTOR 118.

SECTOR 118 IS WHERE MY FATHER IS! I HAVE TO--

NO.

THIS IS WHY WE HAVE LOWLY GRUNTS. I'LL SEND SOME *M.I.T.* GRADS TO TAKE CARE OF IT. YOU'RE TOO IMPORTANT TO *A.I.M.* TO BE CHASING AFTER *"BUGS."*

SUCKERS!

FZAK

I CAN'T *BELIEVE* YOU GUYS FELL FOR THAT. I THOUGHT *A.I.M.* WAS FOR THE SMART GOONS.

WHAT ARE YOU GUYS, LIKE *HYDRA* DROPOUTS? I'M AN AVENGER, MAN! WE'RE LIKE *ANNOYINGLY* GOOD AND PROPER.

I WAS JUST MAKING SURE THE OLD GUY DIDN'T CATCH ANY FIRE WHILE ME AND WASP TOSSED YOU GUYS LIKE A SALAD.

I BET YOU THINK SHRINKING IS A LAME POWER RIGHT?

YOU THINK THAT, BUT YOU'RE WRONG...

BUDDY, I'M BASICALLY A SLIGHTLY SHORTER WOLVERINE.

WHOK

ERIC! IT'S NICE THAT ALL THAT STEVE ROGERS COMBAT-TRAINING IS PAYING OFF.

BUT WE'VE GOT MORE COMPANY!

BWAHAHA! OH, WATCH OUT! THAT'S WHERE *A.I.M.* SOLDIERS KEEP THEIR I.Q.!

WERE YOU IMPRESSED, HANK? DID YA LIKE MY *"BAD COP"* IMPRESSION BACK THERE...

≥SIGH≤

ZAK

I'LL ADMIT YOU MAKE A CONVINCING SELF-CENTERED, POSSIBLY EVIL, RECKLESS JERK.

THIS IS MY *GOOD COP* IMPRESSION.

FWAK

LOOKS LIKE YOU'RE BEEPING US RIGHT TO THAT DOOR.

BEEP!

BEEP!

AGREED.

HEY, I HAVEN'T GOTTEN TO GO BIG SINCE I WAS IN *THE INITIATIVE.*

I'M GOING TO DO MY *G.I.ANT-MAN THING* AND SMASH THIS DOOR OPEN.

NO! YOU COULD END UP DAMAGING THE ¡HEAVEN HALO. I'VE GOT IT.

MY POCKETS ARE ACTUALLY PORTALS TO SUBATOMIC DIMENSIONS. I HAVE A NUMBER OF DEVICES IN HERE THAT WILL GET US IN WITHOUT UNNECESSARY SHOWBOATING.

SHOWBOATING? ME? WHAT DO YOU CALL DIGGING INTO YOUR NIFTY BOTTOMLESS POCKETS?

I CALL IT THINKING AND WORKING EFFICIENTLY AND INTELLIGENTLY.

AND I CALL THIS A PORTABLE HOLE.

OKAY, THAT'S IT. WHAT'S WITH THE CONSTANT STINK EYE AND THE TALKING DOWN?

WHAT HAVE YOU GOT AGAINST ME?

THIS IS HARDLY THE TIME.

ROGERS VOUCHED FOR ME. STARK VOUCHED FOR ME. ISN'T THAT GOOD ENOUGH FOR YOU?

I MEAN, IT'S NOT LIKE I'M THE FIRST GUY TO STEAL AN ANT-MAN SUIT. THAT *SCOTT LANG* DUDE BECAME ANT-MAN THROUGH THE SAME *FIVE-FINGER DISCOUNT METHOD* THAT I DID.

SCOTT DIDN'T *STEAL* THE ANT-MAN SUIT. I *LET* HIM STEAL THE ANT-MAN SUIT.

FOR ALL INTENTS AND PURPOSES, I *CHOSE* HIM TO BE MY SUCCESSOR.

YEAH, WELL, YOU CHOSE WRONG, MAN. IF SCOTT LANG WAS SUCH A GOOD CHOICE FOR ANT-MAN--

--HE WOULDN'T HAVE GOTTEN HIMSELF KILLED.

FUH!

SWOK

WUH. ARE WE GONNA DO THIS? REALLY?

NO. WE'RE NOT. YOU WATCH THE DOOR AND I'M GOING TO GET BILL FOSTER'S *"SOUL"* BACK.

BUTCHERS! LOOK WHAT THEY'VE DONE TO MY WORK.

WE'VE GOT ABOUT FIFTEEN BEEKEEPERS ON THEIR WAY, SLUGGER.

THIS IS A DISASTER. I'M GOING TO TRY AND PUT THIS BACK TOGETHER AND DROP IT INTO ONE OF MY POUCHES.

WE CAN TRY EXITING BACK THROUGH THE MINDSCAPE, AND I'LL DO WHAT I CAN FOR BILL BACK AT THE LAB.

COOL. THE SOONER WE'RE DONE WITH THIS JOB, THE FASTER YOU AND I CAN JUST AWKWARDLY AVOID EACH OTHER AT AVENGERS MEET-UPS--

ALL RIGHT. THAT'S ENOUGH.

I'M CERTAINLY IMPRESSED, AND YOU EXCEEDED MY HIGHEST EXPECTATIONS, DR. PYM. BUT I CAN'T HAVE YOU TAKING THE AUCTION MERCHANDISE.

GUK!

I ASSUME YOU KNOW OF ME, MY PROFICIENCIES WITH NEUROTOXINS, AND THE FACT THAT I'D NEVER HAVE MY FORCE FIELD DOWN AROUND A MAN WHO LIKES TO ZAP PEOPLE WITH HIS OWN BIOELECTRICITY.

MONICA RAPPACINI.

WHAT DID YOU DO TO HIM?!

A NEW TOXIN I'VE BEEN WORKING ON THAT COUNTERACT THE BODY'S ABILITIES TO PROCES YOUR *"PYM PARTICLES."* HIS MUSCLES ARE RESPONDING T(THE PARTICLES AT DIFFERENT RATES AND I'M SURE IT'S QUITE UNCOMFORTABLE.

I IMAGINE HE'LL PASS OUT SOON.

THE SHOW'S OVER...

HNNNGH.

...SO LET'S GET DOWN TO THE REASON YOU'RE HERE.

I'LL LET THE TROOPS IN, JUST TO MAKE SURE YOU'RE IN A MORE COOPERATIVE MOOD--

UNGH!

FWOK

HUNH. MAYBE YOU DIDN'T NEED TO ADJUST THE OL' CYBERLEGS AFTER ALL.

THEY WORK JUST LIKE THEY USED TO.

SUPREME SCIENTIST!

IS SHE OKAY?!

THE SLEEPWALKER WILL BE THROUGH THAT DOOR IN NO TIME.

SO *I'M* TAKING THIS...

AND YOU...

AND GOING SOMEWHERE I CAN THINK.

MONICA! ARE YOU OKAY?!

FIND... PYM.

OH, MAN...IT HURTS...

I KNOW. I'M TRYING TO LOCALIZE THE TOXIN BUT RAPPACINI'S KNOWLEDGE OF BIOCHEMISTRY AND NEUROTOXINS MIGHT EXCEED MY OWN.

DID YOU JUST ADMIT SOMEONE WAS SMARTER THAN YOU?

OH, CRAP, I *MUST* BE DYING.

YOU *ARE* DYING.

HUNF. GOOD THING YOU'RE A SUPER HERO BECAUSE YOU'RE A JERK OF A MEDICAL DOCTOR.

HM. I MAY BE ABLE TO KILL TWO BIRDS WITH ONE STONE.

THE iHEAVEN HALO IS BADLY DAMAGED, AND I DON'T KNOW IF BILL IS STILL EVEN IN HERE.

IF HE IS, I CAN PROGRAM A *"PANIC ROOM"* IN AN UNDAMAGED NODE. BUT I'LL NEED SOMEONE TO GUIDE HIM TO ITS LOCATION.

IF I USE THE HALO'S LIFELOG SOFTWARE AND ATTACH IT TO YOUR MIND, I CAN SEND YOU INSIDE THE VIRTUAL WORLD.

THAT WAY, YOU WON'T BE ABLE TO FEEL THE PAIN YOUR BODY IS GOING THROUGH WHILE I FIND A CURE.

YOU'RE EUTHANIZING ME?

NO. I'M SIMPLY GOING TO ENSURE YOUR MIND WILL BE ABLE TO FOCUS COMPLETELY ON MANIPULATING YOUR VIRTUAL AVATAR WITHOUT ANY DISTRACTION FROM STIMULI IN THE PHYSICAL WORLD.

WHILE YOU FIND BILL, I'LL FIGURE OUT WHERE AND WHEN WE ARE, AND GET THE REST OF THE *AVENGERS* TO RAIN HELL ON RAPPACINI'S ARROGANT ASS.

HUNH. WHAT'S WITH THE BAD TOUCH?

I HAVE TO INDUCE YOU INTO A COMA, ERIC. I'LL MAKE SURE IT DOESN'T HURT.

DOC...

IF I DON'T...WELL... I HOPE YOU'RE WRONG ABOUT GOD.

NO MATTER HOW SMART I AM, OR HOW MUCH I THINK I KNOW, THERE'S ONLY ONE THING I CAN SAY FOR CERTAIN.

FZAAK

HANK PYM IS NOT *ALWAYS* RIGHT.

???

AH! I'M UNDERWATER! I'M--

OH, RIGHT. I'M IN HEAVEN. I DON'T NEED TO BREATHE. DURR.

THIS PLACE HAS TO BE PRETTY BIG IF IT HAS ITS OWN OCEAN.

WHERE DO I START? HOW AM I GOING TO FIND--

...ONE LITTLE MAN.

WHAT THE--?!

DON'T BOTHER TRYING TO ENLARGE YOUR WAY OUT OF THERE.

IT'S COMPOSED OF A WEB OF ATOM-SIZED FIBERS, AND YOU'LL JUST MAKE YOURSELF INTO FINELY DICED BITS IF YOU TRY TO ESCAPE.

NOW, LET'S GET TO THE *REAL* REASON I TOOK YOUR LITTLE HOMEMADE HEAVEN.

CERTAINLY THE FUNDS ATTAINED FROM THE AUCTION OF YOUR DEVICE WILL HELP *A.I.M.* GREEN-LIGHT SOME IMPORTANT PROJECTS.

BUT MORE IMPORTANTLY, STEALING FROM YOU WAS ALMOST GUARANTEED TO BRING YOU HERE. SO, WHILE ANNA FINDS YOUR FRIEND, I'D LIKE TO USE THIS CHANCE...

...TO FORMALLY INVITE YOU TO *JOIN* A.I.M..

#3

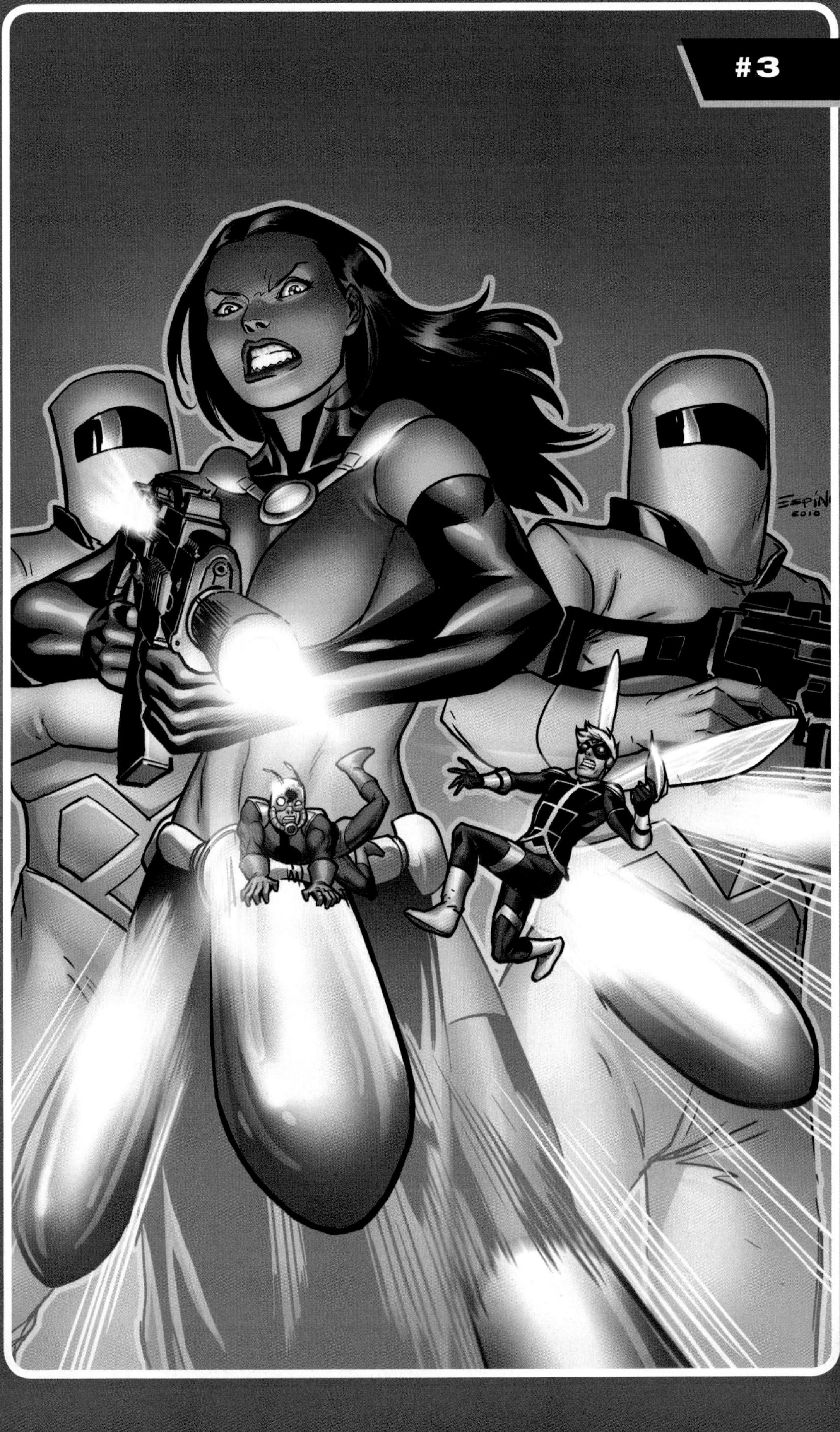
ESPIN
2010

"HAPPINESS IN INTELLIGENT PEOPLE IS THE RAREST THING I KNOW."

ERNEST HEMINGWAY SAID THAT.

NO SMALL WONDER I SUPPOSE THAT HE RECEIVED HIS *LAST KISS* FROM THE BARREL OF HIS FAVORITE SHOTGUN.

I KNOW WHAT IT'S LIKE, *DR. PYM*...BEING TRAPPED INSIDE YOUR OWN HEAD.

I KNOW THE *LONELINESS,* SEEING THE IGNORANT AND STUPID SO EASILY ENTERTAINED BY THE PURSUIT OF MONEY AND SEX.

I KNOW THE FRUSTRATION AT THEIR *SIMPLICITY.* THEY NEED LOOK NO FURTHER THAN THE ANTICS OF *"REALITY"* STARS ON HIGH DEFINITION, FLAT SCREEN TELEVISIONS FOR HAPPINESS.

STEALING YOUR ELECTRONIC ELYSIUM WAS SIMPLY MY WAY OF GETTING YOUR ATTENTION, DR. PYM.

A.I.M. IS THE HOME OF PEOPLE LIKE US: HYPER-INTELLIGENT OUTCASTS WITH AN OVERRIDING DESIRE TO SAVE THE WORLD FROM THE CLUTCHES OF MONKEYS WHOSE SOLUTION TO PROBLEMS IS HITTING THEM WITH A STICK.

YOU BUILT YOUR "¡HEAVEN" BECAUSE YOU, UNLIKE MOST OF THE CHIMPS, KNOW THAT WHEN WE DIE, THERE IS ONLY PEACE, DARKNESS, AND THE RAPID DECAY OF A BODY INTO ITS BASE ELEMENTS.

JOIN US, AND WE'LL BUILD THEM HEAVEN, HERE AND NOW, SO THEY DON'T HAVE TO WAIT FOR DEATH---

--TO LIVE LIKE ANGELS.

YOU FORGOT "WHETHER THEY LIKE IT OR NOT."

AGHK!

ENERGY DISPERSING JELLY. THE MORE YOU MOVE, THE COLDER IT GETS.

I'VE DEVELOPED ONE HUNDRED AND FIFTY-SEVEN METHODS OF KEEPING YOU HERE LONG ENOUGH TO HEAR MY OFFER.

WE CAN DO THIS ALL DAY.

¡HEAVEN.

FOSTER! DUDE, OVER HERE!

HUGE BLACK GUY! PLEASE LISTEN TO TINY WHITE GUY!

I HAVE TO GET HIS ATTENTION.

I'M NOT ME. NOT REALLY. I'M A PROGRAM. I'M A DIGITAL PROXY.

JUST LIKE ON MY Wii. AND I CAN MAKE MY Wii PROXY LOOK ANY WAY I LIKE...

YES! IF ONLY I HAD TIME FOR A SHOWER...

NOW, TO DO MY BEST BLOWHARD, ARROGANT SCIENCE JERK IMPRESSION.

BILL FOSTER!

HENRY? WHAT ARE YOU DOING HERE?

BILL! I NEED YOU TO COME WITH ME!

HEAVEN IS BURNING MAN, AND WE NEED TO GET YOU OUT!

HEAVEN? OH...

OH... OH, GOD.

I REMEMBER... I'M DEAD.

UH, YEAH. SORRY, MAN.

BUT WE'RE GOING TO GET YOUR HAPPY LITTLE AFTERLIFE BACK ONLINE IN NO TIME.

JUST FOLLOW ME...

WAIT, HANK. I HAVE TO TELL YOU.

WHEN WE BUILT THIS, WE FORGOT ONE THING. WE WERE SO CONCERNED WITH MAKING THE PERFECT PLACE...

WE FORGOT THE MOST IMPORTANT THING ABOUT UTOPIA IS EVERYONE YOU SHARE IT WITH.

FIRST THING YOU DO WHEN YOU GET BACK TO LIFE?

YOU MAKE SURE YOU STOP PUSHING ALL THOSE PEOPLE AWAY.

DAMN YOU, PYM!

I DIDN'T THINK I'D GET AS FAR AS THE *HARD LIGHT TESSERACT*.

I PREDICTED YOU'D SEE THE ERROR OF YOUR WAYS ABOUT THREE PRISONS AGO.

YOU'RE A COMPLEX INDIVIDUAL, MR. PYM. YOU SO VEHEMENTLY DEFEND HUMANITY, DESPITE YOUR DISCONNECT FROM IT.

IF YOU'LL PERMIT A BIOLOGIST TO STEP INTO THE ROLE OF PSYCHOLOGIST FOR A SECOND, I THINK IT'S THIS DISPARITY THAT CAUSES YOU SO MUCH TROUBLE. THE DEPRESSION, THE ANGER, THE ADDICTIONS...

ALL BECAUSE YOU MAKE YOURSELF PUT ON PAJAMAS AND *"AVENGE"* WHEN YOU KNOW YOU SHOULD BE RULING THEM ALL.

TELL ME, DR. PYM. DID YOU BUILD ¡HEAVEN FOR YOUR FRIEND, BILL FOSTER?

OR DID YOU BUILD IT FOR YOURSELF, KNOWING THAT WHAT YOU TRULY DESERVE IS HELL?

♪ HUSH LITTLE BABY, DON'T SAY A WORD... ♪

HUNGH!

♪ MAMA'S GONNA BUY YOU A MOCKINGBIRD... ♪

♪ AND IF THAT MOCKINGBIRD DON'T SING... ♪

AAGGHKK!

THE PAIN YOU MUST FEEL RIGHT NOW.

IT'S...IT'S BEYOND ANYTHING I CAN CONCEIVE OF, AND I'VE SEEN INSIDE SOME OF THE DEEPEST, DARKEST NIGHTMARES A MIND CAN IMAGINE.

≶HUNGHK≷ YOU.

W-WHAT DO YOU WANT? ISN'T IT ENOUGH YOU GOT ME INTO THIS IN THE FIRST PLACE?

PLEASE. CALL ME ANA. MY FATHER DID.

MY FATHER SLEEPS, MR. O'GRADY. HE SLEEPS, AND HE NEVER WAKES UP. HE DOESN'T EVEN DREAM BECAUSE OF ME.

SUPREME SCIENTIST RAPPACCINI VOWED TO HELP ME, IN EXCHANGE FOR MY ASSISTANCE WITH HER CAUSE. BUT I THINK I AM BEING USED.

NO &#*+, SHERLOCK.

I'M ONLY HALF-HUMAN, MR. O'GRADY. I GREW UP IN ANOTHER WORLD, A CHILD OF THE MINDSPAWN.

THERE WERE NO LIES AMONG MY PEOPLE, NO DECEPTION. ONLY THE PURITY OF THE IMAGINATION AND THE SINCERITY OF DREAMS.

UNGGHK.

I SEE NOW THAT HUMANS ARE MOTIVATED TO HELP OTHERS ONLY FOR REWARD.

I WILL HEAL YOU, MR. O'GRADY. I WILL END THIS AGONY. BUT, IN RETURN, YOU MUST LEAVE IMMEDIATELY.

MONICA MAY HAVE BETRAYED ME, BUT I DO NOT WANT TO SEE HER HURT. I WANT YOU TO TAKE FATHER SOMEWHERE FAR AWAY, AWAY FROM THIS FIGHT.

THIS MEANS YOU WILL LEAVE YOUR FRIEND, DR. PYM. CAN I TRUST YOU TO HOLD YOUR END OF THE BARGAIN?

HAH. LADY, YOU'VE WALKED MY MIND. YOU'VE SEEN WHAT'S IN THERE.

ABANDONING PEOPLE IS MY SPECIAL SKILL. AND I'VE DONE IT FOR A LOT LESS.

PYM MEANS ABSOLUTELY NOTHING TO ME.

YOU END THIS TORTURE AND YOU'VE GOT YOURSELF A DEAL.

THE *SLEEPWALKERS* USE THEIR *"GAZE"* TO BREAK THE MENTAL CONTROL OF FOREIGN ENTITIES ON A HUMAN BRAIN.

MONICA'S NEUROTOXINS ARE NOT SO FAR REMOVED FROM A SIMPLE INFECTION OF *"SOUL SLUGS."*

AAAAAAGH!

UNH. IT IS DONE.

HOLY... YOU DID IT.

YOU DID IT!

YES.

YOU ARE TOTALLY AMAZING! AND REALLY, REALLY *HOT*.

SO I FEEL REALLY BAD THAT I HAVE TO DO THIS.

WHU--?

FRZAAAK

HA, WHADDAYAKNOW? SHE'S BALD.

I FEEL A LOT LESS BAD ABOUT THIS NOW.

LOOK, HONEY, I MAY BE A JERK, BUT I KNOW A GOOD THING WHEN I HAVE IT.

I LIKE BEING AN AVENGER. AND AVENGERS DON'T ABANDON THEIR TEAMMATES, NO MATTER HOW BIG OF A STIFF THAT TEAMMATE MAY BE.

"ONLY THE PURITY OF THE IMAGINATION AND SINCERITY OF DREAMS."

HAH!

WHAT A BUMPKIN.

YOU STUBBORN BASTARD...

JUST GIVE UP.

THE DARKFORCE MIST IS IMMENSELY DANGEROUS AND UNSTABLE. YOU CAN'T ESCAPE WITHOUT DESTROYING YOURSELF.

WELL, I'M NOT TRYING TO ESCAPE AT THE MOMENT. IN FACT, I'D LIKE TO THANK YOU, MS. RAPPACCINI.

ALL THIS INTENSE, FREE-FORM PROBLEM SOLVING HAS REALLY GOT MY BRAIN RACING.

WHILE I WAS FIGURING OUT HOW TO BREAK THE PSIONIC SHELL, MY SECONDARY THOUGHT PROCESSES WERE ACTIVELY MAKING CONNECTIONS BETWEEN MY EARLIER ENCOUNTER WITH A CHRONAL ABERRATION, AND THE FACT THAT IT APPEARS THIS "SECRET BASE" DOESN'T EXIST IN PHYSICAL SPACE.

I REALIZED THAT ABERRATION WAS NO NATURAL OCCURRENCE.

YOU USED A.I.M.'S KNOWLEDGE OF ALTERNATE TIMELINES TO FIND ONE THAT HAD BEEN OVERWRITTEN BY TIME TRAVEL. YOU THEN TIED THAT QUANTUM-POCKET TO THIS PHYSICAL SPACE, MAKING YOUR BASE OUT-OF-SYNC, AND THUS, INVISIBLE.

OF COURSE, NATURE ABHORS A VACUUM, BUT YOU KNEW REED AND I WOULD STOP OUR OWN FUTURE FROM FALLING INTO THE DEAD THREAD.

I'M SURE YOU EVEN JUSTIFIED IT AS A "TEST" OF MY OWN APTITUDE.

SO, I JUST FREED THE "IMPRISONED TIMELINE," MEANING YOUR BASE IS GOING BACK INTO SYNCH, BECOMING FULLY "CHRONALLY VISIBLE."

OF COURSE, AS SOON AS I WAS ABLE, I PUT IN A CALL FOR BACKUP.

PYM. I HAD SUCH HIGH HOPES FOR YOU.

YOU'VE BEEN POISONED BY EXPOSURE TO TINY INTELLECTS LIKE THOSE MEAT-HEADED AVENGER TYPES.

ALL THESE CREATIONS...ALL THIS BEAUTIFUL SCIENCE. SPURNED, REJECTED, DESTROYED.

≷SIGH≷ I DO HAVE ONE INVENTION I HAVEN'T TRIED ON YOU.

I MADE THIS FOR MY FIRST SCIENCE FAIR; AN ELECTRIC KNIFE TO HELP MY MOTHER SLICE HAM.

I LOST OUT TO A TOMATO SAUCE SPOUTING VOLCANO MODEL.

I NEVER DID GET OVER THAT.

NRRRRRR

COULD HAVE BEEN WORSE.

COULD HAVE BEEN A STYROFOAM MODEL OF URANUS!

PKGW

NEVER GETS OLD!

THE HALO? BILL?

DONE AND DONER.

WE SHOULD GO.

CHRONAL READJUSTMENT QUAKES ARE ABOUT TO MAKE THIS A VERY DANGEROUS PLACE.

OH, JEEZ, NOT THIS AGAIN.

PYM AND ANT-MAN ARE ESCAPING!

I NO LONGER WANT THEM CAPTURED! I WANT THEM DEAD!

YOU EVER FIGURE OUT WHERE WE ARE, SMART GUY?

COORDINATES PLACED US OFF THE COAST OF NORWAY.

OR, RATHER...

"...DIRECTLY ABOVE IT."

COME ON, MAN! WE GOT WHAT WE WANTED!

TIMEQUAKES EMIT AN IMMENSE AMOUNT OF ELECTROMAGNETIC ENERGY.

"IF I DON'T DO SOMETHING ABOUT IT, THIS SHIP'S SYSTEMS WILL FAIL AND IT'LL FALL DIRECTLY ON MARKEN!"

DAMN IT. IF IT'S NOT ONE THING--

SHRAK

IT'S SOMETHING WORSE!

UNGH!

FZZAK

A.I.M. HIGH!

CRAAAAAAAAAAP!

DAMN IT! I DON'T HAVE TIME FOR INTERRUPTIONS.

SHRAK

PYM!

I'M GOING TO STUDY YOUR DEAD, CLEARLY ABNORMAL BRAIN.

HUK!

AAAAAHHH!

WOOF!

GOT 'IM! NOT BAD FOR A "FRAT BOY," EH, JERKWAD?

OH, JESUS. THANK YOU THANK YOU THANK YOU.

I VOW TO NEVER AGAIN UNDERESTIMATE AN ELECTRIC-POWERED JOCK OR THE EYESIGHT OF A KID WITH A T-REX FOR A HEAD.

WHAT THE HELL ARE YOU GUYS DOING HERE?!

WE'RE STUDENTS.

"WE'RE HERE TO WATCH AND LEARN."

DA-YUM.

OH, NO.

"ANA."

YOU CAN'T SHRINK AWAY WITH THIS KNIFE STUCK IN YOU, CAN YOU, DR. PYM?

ALL THAT HIGH TECHNOLOGY, AND YOU'RE ABOUT TO BE BROUGHT LOW BY ONE OF MAN'S EARLIEST TOOLS.

HRRN. MAN'S EARLIEST TOOL, RAPPACCINI...

...WAS HIS HEAD.

YOU'VE FORCED MY HAND. I AM SORRY.

THERE'S ONLY ONE WAY FOR ME TO STOP THIS SHIP FROM FALLING ON MARKEN...

SHRZZAK

DAMN IT!

I WON'T LEAVE YOU HERE!

ANA!

I'M HERE TO HELP YOU! TRUST ME!

MR. O'GRADY.

TRUST YOU?!

YOU SOULLESS COWARD--

OH...NO.

NOOO!

FWAASH

YOU DID IT.

BUT WHERE'D YOU SEND THEM?

THEIR OWN PERSONAL HELL.

EARTH 9939. ALSO KNOWN AS EARTH-CHARNEL.

THE YEAR 2020.

I NEED A MEDTECH OVER HERE!

DAMN IT.

WHERE?! WHERE DID YOU SEND US, MONICA?!

AN ALTERNATE FUTURE. ONE IN WHICH *A.I.M.* CREATED A PERFECT ASSASSIN.

AN ENEMY USED THAT PERFECT ASSASSIN AND TURNED HIMSELF INTO THE DEVIL INCARNATE.

"THIS IS A WORLD WHERE FEAR, BARBARISM, AND SUPERSTITION RULE. IT IS A PLACE WHERE SCIENCE IS DEAD, AND PROGRESS HAS GROUND TO A STANDSTILL.

"IT IS A WORLD IN WHICH *A.I.M.* HAS UTTERLY FAILED. AND IT IS A WORLD THAT *A.I.M.* IS RESPONSIBLE FOR.

"IT IS OUR HOME FOR THE FORESEEABLE FUTURE.

"PRAY WE ARE ALONE."

JANET VAN DYNE CENTER FOR WOMEN. MANHATTAN.

LATER.

I'VE SEEN A LOT OF THINGS IN MY LIFE.

ALIENS, ALTERNATE REALITIES, THE BIRTH OF UNIVERSES...

JANET VAN DYNE CENTER FOR WOMEN

BUT *THIS* MAY BE THE MOST AMAZING.

ERIC O'GRADY, VOLUNTEERING HIS TIME. THERE IS A GOD.

YEAH, YEAH, LAUGH IT UP.

WAY TO OVERCOMPENSATE FOR DRESSING LIKE YOUR WIFE, *"GIANT" MAN.*

WE APPRECIATE THE HELP, ERIC.

IT'S THE LEAST I CAN DO.

YOU SENT ME TO HEAVEN. I MEAN, THAT'S PROBABLY THE CLOSEST EITHER OF US WILL *EVER* GET, RIGHT?

BESIDES, IT'S NOT ENTIRELY SELFLESS.

THIS IS ALLOWING ME TO SPEND SOME TIME WITH MY FAVORITE GI--

ERIC!

ANY PARTICULAR REASON I FOUND A SLIP OF PAPER WITH YOUR PHONE NUMBER ON IT IN CANDY'S ROOM?

WHAT? UH. I--NO!

THAT WAS FOR... COUNSELING?

ARE YOU TRYING TO PICK UP WOMEN AT A DOMESTIC ABUSE SHELTER?

WHAT KIND OF SLEAZEBAG WOULD DO THAT, ABIGAIL?

DR. PYM ONLY
EXTRADIMENSIONAL PORTAL INSIDE

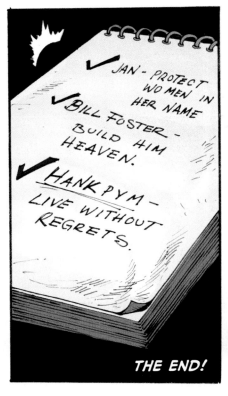

✓ JAN - PROTECT WOMEN IN HER NAME

✓ BILL FOSTER - BUILD HIM HEAVEN.

✓ HANK PYM - LIVE WITHOUT REGRETS.

THE END!

TALES TO ASTONISH

APPROVED BY THE COMICS CODE AUTHORITY

44 JUNE

MARVEL COMICS GROUP 12¢

ANT-MAN and the THE WASP BATTLE "THE CREATURE FROM KOSMOS"!!

MEET THE FLYING WASP, ANT-MAN'S GORGEOUS, NEW PARTNER-IN-PERIL!

A DOUBLE-LENGTH ANT-MAN SUPER EPIC!

ANT-MAN and the WASP! VS "the CREATURE from KOSMOS!"

THROUGHOUT HISTORY THERE HAVE BEEN MEN WHO HAVE BECOME LEGENDS, MEN WHO HAVE POSSESSED POWERS BEYOND MORTAL KEN, SO THAT, IN TIME, THOSE MEN HAVE BECOME SUPER-HEROES WHO THRILL THE ENTIRE WORLD! WE ARE ABOUT TO TELL YOU OF SUCH A MAN, THE SCIENTIST KNOWN TO THE WORLD AS HENRY PYM, BUT, KNOWN TO *YOU* AS THE ASTONISHING *ANT-MAN!* AND YOU WILL LEARN HERE, FOR THE FIRST TIME, THE REASON THAT HENRY PYM *BECAME* THE ANT-MAN, THE PAST THAT GNAWS LIKE A CANCER AT THE SOUL OF THIS MAN, GIVING HIM NO REST, DRIVING HIM TO THE STRANGEST ADVENTURES ANY HUMAN BEING HAS EVER KNOWN! YOU WILL SEE HIM FIND A COMPANION TO AID IN HIS SOLITARY FIGHT AGAINST INJUSTICE, TYRANNY, AND CRIME, THE COMPANION WHO WILL BECOME KNOWN AS... *THE WASP!* COME WITH US NOW, AS ANT-MAN AND THE WASP BATTLE THE UN-HUMAN THING FROM BEYOND SPACE AND TIME... *THE CREATURE FROM KOSMOS!*

PLOT....STAN LEE   ART.......JACK KIRBY
SCRIPT..H.E. HUNTLEY   INKING..DON HECK
          LETTERING...ART SIMEK

X-192

A HUGE SOLDIER ANT CLACKS ITS MANDIBLES AS THE ANT-MAN DISMOUNTS ON THE WINDOW SILL OF HENRY PYM'S LABORATORY!

THROUGH HIS CYBERNETIC HELMET THE TINY MAN SENDS ELECTRONIC-WAVE COMMANDS TO HIS HYMENOPTERA COMPANIONS... AND THE ANTS FAR AWAY!

YOU MUST LEAVE NOW, MY FRIENDS! I WILL CALL YOU WHEN THERE IS NEED AGAIN!

AND NOW, IT IS TIME TO RESUME MY *OTHER* IDENTITY!

ALONE IN HIS LABORATORY, ANT-MAN RELEASES HIS GROWTH GAS...

AND SO, ANT-MAN BE-COMES THE SCIENTIST HENRY PYM, A MAN DRIVEN TO RESTLESSNESS BY BITTER MEMORIES!

HE IS TIRED... SO VERY TIRED! IF ONLY HE HAD HELP... HUMAN HELP! BUT IT IS HIS DESTINY NEVER TO REVEAL HIS SECRET TO ANY OTHER HUMAN...

I MUST ALWAYS BE ALONE! IT IS MY FATE! IF ONLY *MARIA* WERE HERE BY MY SIDE! TOGETHER WE COULD... BUT... MARIA IS *GONE*...

AND SO HE SITS, THIS MAN OF SCIENCE, OF LEGEND, AS HIS THOUGHTS GO BACK TO THE PAST...

HELLO, MRS. PYM ...MY BEAUTIFUL MARIA, MY LOVELY WIFE!

HELLO, MR. PYM, MY HANDSOME HUSBAND!

DARLING, DO YOU THINK IT WISE FOR US TO COME BACK TO HUNGARY ON OUR HONEYMOON! YOU AND YOUR FATHER WERE POLITICAL PRISONERS AND...

HUSH, MY LOVE! WE ESCAPED TO YOUR WONDER-FUL COUNTRY! THEY WILL NOT KNOW ME NOW THAT I AM THE WIFE OF AN AMERICAN! I AM MRS. PYM NOW, NOT MARIA TROVAYA!

2

MY FATHER IS SAFE IN AMERICA, WORKING FOR YOUR WONDERFUL COUNTRY! AND I MERELY WISH TO SEE THE PLACES WHERE I SPENT MY CHILDHOOD!

FASTEN YOUR SEAT BELTS, PLEASE, WE ARE ABOUT TO LAND!

Y'KNOW, DARLING, THIS HONEYMOON IS THE FIRST VACATION I'VE TAKEN IN YEARS! NOW I FEEL AS THOUGH I NEVER WANT TO WORK AGAIN...JUST SPEND EVERY MOMENT OF MY LIFE WITH YOU!

HA! YOU ARE BECOMING A LAZY HUSBAND! MY FATHER ALWAYS USED TO SAY, "GO TO THE ANTS, THOU DULLARD!" BUT YOU ARE NOT AN INDUSTRIOUS ANT, ARE YOU, MY LOVE!

I AM MERELY A MAN IN LOVE, MY DARLING!

HERE'S A TAXI TO TAKE US TO THE HOTEL! AND, PERHAPS YOU ARE RIGHT! NO ONE WILL KNOW YOU WERE ONCE MARIA TROVAYA NOW THAT YOU ARE MRS. HENRY PYM!

BUT, SUDDENLY...

YOU WILL NOT MAKE A SOUND, MARIA TROVAYA, OR YOUR AMERICAN HUSBAND WILL BE SHOT!

HENRY!

WHAT IS THIS?

SILENCE, AMERICAN!

HEY! WAIT! YOU CAN'T... -UGH-

AN HOUR LATER, AT THE AMERICAN EMBASSY!

NEVER MIND MY HEAD! IT'S BEEN AN HOUR NOW...

I KNOW MR. PYM! WE ARE DOING ALL WE CAN TO FIND YOUR WIFE! YOU MUST BE PATIENT!

RRR HING

YES! THIS IS HE! YES? OH! I SEE! YES, I--I'LL TELL HIM!

3

YOU MUST BE BRAVE, MY FRIEND! MY PEOPLE HAVE FOUND YOUR WIFE! THERE WAS A NOTE ON HER BODY SAYING THAT THIS IS WHAT HAPPENS TO THOSE WHO ATTEMPT TO ESCAPE FROM BEHIND THE IRON CURTAIN!

MARIA... DEAD? NO! SHE... SHE WAS SO YOUNG, SO BEAUTIFUL, SO WONDERFUL! NO! IT CAN'T BE!

THERE IS MORE! A MESSAGE FROM AMERICA! THE LABORATORY IN WHICH HER FATHER WAS WORKING BLEW UP! SABOTAGE IS FEARED!

THE FIENDS!! THE MERCILESS MURDERERS! WE MUST MAKE THEM PAY!

YOU HEAR? WE MUST MAKE THEM PAY!

CONTROL YOURSELF! MY PEOPLE WILL DO THEIR BEST...

DO THEIR BEST? I'LL FIND THEM! I'LL FIND THE ONES WHO DID THIS! I'LL MAKE THEM PAY! MARIA, I'LL FIND THEM... I SWEAR IT!

WAIT! PYM, YOU CAN'T!

THE YOUNG SCIENTIST WENT BERSERK, AND, WITHIN A FEW DAYS, LANDED IN JAIL ON THE VERGE OF A MENTAL AND PHYSICAL BREAKDOWN!

I... I COULDN'T FIND THEM! I DIDN'T KNOW... DIDN'T KNOW WHERE TO LOOK...

I'VE COME TO HAVE YOU RELEASED AND YOU WILL BE SENT HOME, MY BOY!

IN HIS LABORATORY IN AMERICA, HENRY PYM LIVED WITH THE TERRIBLE TRAGEDY THAT HAD MARRED HIS LIFE, STARING INTO SPACE, TRYING TO RECAPTURE EVERY MOMENT OF THAT WONDERFUL PAST THAT WAS NOW GONE FOREVER!

SHE SAID SOMETHING... MARIA SAID SOMETHING, BUT I CAN'T REMEMBER! WHY DID THIS HAVE TO HAPPEN? OH, MARIA, I... WAIT! I REMEMBER NOW!

I REMEMBER WHAT SHE SAID... "GO TO THE ANTS, THOU SLUGGARD!" YES, SHE WAS RIGHT! I SIT HERE DOING NOTHING WHILE THROUGHOUT THE WORLD, CRIMINALS PROWL, INJUSTICE IS RAMPANT, TYRANNY TRAMPLES THE UNDERDOG!

4

SO I WILL STRIKE *BACK* AT ALL OF IT, WHEREVER ROTTENNESS EXISTS! I AM A SCIENTIST! I WILL USE MY TALENTS, MY KNOWLEDGE TO FIND A WAY...

AND SO, ALONE, HE THREW HIMSELF INTO HIS WORK, DRIVING ALWAYS TO KEEP THE PAINFUL PAST FROM HIS MIND, A MAN POSSESSED, A MAN PUSHED BEYOND THE LIMITS OF SCIENTIFIC REASON BY MEMORIES...

IT WORKS... THE REDUCING GAS WORKS! MY THEORY IS CORRECT! LIVING CELLS *CAN* BE REDUCED IN SIZE BY CHEMICAL MEANS... AND MY GROWTH GAS WILL ENLARGE THEM AGAIN...

"GO TO THE ANTS, THOU SLUGGARD!" IT RANG IN HIS BRAIN, OVER AND OVER, UNTIL THAT FATEFUL DAY WHEN HENRY PYM BECAME...*THE ANT-MAN!*

THE SKEIN OF MEMORY BREAKS AND BRINGS OUR HERO BACK TO THE PRESENT!

YES... I BECAME THE ANT-MAN AND DEVELOPED CLOTHING OF UNSTABLE MOLECULES TO WEAR... THE CYBERNETIC HELMET, COMMUNICATION WITH THE ANTS! ALL THIS AND MORE! BUT IT'S *STILL* NOT ENOUGH!

TOO OFTEN HAVE I COME CLOSE TO DEFEAT! I NEED A *PARTNER!* SOMEONE TO STAND BY, TO CARRY ON IF SOMEDAY I MEET DEFEAT AND DEATH! BUT *WHO?* WHO COULD I EVER TRUST TO KNOW THE SECRETS OF THE ANT-MAN... KNOW MY *TRUE IDENTITY?*

I DON'T KNOW! BUT, PERHAPS SOMEDAY, I SHALL FIND THE ONE, AND WHEN I DO I MUST BE READY! WORK! YES, I WILL WORK, FIND THE WAY TO EQUIP THAT PARTNER TO AID ME IN MY WORK...

FOR WEEKS THE SCIENTIST WORKS, TAKING LITTLE NOURISHMENT OR SLEEP... NEVER PAUSING FOR THE MEMORIES TO COME AGAIN!

YES, IT'S TRUE... THE CELLS OF THE WASP CAN BE MADE TO SPECIALIZE, TO GROW AS LEGS, OR WINGS, OR ANTENNAE... BUT ONLY IN A LIFE FORM OF *MINIATURE* SIZE! *WAIT!* WHAT IS THAT NOISE? OH, IT'S THE DOORBELL...

IMPATIENT AT THE INTERRUPTION, HENRY PYM GOES TO THE DOOR!

WHAT IS IT?

AH, YOU ARE HENRY PYM! I AM DR. VERNON VAN DYNE! YOU ARE QUITE FAMOUS, MR. PYM! SO, I HAVE COME TO VISIT, FOR WE ARE *BOTH* SCIENTISTS AND PERHAPS HAVE MUCH IN COMMON!

5

ER...YES, OF COURSE! COME IN!

THIS IS MY DAUGHTER, JANET!

HOW DO YOU DO, DOCTOR PYM?

SHE...SHE LOOKS SOMEWHAT LIKE *MARIA!* BUT SHE'S MUCH YOUNGER! NOT MUCH MORE THAN A CHILD!

HMMMM, HE'S QUITE HANDSOME! BUT SCIENTISTS ARE SUCH BORES! I PREFER THE *ADVENTUROUS* TYPE, NOT THOSE DULL, INTELLECTUAL BOOK-WORMS!

MR. PYM, I MUST CONFESS THAT MY VISIT IS NOT MERELY SOCIAL! I THINK PERHAPS YOU CAN HELP ME! I HAVE BEEN WORKING ON A GAMMA-RAY BEAM TO PIERCE SPACE AND DETECT SIGNALS FROM OTHER PLANETS! IF THERE *IS* LIFE OUT THERE IN THE GALAXY PERHAPS, THROUGH MY BEAM, WE CAN MAKE CONTACT!

I'VE *HEARD* OF YOUR WORK!

DOCTOR, I'M AFRAID I CAN'T BE OF HELP TO YOU! MY FIELD IS MOLECULAR CELL TRANSITION AND CELL SPECIALIZATION!

I KNOW! BUT I THOUGHT... YOU SEE, THE BEAM NEEDS STRENGTHENING TO REACH....! AH, BUT I SEE YOU ARE NOT INTERESTED! I UNDERSTAND, MR. PYM! EACH MAN TO HIS OWN FIELD! WELL, IT WAS A PLEASURE MEETING YOU!

LET'S GO, DADDY!

YES, YES OF COURSE! GOOD-NIGHT, MR. PYM!

SO MUCH LIKE MARIA! IF SHE WERE NOT SUCH A CHILD....!

SO, HENRY PYM RETURNS TO HIS WORK ON SPECIALIZED CELLS, PAUSING ONLY TO TUNE IN WITH HIS FANTASTIC CYBERNETIC MACHINE TO ELECTRONIC IMPULSE MESSAGES FROM THE VAST ARMY OF ANTS THAT ROAM THE CITY!

TROUBLE ON TEMPLE STREET ...BUT THE POLICE HAVE IT WELL IN HAND! NO NEED FOR THE ANT-MAN!

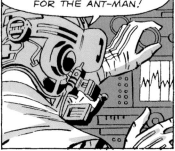

AND DR. VERNON VAN DYNE CONTINUES WITH HIS OWN EXPERIMENT!

I'VE GOT IT! YES, THE BOOSTER IS PUSHING THE RAYS DEEP INTO SPACE...

DADDY, I'M GOING OUT... SOMEPLACE WHERE THERE IS MUSIC AND LAUGHTER AND GAIETY!

BUT, THESE THREE HUMANS DO NOT SUSPECT THAT SOON THEY WILL BE TANGLED TOGETHER IN THE WEB OF FATE, AS THEY CONFRONT THE MOST AWESOME MENACE EVER LET LOOSE UPON OUR UNSUSPECTING WORLD... 6

AH, MY RAYS ARE GOING BEYOND OUR OWN GALAXY...REACHING INTO THE DEPTHS OF SPACE TO OTHER GALAXIES, OTHER WORLDS, STAR WORLDS WE CANNOT EVEN SEE...

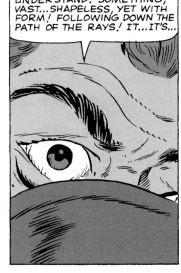

WHAT IS THAT? A DARKNESS... A FLUIDITY...FLUX, WHIRLING ...COMING CLOSER! I DON'T UNDERSTAND! SOMETHING, VAST...SHAPELESS, YET WITH FORM! FOLLOWING DOWN THE PATH OF THE RAYS! IT...IT'S...

OHHHHHHHH...

THE DOCTOR LOOKS AT THE THING THAT IS IN THE ROOM WITH HIM! HIS SENSES REEL, HIS FACE TURNS ASHEN AND EVERYTHING HUMAN WITHIN HIM CRIES OUT IN AGONY AGAINST THIS ALIEN THING...A CREATURE SO UNEARTHLY THAT IT IS ALMOST MORE THAN HUMAN EYES CAN BEAR!

WHAT...WHAT *ARE* YOU?

MALEABLE, A VISCOUS FLOWING, A PRESENCE THAT FILLS THE ROOM, CONSCIENCELESS, HOSTILITY EMANATING FROM IT LIKE A CLOUD OF SNAKES, THE THING ANSWERS IN A SLITHERING VOICE THAT IS NO VOICE, THAT IS A TOUCHING OF THE HUMAN BRAIN WITH WAVES OF MEANING!

I AM FROM THE PLANET KOSMOS, DEEP IN SPACE! WE OF KOSMOS ARE A FLUID FORM OF LIFE! I ESCAPED DOWN THE PATH OF YOUR RAY TO THIS, YOUR PLANET!

E-ESCAPED? YES! I AM A CRIMINAL... THE GREATEST KOSMOS HAS EVER SEEN ...ALONE, I ALMOST SUCCEEDED IN SMASHING KOSMOSIAN SOCIETY, MAKING SLAVES OF THEM ALL! BUT I FAILED! NOW I AM SAFE HERE! HERE I CAN DO WHAT I FAILED TO DO ON KOSMOS! OF COURSE I MUST SMASH YOUR MACHINE TO KEEP ANY FROM *FOLLOWING* ME, FROM MY OWN PLANET AND... I MUST DISPOSE OF YOU, SO NO ONE KNOWS OF MY PRESENCE HERE! LOOK AT ME, EARTHMAN...LOOK... LOOK...

SILENTLY THE SCIENTIST FIGHTS, KEEPING HIS HEAD TURNED FROM THE MONSTER, KNOWING THAT TO LOOK IS TO DIE! BUT THE ALIEN POWER OF THE CREATURE FROM KOSMOS IS NOT TO BE DENIED! VAN DYNE'S HEAD TURNS...SLOWLY...SLOWLY... UNTIL...

IT IS DONE!!

7

LATER, JANET RETURNS HOME...

WHAT IS THAT AWFUL MIST!? SEEMS TO BE COMING FROM DADDY'S LAB! DAD... ARE YOU THERE?

DAD!!! OH, NO!!

I... I MUST HAVE HELP! I MUST CALL SOMEBODY! BUT WHO?? I DON'T KNOW ANYONE WHO...! WAIT... PYM! HENRY PYM! HE'S A SCIENTIST, TOO! DAD TRUSTED HIM...

YES, THIS IS HENRY PYM! JANET VAN DYNE! WHAT? YOUR FATHER...! OH, COME NOW!

THOSE BORED SOCIETY PLAYGIRLS ARE ALL ALIKE! BUT IT'S PRETTY GRUESOME FOR HER TO GET HER KICKS BY MAKING UP A HORROR STORY ABOUT HER FATHER!

LIGHTS FLASHING ON THE CYBERNETIC BOARD...IT MEANS A MESSAGE IS COMING FROM THE ANTS! I HAVE NO TIME TO PLAY GAMES WITH A SPOILED BRAT LIKE JANET VAN DYNE!

WHAT? VAN DYNE KILLED...! THEN SHE WASN'T ACTING... IT'S TRUE!

QUICKLY HENRY PYM RELEASES HIS REDUCING GAS...

BUT THIS IS NOT A JOB FOR HENRY PYM...

IT'S A MISSION FOR... ANT-MAN!

8

I'LL SEND ELECTRONIC WAVES THROUGH MY CYBERNETIC HELMET TO SUMMON ALL THE ANTS IN THE VICINITY TO MEET ME AT VAN DYNE'S LABORATORY!

THE CATAPULT WILL GET ME TO MY DESTINATION IN A HURRY! JUST SET THESE DIALS...

ANT-MAN TRIGGERS THE INGENIOUS CATAPULT MECHANISM AND, A MOMENT LATER, SHOOTS SWIFTLY THROUGH THE AIR!

THE ANTS WILL BE WAITING FOR ME TO FORM A SOFT PLATFORM FOR ME TO LAND ON!

GOOD! NOW TO FIND THE GIRL AND SEE WHAT CAUSED DR. VAN DYNE'S DEATH!

THERE SHE IS... UNAWARE OF MY PRESENCE!

HELLO! I'M ANT-MAN! PERHAPS YOU'VE HEARD OF ME! I'VE COME TO HELP YOU!

I HAVE HEARD OF YOU BUT... I THOUGHT YOU WERE ONLY A MYTH! MY FATHER... HE'S DEAD... IN HIS LABORATORY...

THERE WAS A STRANGE MIST... I CAME IN AND FOUND HIM...

HE'S BEEN MURDERED... ALMOST LOOKS LIKE HE DIED OF FRIGHT! THERE'S SOMETHING STRANGE... SOMETHING EERIE HERE! I CAN SENSE IT!

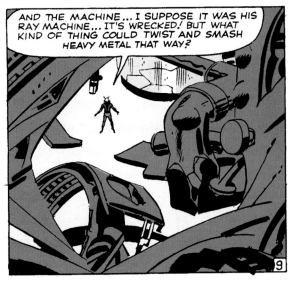
AND THE MACHINE... I SUPPOSE IT WAS HIS RAY MACHINE... IT'S WRECKED! BUT WHAT KIND OF THING COULD TWIST AND SMASH HEAVY METAL THAT WAY?

9

SOMETHING UNEARTHLY, OF AWFUL MENACE AND TERRIBLE POWERS...COMPLETELY **ALIEN**, WAS HERE! BUT **WHAT**... AND HOW DID IT **GET** HERE?

I LOVED MY FATHER! HE WAS THE FINEST MAN ON EARTH! I NEVER SHOWED HIM HOW MUCH I LOVED HIM! I THOUGHT IT WASN'T SOPHISTICATED! NOW I'LL NEVER HAVE THE CHANCE! BUT, THERE IS **ONE** THING I CAN DO... **AVENGE** HIM!

THIS IS SO LIKE MARIA...

CALL IT A WOMAN'S INTUITION IF YOU WISH, BUT I KNOW THAT IT WAS HIS EXPERIMENT TO REACH OUTER SPACE, TO COMMUNICATE WITH OTHER LIFE FORMS ON OTHER PLANETS, THAT WAS THE CAUSE OF HIS DEATH! SOMEHOW I'LL FIND OUT... IF IT TAKES THE REST OF MY LIFE TO DO IT!

SHE'S CHANGED! THE BORED FLIGHTY SHELL SHE WORE IS GONE! SHE HAS DETERMINATION, STRENGTH OF CHARACTER! I WONDER IF **SHE**...?

LISTEN TO ME AND ASK NO QUESTIONS! PHONE THE F.B.I.! ASK FOR LEE KEARNS AND TELL HIM WHAT HAPPENED HERE! THEN GO TO HENRY PYM'S LABORATORY IMMEDIATELY! TRUST ME AND DO AS I TELL YOU!

I **DO** TRUST YOU, ANT-MAN!

TEMPLTON 47900

TUV 8

WXY 9

OPERATOR 0 Z

THAT'S STRANGE... THE ANTS HAVE GONE! THEY'RE ALL DOWN BELOW! THIS IS THE FIRST TIME THEY'VE EVER LEFT ME! WELL, GUESS I'LL HAVE TO SHINNY DOWN THE WATER PIPE...

F.B.I.? I WANT TO SPEAK TO LEE KEARNS...

SECONDS LATER...

WHY DID YOU DESERT ME, MY FRIENDS?

SUDDENLY, THERE IS A STRANGE STIRRING AMONG THE ANT HORDE! MANDIBLES CLICK, AND THE OUTER SKELETON ARMOR OF THE INSECTS MOVES WITH SELF-CONSCIOUS MUSCLE PULL! THEN THE HUGE SOLDIER ANT SENDS OUT ITS MESSAGE WAVES...

THE CREATURE THAT WAS IN THERE... THE MIST IT LEFT... IT CONTAINS TRACES OF FORMIC ACID! IT MUST BE KIN TO US, THE ANTS, FOR WE SECRETE FORMIC ACID, TOO! BUT, IT IS ALIEN AND WE ARE AFRAID!

10

WELL THEN, TAKE ME BACK TO MY LABORATORY, QUICKLY! THEN YOU WILL SPREAD OUT, TRY TO FIND SOME TRACE OF THIS CREATURE! AND SOME OF YOU WILL GO TO THE F.B.I. OFFICES AND SEND ME A MESSAGE OF WHAT THEY FIND OUT!

BACK IN HIS LABORATORY, ANT-MAN RELEASES HIS GROWTH GAS...

AND NOW TO WAIT FOR JANET'S ARRIVAL! I MUST GREET HER AS HENRY PYM!

SECONDS LATER...

JANET... AT THE DOOR! PERHAPS I WAS WRONG IN ASKING HER TO COME HERE, TO CARRY OUT THE PLAN I HAVE IN MIND! PERHAPS,...

DOCTOR PYM! MY FATHER --HE--

I KNOW! AND I KNOW YOU WANT TO AVENGE HIS DEATH! ARE YOU REALLY SERIOUS? WOULD YOU RISK ANYTHING FOR JUSTICE? I MUST KNOW!

I MEANT WHAT I SAID! I SHALL DEDICATE MY LIFE TO FINDING HIS MURDERER! COMING HERE, I HAD TIME TO THINK! I WISH I COULD HELP TRACK DOWN ALL THE CRIMINALS, THE HUMAN WOLVES WHO PREY ON HONEST PEOPLE! I SUPPOSE YOU THINK I'M JUST A FOOLISH FEMALE, BUT...

COME IN HERE, INTO MY LABORATORY, AND SHUT THE DOOR!

I'M GOING TO TELL YOU WHAT NO ONE ELSE IN THE WORLD KNOWS! IN SO DOING, I PUT MY LIFE IN YOUR HANDS! BUT, I TELL YOU BECAUSE I NEED A PARTNER... AND I HAVE CHOSEN HER! I AM... THE ANT-MAN!

YOU...? BUT, OF COURSE! HOW ELSE COULD YOU HAVE KNOWN ABOUT... BUT YOU SAID YOU HAVE CHOSEN A... PARTNER?

YES! I CAN MAKE YOU SMALL AS ANT-MAN WITH MY SHRINKING GAS! AND, DUE TO MY RESEARCH IN CELL SPECIALIZATION, I CAN GIVE YOU WINGS, ANTENNAE, I CAN MAKE YOU A HUMAN WASP! YES! ANT-MAN AND THE WASP! WE WILL FIND YOUR FATHER'S MURDERER AND BRING JUSTICE TO ALL WHO NEED IT! WHAT IS YOUR ANSWER, JANET VAN DYNE?

YES! I SAY, YES! SHOW ME HOW AND I WILL STAND BESIDE YOU ALWAYS... TO AVENGE MY FATHER'S DEATH! I SWEAR IT!

11

DO YOU SEE THOSE SYNTHETIC CELLS IN THE MICROSCOPIC FIELD? THEY ARE SPECIALIZED CELLS! I CAN IMPLANT THEM BELOW YOUR SKIN TISSUE! IT WILL LEAVE NO SCAR, BUT WHEN YOU ARE REDUCED TO THE SIZE OF A WASP YOU WILL GROW WINGS AND TINY ANTENNAE!

IT...IT ALL SOUNDS SO UNBELIEVABLE... SO WONDERFUL!

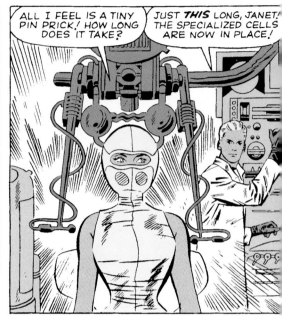

ALL I FEEL IS A TINY PIN PRICK! HOW LONG DOES IT TAKE?

JUST THIS LONG, JANET! THE SPECIALIZED CELLS ARE NOW IN PLACE!

MEANWHILE, AT THE BUILDING THAT HOUSES DR. VAN DYNE'S LABORATORY...

RUN! IT'S AN EARTHQUAKE!

HELP!!

KEEP BACK! THE BUILDING IS COLLAPSING!

AND, AT THE DOCKS NEARBY, A FEW MINUTES LATER...

HEY, FEEL THAT, JOE? THE WHOLE DOCK'S SHAKIN'!

SEEMS TO BE COMIN' FROM BEHIND US!

LOOK! OVER THERE... WHA--WHAT IS IT?

RUN! RUN... YELL TO THE OTHERS TO GET OFF THE DOCKS...

AND SO THE WORLD FIRST MEETS THE CREATURE FROM KOSMOS!

WHILE, IN HENRY PYM'S LABORATORY...

ELECTRONIC IMPULSES COMING FROM MY ANT SCOUTS! JANET, IN THE CLOSET IS A COSTUME WOVEN FROM UNSTABLE MOLECULES THAT WILL EXPAND AND SHRINK AS YOU DO! I HAVE A FEELING THIS IS OUR FIRST MISSION!

12

CYBERNETIC UNITS IN THE MACHINE TRANSLATE THE INCOMING SIGNALS INTO HUMAN SPEECH, AS JANET VAN DYNE DONS HER NEW COSTUME...

F.B.I. SAYS VAN DYNE KILLED BY STRANGE ELEMENT AKIN TO FEAR... ENTIRE SYSTEM RUPTURED! F.B.I., POLICE, MILITARY CALLED OUT TO FIGHT ALIEN MENACE! VAN DYNE HOUSE SMASHED AS THOUGH BY GIANT HAND! DOCKS NEARBY UPROOTED, SMASHED!

ALIEN THING ADVANCING TOWARD GEORGE WASHINGTON BRIDGE! POLICE CLEARING MANHATTAN! MILITARY STANDING BY, READY TO FIRE!

THIS IS IT, JANET! THAT IS THE THING THAT KILLED YOUR FATHER! SOMEHOW YOUR FATHER'S SPACE PROBE MACHINE BROUGHT THAT UNEARTHLY MENACE DOWN TO OUR PLANET!

HERE, DON THIS BELT! THE CYLINDERS CONTAIN YOUR REDUCING AND GROWTH GASSES! PRESS THE BOTTOM BUTTON...LIKE THIS!!

I SEE!

THE MIRACULOUS VAPOR ENGULFS THEM AND THEY SHRINK... SMALLER... SMALLER... SMALLER...

OH! IT FEELS SO--SO WEIRD!

YOU'LL GET USED TO IT, JANET!

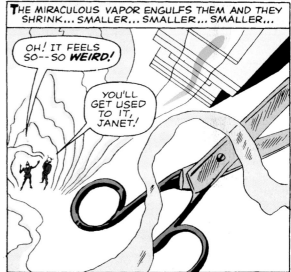

AND, AS SHE SHRINKS TO MINUTENESS, GOSSAMER, DAINTY WINGS SPROUT FROM JANET'S SHOULDERS AND TINY, DELICATE ANTENNAE ADORN HER FOREHEAD! THE LOVELY GIRL HAS TRULY BECOME... THE WASP!

THE SPECIALIZED CELLS... THEY WORK!! I CAN HEAR THINGS THROUGH MY ANTENNAE!

THE VOICES OF THE INSECT WORLD... AS I HEAR THEM THROUGH MY CYBERNETIC HELMET! COME, NOW YOU WILL TRY YOUR WINGS!

SHOT INTO SPACE BY HIS CATAPULT, ANT-MAN FINDS HIS COMPANION CLOSE BESIDE HIM AS HE FLIES SWIFTLY THROUGH THE AIR!

THIS IS EXHILIRATING! WHERE ARE WE GOING?

TO THE GEORGE WASHINGTON BRIDGE! I'VE ORDERED THE ANTS TO GATHER THERE!

ANT-MAN... I THINK YOU'RE WONDERFUL! I WANT YOU TO KNOW, IN CASE THIS CREATURE KILLS US, AS IT DID MY FATHER, I-I'M FALLING IN LOVE WITH YOU!

13

NO! YOU MUSTN'T **SAY** THAT, JANET! YOU'RE ONLY A CHILD! LET'S GET THIS STRAIGHT... I CHOSE YOU AS MY PARTNER SIMPLY BECAUSE I THOUGHT YOU HAD A REASON, AS **I** HAVE, TO FIGHT FOR MANKIND!

I NEVER WANT TO LOVE AGAIN! I--I COULDN'T BEAR IT IF I HAD TO LOSE A LOVED ONE-- TWICE!

SO I'M ONLY A **CHILD**, AM I?? WELL, MISTER ANT-MAN... WE SHALL **SEE!**

SHE IS SO LIKE MARIA...HER BEAUTY... HER SPIRIT!! I MUST BE CAREFUL LEST I **DO** FALL IN LOVE WITH HER!

THIS IS MY PARTNER, **THE WASP!** YOU WILL BE TO HER AS YOU ARE TO ME! NOW, MY FRIENDS, TOGETHER WE WILL DEFEAT THIS STRANGE MENACE FROM SPACE!

WE **CANNOT** AID YOU THIS TIME, ANT-MAN! THIS CREATURE... THERE IS SOMETHING ABOUT IT THAT PREVENTS US FROM APPROACHING IT! WE CANNOT!

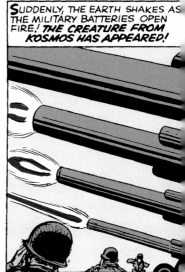

SUDDENLY, THE EARTH SHAKES AS THE MILITARY BATTERIES OPEN FIRE! **THE CREATURE FROM KOSMOS HAS APPEARED!**

NOTHING STOPS IT! SHELLS, BULLETS, MEAN NOTHING TO IT! IT...IT'S TERRIBLE... FORMLESS! I CAN'T **LOOK** AT IT!

DON'T LOOK AT IT, OR YOU'RE LOST! RETREAT! PULL BACK! PASS THE WORD!

THE MOST MODERN WEAPONS WON'T STOP IT! AND WITH-OUT THE ANTS WE HAVE HARDLY A CHANCE!

THAT AWFUL THING KILLED MY FATHER! IF **YOU'RE** AFRAID, I'M NOT!

THE WASP FLIES STRAIGHT TOWARD THE TOWERING, SOULLESS MONSTROSITY...

WASP, COME BACK! YOU FOOL CHILD! **COME BACK!**

I'LL **SHOW** HIM I'M **NOT** A CHILD!

14

...LIEN, MIASMIC TENTACLES LICK OUT AT THE TINY FLYING FIGURE, REACHING FORMLESS FOG-FINGERS, LIKE TRICKLES OF DOOM... BUT STILL SHE FLIES CLOSER--CLOSER--UNTIL HE SEEMS TO DRAW HER TO HIM...

DESPERATELY ANT-MAN CLIMBS ATOP THE STEEL GIRDERS...

DON'T **LOOK** AT THE THING! TURN YOUR HEAD! I'M COMING...

I CAN'T **HELP** MYSELF! I'M BEING DRAWN TOWARDS HIM!

HURLING HIMSELF INTO SPACE, **ANTMAN** SEIZES THE WASP'S HAND, HIS WEIGHT CARRYING HER DOWN, AWAY FROM THE CREATURE FROM KOSMOS...

GOT YOU!

DON'T YOU TRY ANYTHING LIKE THAT AGAIN! I DIDN'T SAY I WAS QUITTING! I'VE JUST GOT TO FIND A **WAY** TO FIGHT THAT THING! AND I THINK I'VE **FOUND** IT NOW!

GOT TO RUSH BACK TO THE LABORATORY! THE MIST... WHAT THE ANTS SAID... IT ALL ADDS UP! THIS CREATURE IS NOT MADE AS WE ARE! IT IS AN ACID SPECIES, COMPOSED MAINLY OF FORMIC ACID...

MINUTES LATER, IN HENRY PYM'S LAB...

ON THE SHELF IN THE CLOSET YOU'LL FIND A 12 GAUGE SHOTGUN AND SOME SHELLS! BRING THEM HERE AND EMPTY OUT THE SHELLS!

YES SIR, BOSS MAN!

MAN USES FORMIC ACID AS A DYE! MEDIEVAL DOCTORS DISTILLED THE ACID FROM ANTS, BUT MODERN MAN USES AN OXALIC BASE... AND THE ANTIDOTE? YES, HERE IT IS...

15

HELP ME FILL THESE SHELLS ...*HURRY!*

WHAT *IS* THIS STUFF?

THE *ANTIDOTE* TO FORMIC ACID! CERTAIN SPECIES OF ANTS USE THE ACID TO STING AND KILL ENEMIES! WE ARE FILLING THESE SHELLS WITH THE ANTIDOTE! AND, JANET...

YES?

PRAY THAT MY THINKING IS RIGHT! IF IT ISN'T, THIS COULD VERY WELL BE THE END OF OUR WORLD, THE END OF MANKIND AS WE KNOW IT! NOW, WE MUST BECOME *ANT-MAN* AND *THE WASP* AGAIN! ARE YOU READY?

YOU *KNOW* I AM!

AND SO...

BUT NOW, HOW CAN WE CARRY THE RIFLE AND THE SHELLS?

MY FRIENDS, THE ANTS SHALL DO THAT *FOR* US!

ANT-MAN SENDS OUT SIGNALS TO THE ANTS, AND...

CARRY THOSE! WE MUST HURRY! WHERE IS THE ALIEN *NOW?*

WALL STREET! NOTHING STOPS HIM! EVERY WEAPON HAS FAILED!

*S*O THE STRANGE PROCESSION BEGINS ITS MARCH, AS THE FATE OF MANKIND RESTS ON THE TINY SHOULDERS OF ANT-MAN AND THE WASP!

SHELLS

16

THERE IT *IS*, AHEAD! NOW, MY HEXAPODA FRIENDS, I DO NOT ASK YOU TO FIGHT THIS CREATURE! JUST OBEY MY COMMANDS AND YOU WILL ONLY TAKE A PASSIVE PART IN THIS! UP THE BUILDING HERE TO THE ROOF!

BUT, *ANT-MAN*, WHAT...?

QUIET, GIRL! I'VE GOT TO THINK THIS OUT!

BUT HOW CAN YOU *LOAD* IT... PULL THE TRIGGER? EVERYTHING IS SO *HUGE*...

YOU WILL FIND, AS I HAVE, THAT THOUGH YOU ARE REDUCED IN SIZE, YOU STILL RETAIN MUCH OF THE STRENGTH OF A FULL-GROWN HUMAN! SEE?

AND NOW, STAND BY WITH OTHER SHELLS READY FOR ME TO LOAD!

HERE IT COMES! OH, THE LOATHSOME THING...

ANT-MAN PULLS THE TRIGGER AS THE ANTS ABSORB THE RECOIL... AND, WITH THE BLAST AND CHARGE GO A FERVENT PRAYER...

BOOOM

NOTHING'S HAPPENED! IT'S *STILL* ADVANCING!

DON'T *LOOK* AT IT!

BOOOMM

17

SUDDENLY THE HORRIBLE MIST FILLS THE AIR... A SOUNDLESS SCREAMING VIBRATED INTO NOTHINGNESS...

IT--IT'S STOPPED! IT SEEMS TO BE FALLING APART... WAVERING... SECTIONS ARE BLOTTING OUT...

IT WORKED! YOUR ANTIDOTE WORKED!

LIKE ROTTING TENDRILS OF SOME EVIL, ALIEN PLANT, THE CREATURE FALLS, WRITHING, VANISHING AS THE FORMIC ACID ANTIDOTE CHARGES ENTER THE NOXIOUS SUBSTANCE THAT WAS THE ALIEN BEING OF THE CREATURE FROM KOSMOS...

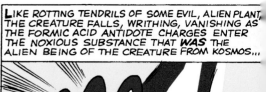

BOOOOOOM!

IT--IT'S VANISHING! IT'S FADING AWAY!

YES! WE'VE WON... WE'VE WON!

ER... WE--WE'D BETTER GET BACK TO THE LAB! AND FROM NOW ON YOU MUST NOT DISPLAY SUCH EMOTION! IT-- IT ISN'T PROPER!

HE'S BLUSHING... AND PRETENDING THAT HE DIDN'T FEEL ANY EMOTION AT ALL!

ONCE AGAIN NORMAL-SIZED, HENRY PYM PUTS IN A CALL TO THE F.B.I. ON A TELEPHONE WITH A SCRAMBLER SO THAT THE CALL CANNOT BE TRACED!

HELLO! LEE KEARNS! THIS IS THE ANT-MAN! THE MENACE IS OVER! THE PEOPLE CAN BE BROUGHT BACK TO THEIR HOMES AND BUILDING CAN RESUME...

ANT-MAN, LISTEN... I WANT TO MEET YOU, TALK TO YOU! WE'RE BOTH FIGHTING THE SAME THINGS! WE CAN HELP EACH OTHER! LOOK, YOU CAN'T KEEP ON GOING IT ALONE..

I'M NOT GOING IT ALONE, KEARNS ...NOT ANYMORE... NOT EVER AGAIN!

NO, MY DARLING! I WILL ALWAYS BE BESIDE YOU! AND SOMEDAY I WILL MAKE YOU REALIZE THAT YOU LOVE ME AS I LOVE YOU! BUT, UNTIL THAT DAY COMES, IT WILL BE AS YOU WANT IT...JUST PARTNERS... THE ANT-MAN AND THE WASP FIGHTING SIDE BY SIDE!

THE END

TALES TO ASTONISH

APPROVED BY THE COMICS CODE AUTHORITY

45 JULY

MARVEL COMICS GROUP 12¢

NO, NO, ANT-MAN! STAY BACK!! IT'S A *TRAP!* DON'T TRY TO SAVE ME!

IT'S NO USE! *GASP!* HE CAN'T HEAR ME! *NOTHING* CAN SAVE US NOW!

THAT'S *IT*, ANT-MAN! YOU'VE BLUNDERED INTO MY TRAP! AND NOW, WHEN I PULL THIS SWITCH, I'LL BE RID OF YOU-- *FOREVER!*

MORE VILLAINOUS, MORE DEADLY THAN EVER! DON'T DARE MISS..... "THE *RETURN* OF EGGHEAD!"

ANT-MAN and THE WASP CAUGHT IN "THE TERRIBLE TRAPS OF EGGHEAD!"

THIS TIME YOU LOSE, ANT-MAN! THIS TIME YOU DIE! THE MOST PERFECT ANT KILLER IN THE WORLD... THE ANT-EATER! LOVELY, ISN'T IT, ANT-MAN? A LOVELY, INTRICATE SCHEME TO TRAP YOU, AND THEN... THE SIMPLE, FOOL-PROOF, ESCAPE-PROOF END OF ANT-MAN!

FEAR IS RUNNING THROUGH THE ANTS LIKE WILDFIRE! THEY CAN'T HELP US THIS TIME, ANT-MAN! WHAT ARE WE GOING TO DO?

IT'S THE MOST DEADLY TRAP WE'VE EVER BEEN IN! BUT THERE HAS TO BE A WAY OUT... THERE HAS TO!

PLOT.............STAN LEE
SCRIPT.........H.E. HUNTLEY
ART.............DON HECK
LETTERING...ART SIMEK

EGGHEAD, THE MOST BRILLIANT ANTAGONIST THE ANT-MAN HAS EVER FACED, RETURNS AGAIN, HIS TWISTED MIND EATEN WITH BITTERNESS AND THE GALLING ACHE FOR VENGEANCE! NO LIVING MAN HAD EVER DEFEATED THE SINISTER SCIENTIST BEFORE, EXCEPT THE *ANT-MAN,* AND THAT DEFEAT MUST BE WIPED OUT...

LET US GO BACK FOR A MOMENT AND RECAPTURE THE THRILLS OF THE FIRST TIME THAT EGGHEAD AND ANT-MAN CLASHED! REMEMBER, IT BEGAN WHEN THE EVIL MENTAL MASTER WAS DISCHARGED FROM THE GOVERNMENT'S ATOMIC RESEARCH CENTER...

YOU ARE BENEATH CONTEMPT! A MAN WITH YOUR GREAT MENTALITY AND SCIENTIFIC GENIUS, ATTEMPTING TO SELL SECRET ATOMIC INFORMATION...

BAH! TO A GENIUS LIKE ME, YOUR INSIPID PATRIOTIC PHRASES ARE LAUGHABLE! I SNEER AT YOU ALL!

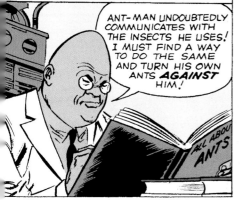

CONTACTED BY THE UNDERWORLD, EGGHEAD AGREED TO CONCENTRATE HIS GREAT BRAINPOWER ON DESTROYING THE ANT-MAN! WITH COLD, SCIENTIFIC PRECISION HE UNDERTOOK HIS DANGEROUS TASK...

ANT-MAN UNDOUBTEDLY COMMUNICATES WITH THE INSECTS HE USES! I MUST FIND A WAY TO DO THE SAME AND TURN HIS OWN ANTS *AGAINST* HIM!

ALL ABOUT ANTS

FINALLY...

COMPLETED... A MACHINE THAT CAN TRANSLATE WORDS INTO ELECTRONIC IMPULSES WHICH THE ANTS WILL PICK UP THROUGH THEIR ANTENNAE! NOW I WILL INVADE THE ANT-MAN'S OWN DOMAIN!

EGGHEAD QUICKLY PUT HIS SCHEME TO WORK! HE COMMUNICATED WITH THE ANTS!

OBEY MY INSTRUCTIONS, YOU OF THE ANT KINGDOM, AND I SHALL FREE YOU FROM ANT-MAN'S RULE!

WITH THE HELP OF THE CRIMINALS WHO EMPLOYED HIM, EGGHEAD COMMITTED A COLORFUL ROBBERY TO LURE ANT-MAN TO THE SCENE! AND THEN...

HA, THE BELLOWS SUCKED YOU UP AND DROPPED YOU IN THE BOX LINED WITH *FLYPAPER!* YOU'RE HELPLESS!

NOT QUITE, EGGHEAD! THESE ELECTRONICALLY CONTROLLED SPRINGS IN THE BOTTOM OF MY SHOES CAN BREAK THE FYYPAPER'S HOLD!

SPOOIINGG!

2

THEN, AIDED BY HIS ANTS, ANT-MAN USED SOME FLYPAPER OF HIS OWN... A HUGE SHEET THE ANTS DROPPED UPON THE FLEEING CRIMINALS!

EGGHEAD HAD MADE HIS ESCAPE AND, IN HIDING, LISTENED TO ANT-MAN EXPLAIN HOW HE HAD DEFEATED THE UNSCRUPULOUS SCIENTIST...

EGGHEAD TRIED TO APPEAL TO THE ANTS' SENSE OF GREED AND VANITY! BUT INSECTS HAVE NO SUCH EMOTIONS! EGGHEAD MISUNDERSTOOD THE PSYCHOLOGY OF THE ANTS... THEY AREN'T MY SLAVES, THEY ARE MY FRIENDS AND PARTNERS!

DEFEATED, HUNTED, THE ONCE BRILLIANT SCIENTIST, HIS CONFIDENCE SHAKEN, BECAME A BUM IN A BOWERY FLOP-HOUSE!

ALL HE DOES IS MUTTER ABOUT ANTS! MUST BE SOME KINDA NUT!

THE ANTS... THEY WERE TOO SMART FOR ME... THEY DEFEATED ME... THE ANTS DEFEATED ME!

YES, IT ALL HAPPENED MONTHS AGO! BUT LAST NIGHT, IN THAT SAME FLOPHOUSE...

HE GOT ALL THE OTHERS! WE WERE LUCKY TO GET AWAY, TWISTER!

YEAH! I TELL YUH, APE WITH THE ANT-MAN LOOSE, AN HONEST CRIMINAL DOESN'T STAND A CHANCE! 'SPECIALLY NOW HE'S GOT THE WASP WITH HIM...

WHAT WAS THAT YOU SAID? YOU SPOKE OF THE ANT-MAN!!

LET GO, YUH KOOK! FORGET WHAT I SAID! ME AN' APE AIN'T BEEN HERE IF THE COPS ASK YOU! GET IT?!!

YOU DON'T UNDERSTAND! THE ANT-MAN DEFEATED ME, TOO! LISTEN, WE CAN HELP EACH OTHER!

SHOULD I SQUASH THIS BUM, TWISTER?

HOLD IT, APE! IT WON'T HURT TO LISTEN!

IT HAD BEEN BUILDING UP INSIDE HIM, THE HATE, THE NEED FOR REVENGE AND SUDDENLY DESPAIR LEFT EGG-HEAD TO BE REPLACED BY A DRIVING VICIOUS NEED TO ENCOUNTER AGAIN THE MAN WHO DEFEATED HIM!

I'M GOING TO TELL YOU WHO I AM AND THEN YOU'LL UNDERSTAND! A PLAN IS BEGINNING TO FORM IN MY MIND! YOU MENTIONED THE WASP! TELL ME ALL ABOUT HER...

"...AND THAT'S THE WHOLE STORY! ANT-MAN AND THE WASP ARE PARTNERS NOW!...LOOK, I REMEMBER HOW YOU ALMOST BEAT THE ANT-MAN! APE AND ME'LL WORK WITH YOU!"

GOOD! FIRST, WE MUST FIND SOME HIDDEN PLACE WHERE I CAN SET UP A LABORATORY...AND I MUST TAKE A NEW IDENTITY! YES, THE PLAN IS BEGINNING TO FORM...

EVERY MAN HAS HIS ACHILLES HEEL! WE WILL STRIKE AT ANT-MAN THROUGH HIS... THE WASP! WE WILL CAPTURE HER AND USE HER AS THE BAIT FOR OUR TRAP TO CAPTURE THE ANT-MAN!

AND THIS TIME I SHALL NOT FAIL! I KNOW MY ANTAGONIST BETTER, AND I AM MORE FULLY AWARE OF HIS POWERS! THROUGH THE WASP I SHALL CRUSH HIM FOREVER! FIRST, I SHALL NEED SOME SCIENTIFIC EQUIPMENT...

IN THE CELLAR OF A DESERTED BUILDING THE SINISTER TRIO MAKE THEIR HEADQUARTERS AS EGGHEAD SETS UP HIS LAB...

WITH THIS MACHINE, I'LL BE ABLE TO INTERCEPT, EVEN SCRAMBLE, MESSAGES THE ANTS SEND TO ANT-MAN...

OKAY, OKAY! BUT WHEN WE GONNA GET INTO HIGH GEAR?

SOON! FIRST, I MUST COMPLETE MY DISGUISE AND ESTABLISH MYSELF AS PROFESSOR CARL STRIKER, ZOOLOGIST! BE PATIENT...OUR FOE IS POWERFUL...WE MUST NOT FAIL A SECOND TIME!

THUS, EGGHEAD PUTS HIS PLAN INTO ACTION, STEP BY CAUTIOUS STEP!

...SO YOU SEE, DEAR LADIES, INSECTS CAN BE OUR FRIENDS, AS WELL AS OUR ENEMIES! THE PROBLEM IS TO UNDERSTAND THEM, TO STUDY AND APPRECIATE THE INTRICACIES OF THE INSECT WORLD! I THANK YOU!

WONDERFUL! A BRILLIANT LECTURE!

MOST INTERESTING MEETING WE'VE EVER HAD! SUCH A FASCINATING MAN!

CLAP CLAP CLAP CLAP

4

AMONG THE LARGE AUDIENCE AT ONE OF PROFESSOR STRIKER'S LECTURES, ARE THE FAMOUS SCIENTISTS, HENRY PYM AND YOUNG JANET VAN DYNE, DAUGHTER OF THE DECEASED SCIENTIST, DR. VERNON VAN DYNE!

SOMEHOW THAT MAN, PROFESSOR STRIKER, SEEMS FAMILIAR! BUT I CAN'T REMEMBER WHERE OR HOW WE MET!

HE MUST BE A VERY BRILLIANT MAN... HE SOUNDS SO SURE OF HIMSELF!

TO THOSE WHO SURROUND THEM IN THE CROWD THEY SEEM TO BE JUST A HANDSOME, SERIOUS, INTELLIGENT YOUNG MAN AND A LOVELY YOUNG GIRL! BUT, IN REALITY, THEY ARE--

ANT-MAN and-- --the WASP!

THE TIME HAS COME! I'VE BEEN ASKED TO LECTURE AT THE CITY ZOO! IT'S WHAT I'VE BEEN WAITING FOR! WE WILL BUILD A FASCINATING EXHIBIT ABOUT... WASPS! I DON'T THINK THE REAL WASP... WHOEVER SHE IS... WILL BE ABLE TO RESIST IT!!

BUT HOW'S THAT GONNA CATCH ANT-MAN?

AND I'VE BEEN THINKIN' EGGHEAD, WHAT'S IN IT FOR US WHEN WE GET ANT-MAN?

FIRST, APE; I WILL USE BAIT TO CATCH THE WASP JUST AS I WILL USE HER AS BAIT TO CATCH ANT-MAN! ONCE THE ANT-MAN IS OUT OF THE WAY, I WILL MASTERMIND A SERIES OF PERFECT CRIMES THAT WILL MAKE US ALL AS RICH AS CROESUS AND COMPLETELY SAFE FROM THE POLICE! THAT SHOULD ANSWER YOUR QUESTIONS!!

IN HIS LABORATORY, EGGHEAD AND HIS CRIMINAL COHORTS BEGIN THEIR WORK, AS THE RADIO BLARES...

EACH OF THESE EXHIBITS MUST BE PERFECT... POTTER WASP, MUD DAUBER, MASON WASP, PAPER WASP, BALD FACE HORNET...

...AND THE MIDDLETON DIAMOND HAS BEEN PLACED IN THE HANDS OF THE FAMOUS DIAMOND CUTTER, ANTON MYERS, TO CUT INTO A PENDANT FOR THE PRICELESS LADY ELIZABETH NECKLACE!

HEAR THAT? WE SHOULD BE...

YES, APE... AND WE WILL! THAT IS THE BAIT WE WILL USE TO LURE THE WASP INTO OUR CLUTCHES!

SEVERAL DAYS LATER AT THE ZOO...

PLACE THAT ONE OVER THERE!

DON'T KNOW WHY YOU CHOOSE THE REPTILE HOUSE FOR YOUR EXHIBIT AND LECTURE, PROFESSOR!

'CAUSE IT'S WARM! NOW LET'S HAVE LESS LIP, EH?

AFTER THE ZOO ATTENDANT LEAVES...

THAT GUY HAD A POINT! ONLY ONE THING IN THE WORLD I'M SCARED OF... *SNAKES!*

WE HAVE NO TIME FOR FEAR OF ANYTHING! LET'S GET BACK TO THE LAB...

AN HOUR LATER...

THIS IS A BLUEPRINT OF ANTON MEYER'S DIAMOND-CUTTING ESTABLISHMENT! THE EMINENT PROFESSOR STRIKER VISITED HIM THE OTHER DAY! HA! YOU SEE WHERE THE BURGLAR ALARM WIRES ARE SITUATED...

WOW! WITH A BLUEPRINT LIKE THAT, WE CAN'T MISS! WHEN DO WE HIT THE JOINT?

TONIGHT! TWISTER, THIS IS AN ELECTRONIC DEWELDING GUN I'VE CREATED! WITH IT, YOU'LL BE ABLE TO BURN THE ALARM WIRES APART WITHOUT SETTING OFF THE ALARM! APE, YOU WILL CARRY MY INSECT MESSAGE INTERCEPTOR!

THAT NIGHT, A SLEEPING-GAS GUN TAKES CARE OF THE WATCHMAN IN THE DIAMOND CUTTER'S BUILDING

QUICKLY, APE! GIVE ME THE MACHINE...

I'LL GET TO WORK ON THE ALARM WIRES!

I THINK IT WOULDA BEEN EASIER IF WE JUST GRABBED THE ICE, AND...

IT'S BEST IF YOU DON'T TRY TO THINK, APE! YOU HAVEN'T THE EQUIPMENT! NOW I'LL SEND OUT ELECTRICAL IMPULSES THAT WILL JAM AND SCRAMBLE THE MESSAGES THE WATCHDOG ANTS WILL SEND THE ANT-MAN!

AND, IN HENRY PYM'S LABORATORY...

MESSAGE COMING IN FROM ANTS BUT I CAN'T MAKE IT OUT! SOMEONE'S FIGURED OUT HOW ANT-MAN GETS HIS INFORMATION AND IS SCRAMBLING THE IMPULSES!

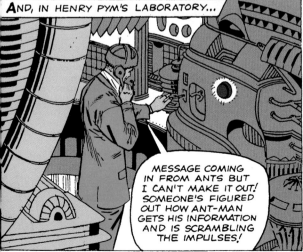

A FEW MINUTES LATER, IN THE APARTMENT OF THE LOVELY SOCIALITE PLAYGIRL, JANET VAN DYNE...

HELLO! YES, THIS IS SHE! *ANT-MAN??!* I'LL BE RIGHT OVER!

6

MINUTES LATER...

WHAT IS IT, HENRY?

IT'S SERIOUS, JANET! I WANT YOU TO WAIT HERE ON STANDBY! THERE MAY BE NEED FOR THE ANT-MAN AND THE WASP TONIGHT! LISTEN, I'LL TELL YOU ALL ABOUT IT...

SAY!! A HUNK OF ICE THIS BIG COULD SET US UP FOR LIFE!

PROFESSOR, I'VE GOT TO HAND IT TO YOU!

BAH! WHEN I FINISH OFF ANT-MAN THIS WILL BE PEANUTS! COME! WE MUST GO NOW!

THEN, IN HENRY PYM'S LAB, AFTER AN HOUR'S VIGIL, THE ELECTRONIC COMMUNICATIONS MACHINE SUDDENLY CLEARS UP...

ROBBERY AT DIAMOND CUTTER'S ...ANTON MYERS...

THE MIDDLETON DIAMOND... THE FAMOUS NECKLACE... WE MUST HURRY...

QUICKLY USING HIS SHRINKING GAS, HENRY PYM BECOMES THE ANT-MAN AND JANET VAN DYNE, THE WASP...

I'LL USE MY CATAPULT TO SHOOT ME THERE! IT'S 22 MAIDEN LANE! MEET ME THERE!

I'LL RACE YOU TO THE SPOT, PARTNER!

A FEW SECONDS LATER...

YOUR CATAPULT IS STILL FASTER THAN MY WINGS!

FOLLOW ME! I'VE SENT A MESSAGE TO THE ANTS... THEY'RE WAITING!

AH! A PERFECT CUSHION FOR MY LANDING, AS USUAL!

A FEW MINUTES LATER, ANT-MAN AND THE WASP ARRIVE AT THE SCENE OF THE CRIME!

TOO LATE! THE DIAMOND AND THE NECKLACE ARE GONE!

I WAS AFRAID OF THAT WHEN THE MESSAGES WERE SCRAMBLED! WHOEVER DID THIS IS REALLY CLEVER! I'LL BET THERE WON'T BE A CLUE TO BE FOUND HERE!

7

AFTER AN EXHAUSTIVE SEARCH, ANT-MAN'S WORDS PROVE TO BE PROPHETIC!

YOU WERE RIGHT, ANT-MAN... NOT A CLUE!

WHOEVER IT WAS IS BOUND TO STRIKE AGAIN... AND NEXT TIME WE'LL BE READY FOR HIM! NOW I'VE GOT SOME *THINKING* TO DO!

AND, AT THE SECRET LAB OF *EGGHEAD*, ALIAS PROF. CARL STRIKER...

WE *DID* IT! NOW WE GOTTA FENCE THESE THINGS AND LAY LOW UNTIL...

FOOLS! ALL YOU SEE IS WHAT IS IN FRONT OF YOUR EYES! THESE ARE MERELY THE *BAIT* TO CATCH THE WASP, AND ANT-MAN!

BAIT? NO YUH DON'T! HAND 'EM BACK, BIG BRAIN OR I'LL PULVERIZE YA!

I'M WITH APE! WE GOT THE LOOT, WORTH MORE DOUGH THAN WE EVER DREAMED OF! WHO CARES ABOUT THE WASP AND ANT-MAN *NOW?!*

IDIOTS! ANT-MAN WILL EVENTUALLY TRACK YOU DOWN! YOU'LL NEVER BE FREE TO SPEND YOUR MONEY! YOU MUST TRUST ME! HAVEN'T I DONE WELL SO FAR?

...I GUESS SO..., ALL RIGHT, WE'LL STRING ALONG!

GOOD! NOW GET THAT FINE WIRE! WE'VE GOT WORK TO DO AT THE ZOO...

FOR THE REST OF THE NIGHT THE STRANGE TRIO WORK IN THE REPTILE HOUSE OF THE ZOO...

WHAT'S IN THIS BOX? IT'S SOMETHIN' ALIVE... AND IT WEIGHS PLENTY!

A SURPRISE FOR *ANT-MAN!* THERE, THE SWITCH IS IN PLACE! ONCE ANT-MAN ENTERS, I'LL PULL THE LEVER AND SEND ELECTRICAL CURRENT THROUGH THE WIRES WE'VE STRUNG AT EVERY CRACK THAT AN ANT CAN CRAWL THRU!

PUT THAT AQUARIUM UNDER THE NEST! NOW TO WIRE THE LITTLE TRAP DOOR AT THE BOTTOM!

THIS IS A WASTE OF TIME! WHY DON'TCHA JUST STEP ON HIM WHEN HE SHOWS UP?

8

HE'S NOT THAT EASY TO STEP ON, MY FRIEND! BESIDES, IT'S PART OF MY PLAN! THE JEWELS SHALL LURE THE WASP HERE...

HOW DO YOU KNOW THE WASP WILL SHOW UP?

HOW COULD SHE RESIST COMING TO AN EXHIBITION ABOUT WASPS? THEN, SHE'LL SEE THE JEWELS AND RECOGNIZE THEM... AND WHEN SHE TRIES TO RETRIEVE THEM... WE'LL *HAVE* HER!

THE NEXT DAY...

MANY WASPS USE THEIR STING TO RENDER OTHER INSECTS UNCONSCIOUS, THEN DRAG THEM TO THEIR NEST FOR THEIR YOUNG TO FEED UPON! NOW, HERE'S AN INTERESTING OVERSIZED REPLICA OF A WASP'S NEST!

SOMETHING INSIDE THE NEST... SPARKLING! *JEWELS!* THEY LOOK LIKE... THEY *ARE!* THE *STOLEN GEMS!* BUT WHY WERE THEY PUT IN *THERE?*

SHOULD I NOTIFY THE POLICE? *NO!* I'LL TELL HENRY AND WE'LL...! NO, I WON'T DO *THAT*, EITHER! HE TREATS ME LIKE A SCATTERBRAINED LITTLE GIRL, AND I WANT HIM TO THINK OF ME AS A FULL-FLEDGED WOMAN... A WOMAN IN LOVE!

THE WASP IS SOME-WHERE IN THIS CROWD! I CAN *SENSE* IT!

I'LL SHOW HIM I CAN DO A JOB ON MY OWN! FIRST, I'LL GET THE JEWELS AND THEN TRACK DOWN THE THIEVES... FOR THEY CAN'T BE FAR FROM WHERE THE JEWELS ARE HIDDEN!

THAT NIGHT, IN HER APARTMENT, THE LOVELY JANET VAN DYNE, BECOMES... *THE WASP!*

THERE'S THE REPTILE HOUSE JUST AHEAD!

9

WONDER WHAT THIS **WIRE** IS FOR? OH, WELL, IT DOESN'T MATTER!

SO INTENT IS SHE UPON HER PURPOSE THAT SHE FAILS TO SEE THE EYES WATCHING FROM THE SHADOWS!

BE READY TO MOVE FAST NOW...

I'M INSIDE THE WASP'S NEST! BUT... WHAT **IS** THIS? SOME STRANGE SORT OF **MAZE!**

SHE'S **TRAPPED!** TWISTER, GET THE SHOES I'VE WIRED SO THE ANTS CAN'T CRAWL UP ON US! APE, GET THAT IGUANA AND PUT IT IN THE AQUARIUM! IN A FEW MINUTES THE WASP WILL BECOME FRANTIC AND SEND OUT HER SIGNALS TO ANT-MAN! WHEN HE ARRIVES WE'LL INTRODUCE HIM TO THE DEADLY SURPRISE WE'VE ARRANGED FOR HIM!

INSIDE THE NEST, THE WASP KNOWS THAT SHE HAS SOMEHOW BEEN TRAPPED BY THE JEWEL THIEVES, AND, AFTER A FRANTIC EFFORT...

THERE IS NO WAY OUT! I--I DIDN'T WANT TO DO IT, BUT I'LL HAVE TO SEND OUT A CALL FOR HELP TO **ANT-MAN!**

HER DELICATE ANTENNAE VIBRATE TREMULOUSLY AS THE MESSAGE IS SENT... AND...

FOOLISH GIRL! I'VE **WARNED** HER NOT TO TACKLE JOBS ALONE! IF ANY HARM COMES TO HER--!

MINUTES LATER...

PUT ON THE MAGNIFYING GOGGLES SO WE DON'T LOSE ANT-MAN!

SHE'S INSIDE!

AS ANT-MAN STEPS INSIDE THE NEST, THE MASTER CRIMINAL PULLS A SWITCH AND...

(10)

ANT-MAN, IT IS I, *EGGHEAD!* I HAVE RETURNED TO CONQUER YOU! YOU PLAY THE MODERN KNIGHT, SO I AM GIVING YOU A CHANCE TO PROVE YOUR PROWESS AS DID THE KNIGHTS OF OLD! HERE IS YOUR LANCE AND *THERE* IS... *YOUR DRAGON!*

I WAS A FOOL! I SHOULD HAVE SUSPECTED! ONLY *YOU* COULD HAVE THOUGHT OF SUCH A DIABOLICAL SCHEME!

BUT THERE IS NO TIME FOR MORE CONVERSATION!

HE USED THE WASP TO BAIT THIS TRAP! FOR THAT ALONE I MUST PAY HIM BACK! BUT FIRST, I MUST DEFEAT THIS IGUANA LIZARD.

ANT-MAN COUCHES HIS LANCE AS DID THE KNIGHTS OF OLD, THEN SIGNALS TO HIS ANT MOUNT...

CHARGE!

HISS-S

SWERVING, AVOIDING THE LASHING TONGUE AND SLASHING FEET OF THE LIZARD, ANT-MAN CLOSES IN QUICKLY, HIS LANCE AIMED AT A VULNERABLE SPOT...

I'VE *WON,* EGG-HEAD!

NOT YET!! THIS IS ONLY THE FIRST ROUND! YOU'RE STILL TRAPPED IN THAT GLASS CASE...

THE ANT-SIZED HUMAN CROUCHES LOW, PRESSING A TINY BUTTON IN HIS BOOT, ACTIVATING AN ELECTRONICALLY CONTROLLED SPRING...

BUT NOT FOR *LONG!*

APE, OPEN THE CRATE DOOR! HURRY!

CRASH!

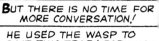

11

WHERE IS THE WASP? **ANSWER ME,** EGGHEAD, IF YOU VALUE YOUR LIFE!

THE WASP MEANS NOTHING TO ME! IT'S **YOU** I WANT, ANT-MAN... AND I'LL GET YOU YET!

HERE I AM, ANT-MAN! I FOUND THE OPENING YOU FELL THROUGH!

THANK, GOODNESS YOU'RE NOT HARMED! NOW, WITH THE AID OF OUR SOLDIER ANTS, WE'LL TACKLE EGGHEAD AND HIS BULLY BOYS!

BUT, WHEN ANT-MAN TURNS AROUND...

THE SECOND TRICK IN MY BAG, ANT-MAN ...AN **ANT-EATER!** THE MOST PERFECT WEAPON AGAINST ANTS EVER DESIGNED! BEAUTIFUL, ISN'T HE, ANT-MAN... THE ULTIMATE WEAPON!

THE CREATURE'S LONG, VISCOUS TONGUE LICKS OUT... THEN FLICKERS BACK, INTO THE SMALL MOUTH OPENING, TAUNTINGLY...

NEITHER YOU NOR YOUR ANTS CAN ESCAPE! I PULL THIS SWITCH AND EVERY CRACK IN THE ROOM HAS A LIVE WIRE ACROSS IT THAT WILL ELECTROCUTE ANY INSECT OR INSECT-SIZED CREATURE THAT ATTEMPTS TO PASS OVER IT! THIS IS YOUR FINISH, ANT-MAN!

THE HUGE ANT-EATER MOVES TOWARDS ANT-MAN, ITS TONGUE DARTING IN ANTICIPATION OF SUCH AN UNUSUAL MORSAL...

ANT-MAN! WHAT CAN WE **DO?**

STAY BACK! I'LL HANDLE THIS!

HIS LASSO, MADE OF TINY STRANDS OF STEEL-STRONG SYNTHETIC FIBER, SNAPS OUT AND LOOPS AROUND THE ELONGATED SNOUT OF THE ANT-DESTROYING CREATURE... THEN, ANT-MAN GIVES A POWERFUL YANK...

WASP, PULL THAT SWITCH TO TURN OFF THE CURRENT AROUND THE CRACKS! **HURRY!**

WILL DO, BOSS MAN!

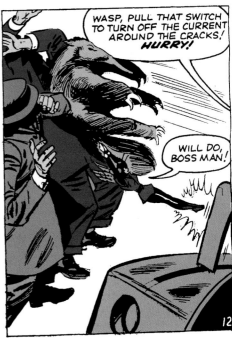

12

IT'S TIME TO USE OUR LAST WEAPON...THE WATER PISTOLS FILLED WITH LIQUID GAS! THIS IS ONE THING EVEN *ANT-MAN* CANNOT FIGHT! *FIRE!!*

THE PIN ANT-MAN USED AGAINST THE LIZARD! I'VE *GOT* IT!

AT LAST I'VE FOUND MY *STING*...THE ONE THING, AS THE WASP, THAT I HAD LACKED!

YEEOOOOOOW

QUICKLY THE WASP FLITS FROM ONE TO THE OTHER, USING HER NEW-FOUND STINGER ON THEIR HANDS TO MAKE THEM DROP THE DEADLY GUNS...

CRASH

IF YOU MOVE, THE SNAKES WILL STRIKE!

I--I AINT MOVIN' A MUSCLE!

EGGHEAD...HE'S *GONE!* GOT AWAY WHILE WE WERE TAKING CARE OF THE OTHER TWO!

THOUGH THEY SEARCH FEVERISHLY, THEY CAN FIND NO TRACE OF THE BRILLIANT ARCH CRIMINAL! THEN, BACK IN THEIR LAB AGAIN...

WELL, THE JEWELS HAVE BEEN RECOVERED AND APE AND TWISTER CAPTURED...BUT EGGHEAD, THE BIGGEST PRIZE OF ALL, IS STILL AT LIBERTY!

13

AS FOR *YOU*, YOUNG LADY, DON'T YOU EVER TRY ANYTHING LIKE THAT AGAIN! WE'RE A *TEAM*-- AND WE'LL WORK AS A TEAM! UNDERSTAND?!

OH, ANT-MAN, CAN'T YOU SEE THAT I'M A WOMAN, AND IN LOVE WITH YOU? HOW CAN A MAN SO BRILLIANT BE SO BLIND?!

AND, IN HIS OWN HIDEAWAY...

I'LL BE BACK! EACH TIME I LEARN A LITTLE MORE AND THE NEXT TIME IT WILL BE DIFFERENT! NEXT TIME I'LL SET A TRAP THAT NO HUMAN CAN ESCAPE! NOT EVEN-- *ANT-MAN!*

THE END

TALES TO ASTONISH

APPROVED BY THE COMICS CODE AUTHORITY

IND.

46 AUG.

MARVEL COMICS GROUP 12¢

ANT-MAN and The WASP FACE A FOE GREATER THAN ANY THEY HAVE EVER KNOWN WHEN "CYCLOPS WALKS THE EARTH!"

CYCLOPS IS *ALIVE!* HE'S AS BIG AS A *MOUNTAIN!* HOW CAN ANYTHING STOP HIM?

AT EASE, HONEY! THIS IS NO TIME FOR GUESSING GAMES!

MARVEL COMICS GROUP *USHERS IN THE MARVEL AGE OF COMICS!*

ANT-MAN and the WASP in

"...WHEN CYCLOPS WALKS THE EARTH"

PLOT:
STAN LEE
SCRIPT:
H.E. HUNTLEY
ART:
DON HECK
LETTERING:
S. ROSEN

WHAT ARE WE GOING TO DO? WE CAN'T FIGHT THE CYCLOPS! HE'S TOO VAST, TOO HUGE! WE'RE JUST MICROSCOPIC SPECKS TO HIM!

IF HE TIGHTENS HIS FINGERS THE SLIGHTEST BIT, HE'LL CRUSH US LIKE GRAINS OF POWDER!

The VEIL OF TIME OPENS, AND FROM THE MYTHOLOGY OF THE DIM PAST IT COMES TO STALK THE EARTH... THE AWESOME **CYCLOPS**, THE ONE-EYED HUMAN MONSTER OF ANCIENT GREECE! AGAINST THIS MENACE TO MANKIND AND MODERN CIVILIZATION THERE STANDS ONLY **ANT-MAN** AND HIS FEMININE PARTNER, **THE WASP!** BUT EVEN THEIR WEAPONS, THEIR DIMINUTIVE SIZE, ARE INADEQUATE THIS TIME AGAINST THE UNFEELING VASTNESS OF THE **CYCLOPS!** SO HUGE IS THIS LEGENDARY CREATURE THAT EVEN **NORMAL-SIZED** HUMANS ARE AS ANTS TO HIM, AND ALL THE WEAPONS OF MANKIND CANNOT MATCH HIS MONSTROUS POWER! HAVE ANT-MAN AND THE WASP AT LAST MET AN OPPONENT TOO **HUGE** FOR THEM TO DEFEAT?

X-326

IT'S A SUNDAY, A QUIET, DROWSY SUNDAY IN THE CITY, AND HIGH ABOVE THE TALL BUILDINGS, ANT-MAN CATAPULTS INTO THE ATMOSPHERE WITH HIS PARTNER, THE WASP, FLYING NEXT TO HIM, AS THEY SURVEY THE STREETS BELOW---

I DON'T SEE ANY TROUBLE STIRRING! ARE YOU PICKING UP ANYTHING ON YOUR ANTENNAE???

NOTHING! ALL'S QUIET!

I'LL CONTACT SOME OF MY FRIENDS, THE ANTS, IN THE VARIOUS CITY DISTRICTS! SEE IF THEY HAVE ANYTHING TO REPORT!

ANT-MAN ALTERS THE FREQUENCY OF HIS CYBERNETIC HELMET, SENDING AND RECEIVING ELECTRONIC IMPULSES...THE LANGUAGE, THROUGH ANTENNA PROJECTION, OF THE ANTS!

ALL IS QUIET!

PEACE REIGNS!

THERE IS NO TROUBLE! ALL IS QUIET!

APPARENTLY THERE IS NO TROUBLE ANYWHERE! LET'S RETURN HOME!

ROGER! THOUGH ACTUALLY, IT'S SO PEACEFUL AND QUIET HERE, THAT I FEEL TOO LAZY EVEN TO FLY! I'LL MEET YOU IN THE LAB!

THEN, THE SMALLEST OF ALL HUMANS SENDS OUT HIS CALL TO THE ANTS...

ANT-MAN CALLING! MEET ME AT MY HOUSE, LITTLE FRIENDS! I'M COMING DOWN!

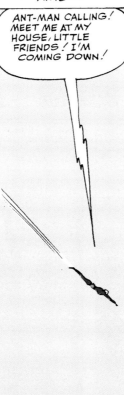

AND A GROUP OF HEXAPODA* HEAR AND... ANSWER!

MESSAGE RECEIVED! ACKNOWLEDGED! WE ARE ON OUR WAY, ANT-MAN!

* HEXAPODA-FROM THE GREEK HEX (SIX) AND PODA (FEET).

WHEN ANT-MAN DESCENDS AT HIS HOME, A SOFT, LIVING MATTRESS OF ANTS, AWAITS TO CUSHION HIS FALL TO THE GROUND!

THANK YOU, MY FRIENDS!

DO YOU WISH TRANSPORTATION TO YOUR ROOMS?

2.

NOT THIS TIME! I WILL ASCEND IN MY ELEVATOR!

AND SO, IN HIS MINIATURE ELEVATOR, ANT-MAN RISES TO THE CATAPULT COMPARTMENT...

THIS IS A GOOD TIME TO CHECK MY CATAPULT, TO MAKE SURE IT'S IN PERFECT WORKING CONDITION!

EVERYTHING SEEMS IN ORDER! WORKS PERFECTLY!

THROUGH A TINY PANEL IN THE CATAPULT ROOM, ANT-MAN ENTERS THE SECRET LAB OF THE SCIENTIST, HENRY PYM, HIS "ALTER EGO"!

WHAT DETAINED YOU? I'VE RETURNED TO MY NORMAL SIZE...BEEN WAITING FOR YOU FOR HOURS!

OH, COME NOW, IT'S NOT BEEN THAT LONG! ONLY A FEW MINUTES!

I'LL RELEASE THE GROWTH GAS AND BE RIGHT WITH YOU UP THERE, JAN!

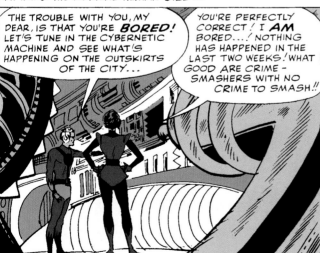

A FEW SECONDS PASS AS ANT-MAN MIRACULOUSLY ATTAINS HIS NORMAL HUMAN SIZE...

THE TROUBLE WITH YOU, MY DEAR, IS THAT YOU'RE BORED! LET'S TUNE IN THE CYBERNETIC MACHINE AND SEE WHAT'S HAPPENING ON THE OUTSKIRTS OF THE CITY...

YOU'RE PERFECTLY CORRECT! I AM BORED....! NOTHING HAS HAPPENED IN THE LAST TWO WEEKS! WHAT GOOD ARE CRIME-SMASHERS WITH NO CRIME TO SMASH!!

EVERYTHING'S PEACEFUL! NO TROUBLE IN THIS AREA!

SEE WHAT I MEAN? ANT-MAN AND THE WASP HAVE MADE CRIME SO UNPOPULAR AND UNPRODUCTIVE THAT THE CRIMINALS ARE AFRAID TO STIR! PEACE! QUIET! HOW GHASTLY!

WHAT YOU NEED... PERHAPS WHAT WE **BOTH** NEED, IS A SHORT **VACATION!** HOW **ABOUT** IT? WHERE WOULD YOU LIKE TO **GO?**

A GREAT IDEA! I'VE ALWAYS WANTED TO GO TO GREECE, THE BIRTHPLACE OF MODERN CIVILIZATION... HELLAS...CRETE.. CYPRUS!

FINE! I THINK IT WILL DO US BOTH GOOD! I'LL MAKE RESERVATIONS IMMEDIATELY ON THE FIRST FLIGHT!

I'LL RUN AND PACK!

TWO DAYS LATER...

THERE IT IS, HENRY... GREECE, THE CRADLE OF MYTHOLOGY! OH, I'M SO EXCITED...

PLEASE FASTEN YOUR SEATBELTS! WE ARE ABOUT TO LAND!

HAPPILY PREPARING TO SEE THE SIGHTS, HENRY PYM AND JANICE ARE UNAWARE THAT THEY ARE ABOUT TO EMBARK ON THEIR MOST DANGEROUS ADVENTURE... AND FACE THE MOST MONSTROUS CREATURE THE WORLD HAS EVER SEEN! AND THEN...

DO YOU **SENSE** SOMETHING... A TENSENESS.. PERHAPS **FEAR,** THAT SEEMS TO EMANATE FROM THESE PEOPLE?

NONSENSE! YOU'RE JUST IMAGINING THINGS! COME ON! LET'S HIRE A BOAT AND CRUISE THE ISLANDS WHERE HOMER SAILED AND HERCULES WALKED!

THAT'S **STRANGE..** THE BOATS ARE ALL **DOCKED!** MOST OF THEM SHOULD BE OUT FISHING, CARRYING CARGO...

WE'D LIKE TO CHARTER A BOAT TO CRUISE THE ISLANDS!

THE **ISLANDS?**

A MURMUR SWEEPS THROUGH THE GROUP OF SEAMEN, AS THOUGH THEY CANNOT BELIEVE THEIR EARS! THEN, HALTINGLY, FEARFULLY, THEY ANSWER...

NO, LADY, WE WILL **NOT** SAIL AMONG THE ISLANDS! NO SEAMAN WILL TAKE HIS VESSEL FROM THE DOCKS! PLEASE ... YOU **GO AWAY** NOW, LADY, EH?

WELL, OF ALL THE NERVE! AND JUST **WHY** WON'T YOU SAIL THE ISLANDS!?

ASK **HIM**... CAPTAIN ANDROPOLUS! HE HAS **SEEN** IT!

SEEN **WHAT?**

THE MONSTER! BIG AS A SIX-STORY BUILDING, COMING AT US AS WE SAILED BY THE ISLAND, BLOCKING OUT THE MOON AND STARS!... WEIRD LIGHTS IN THE ISLAND HILLS!

4.

YOU ACTUALLY SAW A **MONSTER?**

NOT CLEARLY ENOUGH TO KNOW **WHO** OR **WHAT** IT WAS! BUT SO HUGE WAS IT THAT IT CREATED **HIGH WAVES** AS IT CAME TOWARDS US! THEY ROCKED THE SHIP AND MY ARM WAS BROKEN! AND I AM NOT THE **ONLY** ONE WHO SAW IT! ASK **GEORGE** IN THE RADIO SHACK!

RIDICULOUS! NOTHING THAT **LIVES** IS THAT BIG! SILLY SUPERSTITION!

WE'LL SEE! COME ON, WE'LL QUESTION THE RADIO OPERATOR!

NO, THEY DO NOT LIE! **OTHER** MEN ON **OTHER** BOATS HAVE SEEN THE MONSTER, TOO IN FACT, TWO BOATS HAVE **DISAPPEARED ENTIRELY!** ONE OF THEM RADIOED AN ALARM ABOUT A HUGE MONSTER ATTACKING THE SHIP... THEN THE RADIO WENT DEAD! EXCUSE ME, A **MESSAGE** IS COMING IN!

SOUNDS INTERESTING, DOESN'T IT? TOO BAD WE'RE ON A **VACATION**, OR WE COULD HAVE A MONSTER HUNT, AND...

OH, STOP **TEASING!** WE'VE **GOT** TO FIND A BOAT AND SAIL TO THAT ISLAND!

PERHAPS **YOU** KNOW WHERE WE COULD HIRE A BOAT?

YOU CAN HIRE **MINE!** YOU WILL, OF COURSE, HAVE TO SAIL IT **YOUR SELVES!** UNDER THE CIRCUMSTANCE NO SAILOR COULD BE HIRED TO GO **WITH** YOU!

A PRICE IS AGREED UPON, AND THEN...

THANK YOU! OH, THERE IS ONE THING I FORGOT TO MENTION! THE LAST SOUND I HEARD OVER THE AIR FROM THAT ILL-FATED SHIP, JUST BEFORE THE RADIO WENT DEAD, WAS THE WORD... **"CYCLOPS!"** JUST THAT ONE WORD... AND THEN SILENCE!

WITHIN THE HOUR, THEY'RE ON THEIR WAY...

IN THE KNAPSACK YOU'LL FIND OUR COSTUMES AND EQUIPMENT! WE'LL APPROACH THE ISLAND AT DUSK AND, IF THERE **IS** ANYTHING TO THOSE STORIES, WE'LL BE PREPARED! SCARED, JAN?!

WHO, **ME?** YOU'RE TALKING TO THE WRONG GAL, PARTNER! THE ONLY THING **I'M** SCARED OF IS THAT IT'LL BE A FALSE ALARM!

WELL, WE'LL SOON KNOW, MY LITTLE EAGER BEAVER! *CYCLOPS* IS FROM GREEK MYTHOLOGY, KYLOS MEANING "CIRCLE" AND OPS MEANING "EYE", ONE-EYED, LEGENDARY PEOPLE, SAID TO HAVE MIGRATED FROM THRACE! SHEPHERDS LIVING ON AN ISLAND IN THE WESTERN SEA!

I'LL CHANGE INTO MY COSTUME BEFORE YOU DECIDE TO GIVE ME A *TEST*, PROFESSOR!

LATER... YOU CAN COME IN NOW! TELL ME, HENRY, DO YOU THINK A *CYCLOPS* REALLY MIGHT EXIST??

COULD BE, JAN! AFTER ALL, *STRANGER* THINGS HAVE HAPPENED...

THERE IS AN *ANT-MAN!* AND A *WASP!* CREATURES EVERY BIT AS BIZARRE AS ANY OL' *CYCLOPS*, EH?

DON'T YOU DARE CALL ME A CREATURE! INCIDENTALLY, THERE ARE *ANTS* IN THE GALLEY... WINGED ONES!

AS THEY CHANGE TO INSECT SIZE, ANT-MAN IMMEDIATELY CONTACTS THE ANTS ON THE SHIP, A SPECIES OF DRIVER ANTS OF WHICH THE MALES ARE WINGED, FLYING HEXAPODA!

GREETINGS, FRIENDS! I WISH TO ASK YOU SOME QUESTIONS!

LOOK! THERE'S AN ISLAND... AND THERE ARE THE STRANGE LIGHTS IN THE HILLS THE SEAMEN SPOKE OF!

WELL, *THAT* PART AT LEAST, WAS TRUE! WE'LL ANCHOR THE BOAT OFF SHORE AND FLY TO THE ISLAND! I'LL USE ONE OF THESE WINGED ANTS AS A PEGASUS * AND... *LOOK!!* THAT HUGE SHADOW!!

*NOTE: PEGASUS, THE WINGED HORSE OF GREEK MYTHOLOGY.

IT.. IT'S THE *CYCLOPS!!*

THEY DIDN'T LIE! HE *IS* AT LEAST 50 FEET TALL... HE'S *MONSTROUS!*

HE'S REACHING FOR THE *BOAT!*

GET DOWN ON THE DECK! *FAST!*

6.

MONSTROUS HANDS, UNBELIEVABLY HUGE, GRASP THE SMALL CRAFT AS THOUGH IT WERE A SMALL TOY...

BACK... BACK!! HIS THUMB COULD CRUSH US!

HE'S LOOKING RIGHT AT US! DON'T MOVE A MUSCLE!

WE'RE TOO SMALL FOR HIM TO NOTICE... I HOPE!

THE GREAT BULK OF THE ONE-EYE GIANT TURNS AND, HOLDING THE BOAT IN ONE HUGE HAND, WADES BACK TOWARDS THE SHORE...

HE LOOKED RIGHT AT US! I CAN'T UNDERSTAND WHY HE DIDN'T SEE US! WITH AN EYE THAT LARGE, HIS VISION SHOULD BE EXTREMELY KEEN!

OH, ANT-MAN! WHAT DO WE DO NEXT?

CALMLY, ANT-MAN CALLS ONE OF THE WINGED ANTS TO HIM...

THE FIRST THING TO DO IS TO GET FREE OF THIS BOAT! I'LL RIDE ONE OF THESE FLYING ANTS! WE'LL KEEP CLOSE TO THE CYCLOPS! YOU FLY NEXT TO ME! LET'S GO!

SO, YOU WERE AFRAID IT WOULD JUST BE A FALSE ALARM, EH? HOW DO YOU FEEL ABOUT IT NOW, YOUNG LADY?

JUST BETWEEN YOU AND ME, PARTNER... I THINK I TALK TOO MUCH!

I JUST THOUGHT OF SOMETHING, ANT-MAN! ABOUT THOSE EERIE LIGHTS IN THE HILLS... ARE THERE MORE CYCLOPS HERE? AND... WHERE DID HE, OR THEY, COME FROM?

WE'LL FIND OUT SOON ENOUGH, WASP! JUST WAIT!

FOR A MOMENT, THE MOUNTAINOUS CREATURE STARES DOWN AT THE SHIPS! THEN, HIS ENORMOUS ONE-EYED HEAD LIFTS AS THOUGH LISTENING TO SOME SOUNDLESS SUMMONS AND HE BEGINS TO SHUFFLE TOWARD THE HILLS AND THE STRANGE LIGHTS!

THERE'S SOMETHING *STRANGE* ABOUT THE CYCLOPS! HIS MOVEMENTS... THEY'RE SO AWKWARD!

LISTEN! I HEAR VOICES... HUMAN VOICES!

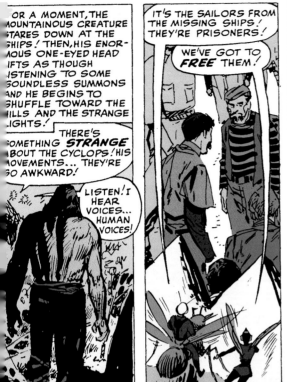

IT'S THE SAILORS FROM THE MISSING SHIPS! THEY'RE PRISONERS!

WE'VE GOT TO *FREE* THEM!

HOLD IT, WASP! FIRST I WANT TO INVESTIGATE THOSE STRANGE LIGHTS IN THE HILLS! THEY SEEM TO HAVE CYCLOPS *SPELLBOUND*!

THERE ARE *PEOPLE* UP THERE! LOOK! THEY HAVE ONE OF THE SAILORS TIED UP... DOING SOMETHING TO HIM!

THOSE ARE *SPACE SHIPS*, GIRL! THIS IS ALL BEGINNING TO TIE TOGETHER NOW!

THOSE "PEOPLE" ARE ALIENS! THEY SEEM TO BE TESTING THE CAPTIVE SAILOR'S BRAIN IMPULSES!

THEY'RE REMOVING THE WIRES FROM HIS HEAD NOW...

SUDDENLY, THE WASP CRIES OUT IN AGONY AND FALLS WRITHING TO THE GROUND! ANT-MAN GRASPS HIS HELMET, AS HIS WINGED ANT TUMBLES ON ITS SIDE IN A HELPLESS FRENZY!

ELECTRONIC IMPULSES!!

SWIFTLY ANT-MAN'S FINGERS MOVE A TINY DIAL ON HIS HELMET, CHANGING HIS ELECTRONIC WAVE PATTERNS!

I..I COULD REMOVE THE HELMET AND THE ALIEN IMPULSES WOULDN'T BOTHER ME... BUT THE WASP *CAN'T* REMOVE HER ANTENNAE! I'VE GOT TO FIND A WAVE LENGTH TO COUNTER-ACT THEIRS ... GOT..TO.. FIND IT FAST! MY MIND IS BURSTING! THE PAIN ...THE AGONY... IT'S UNBEARABLE!

8.

THERE...I'VE **FOUND** IT, AND NOT A MINUTE TOO SOON! WAIT! I'M GETTING NEW IMPULSES NOW... I'M ON THE ALIENS' WAVELENGTH! THEY CONVERSE THROUGH ELECTRONIC IMPULSES EMANATING FROM THEIR BRAINS! I CAN **UNDERSTAND** THEM!

YOU CAN READILY SEE THE MENTAL PATTERNS OF THESE EARTHMEN FROM THOSE WE HAVE MEASURED UNDER THE MENTALSCOPE! THEY ARE INFERIOR CREATURES AND WOULD BE EASILY CONQUERED!

I CA... HEAR THE... NOV... TOO...

YOU ADVISE THEN THAT WE INFORM OUR HOME PLANET, A-CHILTAR III THAT EARTH SHOULD BE CLASSIFIED AS FIT TO BE CONQUERED AND COLONIZED!?

DEFINITE-LY! STEP ON THOSE INSECTS, KRAGLIN! I CANNOT **ABIDE** THE THINGS!

I OBEY YOUR COMMAND, CAPTAIN!

INSECTS! HE MEANS **US!!**

USE YOUR **STINGER**, WASP, WHILE I LASSO HIS FOOT!

THOUGH DIMINUTIVE IN SIZE, THE TINY WARRIOR RETAINS ALL THE STRENGTH OF HIS NORMAL HUMAN SIZE AND MUSCULATURE ---AND, IN THIS CRUCIAL MOMENT, HE USES THAT STRENGTH TO ITS FULLEST...

PERFECT! YOUR STING MADE HIM LIFT HIS FOOT ENOUGH FOR ME TO GET HIM OFF BALANCE!

WHAT IS THIS **FOOLISHNESS**, KRAGLIN? CAN'T YOU OBEY A SIMPLE COMMAND?

I...I DON'T KNOW WHAT **HAPPENED!** I FELT A STINGING PAIN IN MY SOLE, AND THEN... I FLEW THROUGH THE AIR! IT IS VERY STRANGE!

I DON'T SEE THE INSECTS...

NEVER MIND! YOU WILL ALL JOIN ME IN DIRECTING BRAIN IMPULSES TO THE CYCLOPS! WE WILL DIRECT HIM TO DESTROY THE IMPRISONED EARTHMEN! WE HAVE NO FURTHER USE FOR THEM!

NOW I KNOW WHY THE CYCLOPS DIDN'T SEE US AND WHY HE MOVED SO AWKWARDLY! HE'S JUST A ROBOT, BUILT BY THOSE ALIENS TO FRIGHTEN SHIPS AWAY WHILE THEY INVESTIGATE OUR PLANET! THEY MUST KNOW ALL ABOUT OUR CULTURE TO HAVE KNOWN MYTHOLOGY AND...

WHILE YOU'RE LECTURING AGAIN, I'M GOING TO FREE THOSE SAILORS BEFORE THE CYCLOPS KILLS THEM!

WAIT! WASP, DON'T! SHE DOESN'T HEAR ME... OR PRETENDS SHE DOESN'T!

SLOWLY, THE ONE-EYED MECHANICAL BEHEMOTH WALKS TOWARDS THE STOCKADE!

NO TIME TO GO AFTER THE WASP NOW! I'VE GOT TO FIND THE BRAIN CENTER OF THAT KING-SIZED MECHANICAL MAN AND SHUT IT OFF BEFORE IT OBEYS THE ALIENS!

THE MOUTH...IT KEEPS OPENING AND CLOSING ITS MOUTH! I CAN GET IN THROUGH THERE... IF I'M LUCKY!

THANKS, LITTLE FRIENDS! YOU CAN GO NOW! IT'S UP TO ME ALONE FROM HERE ON IN...

I FEEL LIKE ONE OF THOSE LITTLE CARTOON CHARACTERS IN A T.V. COMMERCIAL, SHOWING HOW PILLS DISSOLVE INSIDE THE BODY! WELL, NOW TO HUNT FOR THE CYCLOPS' "BRAIN"!

10

MEANWHILE, THE WASP REACHES THE PRISONERS' COMPOUND...

GUARDS! I'VE GOT TO GET RID OF THEM QUICKLY! WHAT'S THAT? A WASP'S NEST... HANGING FROM THAT TREE?!

FRIENDS, I NEED YOUR HELP! FOLLOW ME!!

THEN, WITH HER ANGRY WASPS BEHIND HER...

BZZ BZZZ ZZ ZZZ ZZZZZ

ATTACK!!

YEEOOOW!

I MUST USE THE GROWTH GAS TO BRING MYSELF TO NORMAL SIZE AGAIN, SO THAT I CAN MORE EASILY COMMUNICATE WITH THE CAPTIVE SAILORS!

THE WASP UNLEASHES THE ENLARGING GAS, AND SECONDS LATER, GROWS TO HER NORMAL HUMAN SIZE! IN THE PROCESS, HER WINGS AND ANTENNAE, WHICH SPROUT ONLY WHEN SHE REACHES WASP SIZE COMPLETELY DISAPPEAR!

HURRY! YOU MUST GET AWAY IMMEDIATELY, BEFORE THE...

LOOK!! THE CYCLOPS— HE COMES!

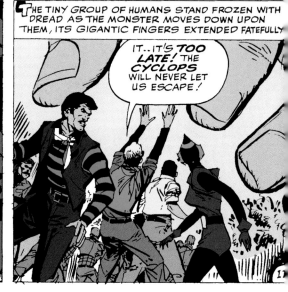
THE TINY GROUP OF HUMANS STAND FROZEN WITH DREAD AS THE MONSTER MOVES DOWN UPON THEM, ITS GIGANTIC FINGERS EXTENDED FATEFULLY

IT...IT'S TOO LATE! THE CYCLOPS WILL NEVER LET US ESCAPE!

11

MEANWHILE, INSIDE THE CREATURE'S MECHANICAL BRAIN...

THERE MUST BE *SOMETHING* HERE THAT TRAPS THE MENTAL IMPULSES OF THE ALIENS, SENDS THE MESSAGE THROUGHOUT THE CYCLOPS' FRAME, CONTROLLING ITS MOVEMENTS!

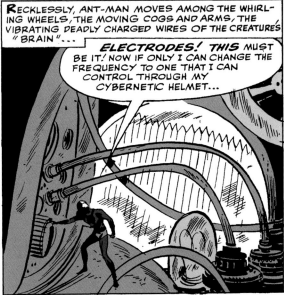

RECKLESSLY, ANT-MAN MOVES AMONG THE WHIRLING WHEELS, THE MOVING COGS AND ARMS, THE VIBRATING DEADLY CHARGED WIRES OF THE CREATURE'S "BRAIN"...

ELECTRODES! THIS MUST BE IT! NOW IF ONLY I CAN CHANGE THE FREQUENCY TO ONE THAT I CAN CONTROL THROUGH MY CYBERNETIC HELMET...

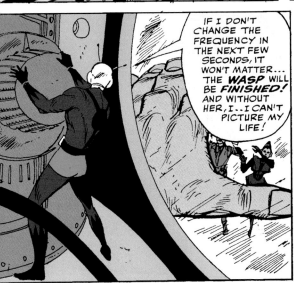

IF I DON'T CHANGE THE FREQUENCY IN THE NEXT FEW SECONDS, IT WON'T MATTER... THE *WASP* WILL BE *FINISHED!* AND WITHOUT HER, I...I CAN'T PICTURE MY LIFE!

ANT-MAN! ANT-MAN! WHERE ARE YOU?

SUDDENLY, AS IF IN ANSWER TO THE GIRL'S ANGUISHED CRY, THE MONSTROUS HAND STOPS, THEN GENTLY FREES THE HUMANS, AS THE *ANT-MAN* EXULTS!

I *DID* IT! NOW THE CYCLOPS OBEYS *ONLY* ME! SO THOSE ALIENS WERE GOING TO CONQUER THE EARTH, WERE THEY?

LOOK! THE CYCLOPS RETURNS... THOUGH WE GAVE IT NO MESSAGE TO DO SO! IT'S CRUSHING ONE OF OUR SHIPS!

IT IS UNDER SOME *OTHER* MENTAL CONTROL EVEN STRONGER THAN *OURS!* IT IS COMING TO *DESTROY* US!

THIS MEANS THAT THE EARTHLINGS HAVE EVEN *STRONGER* MENTAL CONTROL THAN WE! WE HAVE UNDERESTIMATED THEM! HURRY TO THE SHIPS! WE MUST ESCAPE THIS ACCURSED PLANET!

12

THE EARTHLINGS DECEIVED US INTO BELIEVING THEY WERE MENTAL WEAKLINGS...

YES! BUT NOW WE **KNOW** THEIR POWERS! THEY CAN EVEN MOVE MATTER WITHOUT TOUCHING IT, AS WITNESS WHAT HAPPENED TO KRAGLIN! REPORT TO OUR HOME PLANET...EARTH IS TOO STRONG FOR US TO CONQUER!

THE SAILORS, NOW FREE, RUSH TOWARD THE COAST! A TOUCH OF REDUCING GAS AND ONCE AGAIN THE WASP FLIES...DIRECTLY TOWARDS THE EYE OF THE CYCLOPS...

SO **THERE** YOU ARE! I **THOUGHT** SO! WHAT NOW?

I'M GOING TO MAKE CYCLOPS RETRIEVE THE SHIPS AND PUT THEM IN THE BAY AGAIN SO THEY CAN SAIL HOME! SORRY I COULDN'T GET CONTROL SOONER, SO YOU WOULDN'T HAVE BEEN FRIGHTENED!

ME, FRIGHTENED?! DON'T **KID** YOURSELF! ALL I HAD TO DO WAS USE THE REDUCING GAS AND SLIDE RIGHT OUT OF THE ROBOT'S BIG PAWS! I WAS JUST WORRIED FOR THE **OTHERS!**

OKAY, JAN...IF YOU **SAY** SO!

UNDER ORDERS FROM ANT-MAN, THE CYCLOPS DEPOSITS THE VESSELS SAFELY IN THE BAY! THEN, THE MECHANICAL BRAIN RECEIVES ITS FINAL DIRECTIVE FROM ITS NEW MASTER!

WALK INTO THE SEA, CYCLOPS! WALK UNTIL THE WATERS COVER YOU! WALK UNTIL THE SEA SEEPS INTO YOUR MECHANICAL BRAIN AND LIMBS AND RUSTS THEM.. UNTIL YOU TOPPLE TO THE OCEAN'S FLOOR ...AND NEVER MOVE FROM THERE AGAIN!

THE END OF THE CYCLOPS...AND OF THE ALIENS WHO WANTED TO CONQUER THE EARTH! NOW, LITTLE LADY, IF WE WANT TO HITCH A RIDE BACK TO THE MAINLAND, WE'D BEST HURRY TO THE SHIPS!

A FEW DAY'S LATER, IN HENRY'S LAB...

I THINK I'LL CHECK THE CYBERNETIC CONTROL BOARD AND SEE IF ANYTHING IS STIRRING!

MY DEAR PROFESSOR, DO ME A FAVOR, PLEASE! IN THE FUTURE, LET US HAVE **NO MORE VACATIONS!**

I JUST CAN'T STAND THE EXCITEMENT!

TALES TO ASTONISH

APPROVED BY THE COMICS CODE AUTHORITY

IND.

47 SEPT.

MARVEL COMICS GROUP 12¢

SUPER-FANTASY IN THE MARVEL MANNER!! "MUSIC TO SCREAM BY!"

STARRING: ANT-MAN and THE WASP

WHERE CAN THE WASP BE? IF EVER I NEEDED HER, I NEED HER NOW!

FEATURING: TRAGO! ONE OF THE STRANGEST VILLAINS OF ALL TIME!

ANT-MAN and THE WASP
"MUSIC TO SCREAM BY"

FEATURING:
TRAGO!
"THE MAN WITH THE MAGIC TRUMPET!"

THAT MACABRE MUSIC, IT-- IT'S *PIERCING MY BRAIN*, STEALING MY SENSES AWAY! *TRAGO*... HE'LL ENSLAVE *THE WORLD* WITH HIS TRUMPET... AND THERE'S NO WAY TO *STOP* HIM!

IT'S CREATING HORRIBLE IMAGES INSIDE MY BRAIN! I-- I CAN'T *STAND IT!* ANT-MAN,... HELP! HELP ME BEFORE I GO SCREAMING MAD!

IT IS SAID THAT *"MUSIC HATH CHARMS TO SOOTHE THE SAVAGE BEAST"!* BUT THE MUSICIAN KNOWN TO THE JAZZ WORLD AS *TRAGO*, FOUND A *NEW* KIND OF MUSIC, AND TURNED HIS TRUMPET INTO THE PIPES OF PAN! NOTES ISSUED FROM HIS BRASS INSTRUMENT THAT CAME FROM THE ZONE OF MADNESS,... SOUND THAT ENSLAVED THE BRAIN AND BROUGHT A WHOLE CITY UNDER HIS CONTROL ...THE BEGINNING OF A COMPOSITION TO LOOT THE WORLD ...THE START OF A SERENADE OF PILLAGE, A SYMPHONY OF CRIME! HOW COULD *ANT-MAN* AND *THE WASP* FIGHT WAVES OF SOUND THAT STOLE AWAY THEIR SENSES AND HURLED THEM INTO A BOTTOMLESS PIT OF MUSICAL NIGHTMARE?

STORY PLOT..... **STAN LEE**
SCRIPT.......... **H.E. HUNTLEY**
ART.............. **DON HECK**

X-353

1

IN A SWANK SUITE IN ONE OF THE CITY'S FINEST HOTELS, ANT-MAN AND THE WASP BATTLE AGAINST RAMOND THEIS, AN INTERNATIONALLY WANTED CRIMINAL!

IT'S ANT-MAN! GET HIM... HURRY!

IT'S LIKE SHOOTIN' AT THE HEAD OF A PIN!

POW

POW

PUT THAT POP-GUN AWAY, MISTER! BOY FRIENDS ARE HARD TO REPLACE!

YEEOOOOWWW!

A FEW MINUTES LATER...

NOW LET'S UNTIE MR. NEHRADU AND HE CAN TELEPHONE THE POLICE! WASP, DON'T YOU HEAR ME? OH, SHE'S LOOKING AT THAT DIAMOND! JUST LIKE A WOMAN!

THE STAR OF GHANA, LARGEST PRECIOUS GEM IN THE WORLD! IT'S BEAUTIFUL!

TELL ME, JAN... WHAT DO FEMALES FIND SO DOGGONE FASCINATING ABOUT JEWELRY??

IF ONLY YOU'D BUY ME SOME, BIG DADDY, I'D BE HAPPY TO EXPLAIN IT TO YOU!

ACCEPT MY GRATITUDE, MY TINY FRIENDS, FOR RECOVERING MY GEM! EVEN THOUGH INDIA, MY NATIVE LAND, IS KNOWN FOR STRANGE MYSTERIES, AND OCCULT POWERS, I HAD NOT THE SKILL TO DEFEAT THOSE THIEVES BY MYSELF!

2

BUT AREN'T ALL THOSE SO-CALLED INDIAN MAGIC TRICKS, LIKE CLIMBING A ROPE TO NO-WHERE, JUST PHONY STUNTS TO IMPRESS TOURISTS?

PERHAPS *SOME* *ARE*, MY LITTLE WINGED FRIEND, BUT IN INDIA THERE IS ONE MAN, GHAZANDI, WHOSE MAGIC POWER IS MORE THAN JUST SKILLFUL TRICKERY!

HE CAN TRULY HYPNOTIZE COBRAS WITH HIS MUSIC, AND IT IS SAID THAT HE CAN PLAY NOTES WHICH WILL ALSO HYNOTIZE *HUMANS!* BUT THIS HE IS *AFRAID* TO DO, FOR IF HE PLAYS THE WRONG NOTE IT WILL *AFFECT HIM* ALSO, AND IT WILL MAKE GHAZANDI LOSE HIS MYSTIC POWER!

WELL, IT'S AN INTEREST-ING *STORY,* ANYWAY!

NOW I WILL CALL THE POLICE, AND THANK YOU ONCE AGAIN FOR SAVING THE STAR OF GHAMA!

AND IT IS TIME FOR US TO GO:

KORR! *TO ME,* WINGED KORR!

KORR, THE WINGED ANT, FLIES TO ANT-MAN! A FEW MOMENTS LATER, THE TWO CRIME FIGHTERS WING THEIR WAY THROUGH THE CITY TOWARD HOME!

ANT-MAN! LISTEN TO THAT *HORN!* OHH... DO I *LOVE* GOOD JAZZ!! HOW ABOUT US GOING IN TO LISTEN TO *TRAGO AND HIS MAGIC TRUMPET?*

JAN, I DON'T CARE FOR JAZZ! ANY-WAY, WE'VE GOT *MORE* IMPORTANT THINGS TO DO! FORGET IT, KID!

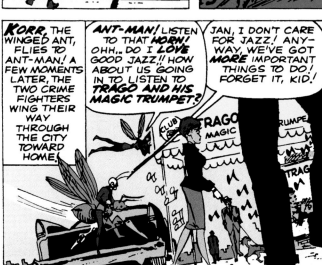

AH, COME ON, HANK! BREAK DOWN AND BE HUMAN FOR ONCE! THE WORLD WON'T COME TO AN END IF WE RELAX FOR A FEW MINUTES!

OKAY--OKAY! I'M JUST PUTTY IN THE HANDS OF A GIRL! WE'LL GO HOME AND CHANGE, THEN WE'LL COME BACK HERE!

AN HOUR LATER... ANT-MAN AND THE WASP HAVE BECOME HENRY PYM, SCIENTIST, AND JANET VAN DYNE, LOVELY YOUNG SOCIALITE!

HE'S NO *COUNT BASIE,* BUT HE'S *GOOD!* HIS TECHNIQUE IS SIMILAR TO WILD BILL DONOVAN'S!

WHOEVER *THEY* ARE!

THEN, WHEN THE MUSICIANS *"TAKE TEN"...*

WELL, I'M GLAD *THAT'S* OVER! HAD *ENOUGH?*

OH, SIT DOWN, YOU BIG, HANDSOME SQUARE! THERE'LL BE LOTS *MORE* MUSIC!

3

SAY! WHAT'S THAT? SOUNDS LIKE A *STRUGGLE!* *COME ON,* JANET!

OH *NO!* NOT ON OUR NIGHT OFF! MAYBE IT'S JUST *MICE!*

MY CASH BOX! YOU CROOK, TRAGO, YOU PETTY CROOK! GIVE IT TO ME!

LET GO, YOU FOOL!

HONEY, THOSE AREN'T *MICE!*

HE STOLE MY CASH BOX! -- RAN THRU THAT DOOR AND LOCKED IT BEHIND HIM! HE'LL BE OUT THE ALLEY AND AWAY BEFORE WE CAN GET HIM! *HELP!! POLICE!!*

QUICK, JAN! FOLLOW ME INTO THE HALL!

HERE ARE MY *REDUCING* AND *ENLARGING GAS* CYLINDERS! I ALWAYS KEEP THEM WITH ME! YOU STILL HAVE YOUR *WASP UNIFORM* UNDER YOUR CLOTHES, I HOPE?

SURE! I JUST WOULDN'T FEEL *DRESSED* WITHOUT IT!

A SLIGHT HISS AND THE RE-DUCING GAS IS RELEASED... AND HENRY PYM AND JANET VAN DYNE SHRINK RAPIDLY TO... *ANT-MAN* AND *THE WASP!*

ONLY SECONDS HAVE ELAPSED SINCE THE ROBBERY AS ANT-MAN RUSHES UNDER THE JAMB OF THE LOCKED DOOR INTO THE ALLEY...

...WHILE *THE WASP* FLIES SWIFTLY THROUGH THE KEYHOLE!

4

THERE HE IS! STING HIS ANKLE! HURRY, WASP! YOU CAN STOP HIM!

-SIGH- A WOMAN'S WORK IS NEVER DONE!

OWWW!

LISTEN! THE MANAGER IS BREAKING DOWN THE DOOR!

NO NEED TO RUSH! TRAGO WON'T BE GOING ANYWHERE NOW!

AH, THERE YOU ARE! DIDN'T GET AWAY WITH IT, DID YOU, TRAGO? WHY, TRAGO? WHY WOULD YOU DO THIS TO ME?

I-I DON'T KNOW, MISTER COSGROVE! I SAW THE SAFE OPEN-- AND THE MONEY --AND I DON'T EARN MUCH WITH MY TRUMPET- SO, IT SEEMED LIKE EASY DOUGH!

YOU MUSICIANS! YOU'RE ALL LUNKHEADS! WELL, THERE IS NO REAL HARM DONE NOW THAT I'VE GOT MY MONEY BACK! COME INTO MY OFFICE...

TRAGO, I'M NOT GOING TO PRESS CHARGES! I'M GOING TO GET YOU A TICKET ON THE FIRST PLANE OUT OF THE COUNTRY... BECAUSE OF OUR FRIENDSHIP! JUST DON'T COME BACK, YOU HEAR? I'LL TAKE THE COST OF THE TICKET OUT OF THE WAGES I OWE YOU!

OKAY BY ME!

HELLO! YOU SAY YOUR NEXT PLANE LEAVES FOR NEW DEHLI, INDIA? THAT'S GOOD ENOUGH! RESERVE ONE SEAT IN THE NAME OF TRAGO! HE'LL BE RIGHT THERE!

WELL, I GUESS THAT'S THE LAST WE'LL HEAR OF THE MAN WITH THE MAGIC TRUMPET! LET'S GO!

AWW... AND HE PLAYED SUCH A MELLOW HORN!

5

NO, ANT-MAN, YOU ARE VERY WRONG! THIS IS BUT THE **BEGINNING!** A PROLOGUE TO THE STORY OF TRAGO, THE MAN WITH THE MAGIC TRUMPET! YOUR LIVES ARE INEXTRICABLY BOUND TOGETHER IN THE WEB OF FATE, AND THE FUTURE WILL BRING ACTION AND DANGER SUCH AS YOU HAVE NEVER DREAMED OF!

WE PICK UP THE TRAIL OF TRAGO AGAIN IN A HUT OUTSIDE OF NEW DELHI, TWO MONTHS LATER!

YOU HAVE BEEN VERY ILL... FEVER, STARVATION! I FOUND YOU ALMOST DEAD! MY NAME IS **GHAZANDI**, A MYSTIC, AND SCHOLAR OF ANCIENT PHENOMENA!

THANKS, DAD, FOR HELPING ME! I COULDN'T FIND WORK ...I WAS STARVING!

I PLAY, TOO! SAY! IS IT **TRUE** THAT YOU CATS CAN CHARM SNAKES AND THINGS LIKE THAT, WITH *MUSIC?*

YES, **GHAZANDI** HAS THE POWER! YOU THINK YOU KNOW HOW TO PLAY THAT TRUMPET, MY FRIEND? AH, THERE ARE NOTES, PASSAGES, THAT YOU HAVE NEVER EVEN **IMAGINED!**

IF THAT'S TRUE, THEN **TEACH** ME! MAN, I WANNA SWING! I WANNA BE THE TOP HORN MAN! YOU'RE NOT **KIDDIN'** ABOUT PLAYIN' NOTES NO ONE **ELSE** CAN, ARE YOU?

I KNOW **MANY** THINGS! I KNOW FROM YOUR MIND THAT YOU STOLE AND THOUGHT YOU SAW TINY HUMAN FIGURES NO BIGGER THAN AN ANT AND A WASP!

YOU *DID* SEE THEM! THERE ARE **MANY** STRANGE THINGS THAT ARE POSSIBLE! I HAVE NEVER BEFORE HAD A STUDENT, BUT IF IT IS WRITTEN IN THE STARS THAT I SHOULD BE YOUR TEACHER, WE WILL BEGIN!

TIME PASSES, AND TRAGO LEARNS MANY THINGS...!

GOOD! YOU HAVE MASTERED THE NOTES THAT HYPNOTIZE THE KING COBRA! I HAVE TAUGHT YOU ALSO THE ART OF HYPNOTISM, USING YOUR **EYES** AS THE POWER MEDIUM!

IF MUSIC CAN HYPNOTIZE A **REPTILE,** WHY CAN'T IT HYPNOTIZE **HUMANS?** GHAZANDI, **TELL ME!** I WANT TO KNOW!

THERE IS GREAT **DANGER** INVOLVED! BUT, YOU ARE **MY DISCIPLE!** I WILL **TEACH** YOU!

6

THE MONTHS FLY BY AND THEN, RETURNING FROM HELPING THE POLICE, ANTMAN AND THE WASP ARE REMINDED OF...

REMEMBER *TRAGO,* THE MAN WITH THE MAGIC TRUMPET? WONDER IF HE'S STILL IN *INDIA?*

CERTAINLY I REMEMBER! IT WAS ONE OF THE FEW TIMES I GOT YOU INTO A NIGHT CLUB! HE WAS A COOL BRASS MAN! BUT YOU JUST DIDN'T DIG 'IM!

JAZZ NITE starring The ALL STARS!

NO, TRAGO *IS NOT* STILL IN INDIA! FOR, AT THAT MOMENT, IN A SMALL NIGHT CLUB IN CONNECTICUT, OFF THE MERRITT PARKWAY, TRAGO HIS APPEARANCE ALTERED, IS PLAYING WITH A SMALL COMBO!

GO, MAN GO!!

NOW IS THE TIME TO TEST MY POWERS! FIRST, I MUST REINFORCE THE HYPNOTIC BONDS WITH WHICH I HOLD MY MUSICIANS ENSLAVED, SO *THEY* WILL NOT BE AFFECTED!!

LOOK DEEP...DEEP! YOU WILL DO ONLY AS MY WILL COMMANDS...YOU WILL HEAR NOTHING BUT THE SOUNDS OF YOUR OWN INSTRUMENTS! NOW... *WE WILL PLAY!!*

THE MUSIC WAILS, SLURRING, JUMPING, SULTRY SOUTHERN JAZZ! THEN, FROM TRAGO'S BLARING TRUMPET, *NEW* NOTES FORM, NOTES NO HUMAN HAS EVER HEARD BEFORE...

HARRY...I...I FEEL STRANGE! I THINK I'M GOING TO *FAINT!*

MY HEAD! MY BRAIN'S WHIRLING!

THE MUSIC GOES ON AND ON, SOME NOTES UNHEARD BY THE EAR BUT HEARD BY THE *SUB-CONSCIOUS!* THEN, *FANTASY* COMES... MIASMIC IMAGES IN THE MIND, FORMED BY THE MUSICAL HYPNOSIS... AS THE STARTLING STRAINS FILL THE ROOM...

AAIEEE EE

TRAGO RAISES HIS HAND! THE MUSIC STOPS! THE AUDIENCE IS MOTIONLESS... HELPLESS... COMPLETELY UNDER TRAGO'S SPELL!

NOW! PASS AMONG THE AUDIENCE AND TAKE THEIR VALUABLES! I *COMMAND* YOU!

7.

MOMENTS LATER...

HA, IT WORKED...THE TEST HAS BEEN A COMPLETE SUCCESS! BUT, *THIS* IS NOT WORTH BOTHERING ABOUT...A HANDFUL OF JEWELS AND BILLS! RETURN THOSE BAUBLES, EACH PIECE TO ITS RIGHTFUL OWNER!

NOW, I'LL BREAK THE HYPNOSIS...AND THEY WON'T EVEN KNOW THAT TIME HAS ELAPSED AND ANYTHING HAS HAPPENED! THEN, ON TO NEW YORK, AND THE *BIG PRIZE!*

I'LL CONTACT A T.V. STATION DIRECTOR, USE MY HYPNOTIC POWERS TO GET MY LITTLE COMBO A BROADCASTING SPOT! THEN, ONCE MY MUSIC IS BEAMED OUT OVER THE AIRWAYS, *EVERYONE* HEARING IT WILL BE HYPNOTIZED! I'LL HYPNOTIZE AN *ENTIRE CITY*...AND LOOT IT AT WILL!

A FEW DAYS LATER, IN THE LAB OF HENRY PYM, AS THE SCIENTIST USES HIS FANTASTIC CYBERNETIC MACHINE TO RECEIVE ELECTRONIC IMPULSE MESSAGES FROM THE VAST ARMY OF ANTS WHILE *THE WASP* LISTENS TO A LOCAL RADIO STATION...

...AND NOW, FRIENDS, WE PRESENT THE MAHARAJAH OF JAZZ... *TRAGO, AND HIS MAGIC TRUMPET!*

TRAGO?

THE ANTS REPORT THAT ALL IS QUIET IN THE CITY...

HENRY, COME HERE! LISTEN TO THIS! *IT'S TRAGO!* REMEMBER HIM?

THEN, SUDDENLY, AS THE MUSIC STARTS...

HENRY!! WHA... WHAT'S *HAPPENING?*

MY EARS! MY BRAIN! JAN, IT'S THE *MUSIC!* QUICK! WE MUST REDUCE OUR SIZE...YOU'VE GOT TO TURN OFF THE RADIO...*GOT TO!*

THE REDUCING GAS SWIRLS AROUND THEM AS THEY SHRINK WITH INCREDIBLE RAPIDITY!

CAN'T *DO* IT! THAT MUSIC! IT'S TOO POWERFUL! *CAN'T RESIST IT!!*

NEED HELP...*FAST!* I'LL CONTACT MY FAITHFUL KORR! KORR...*TO ME, KORR!*

8.

THE DISCORDANT MUSIC WAILS ON, BRINGING HYPNOSIS, BRINGING NIGHTMARE TO THE MINDS OF THE TWO TINY UNCONSCIOUS FIGURES!

THEN, A TINY FORM APPEARS AT THE WINDOW! IT IS *KORR!* KORR, THE FAITHFUL HAS HEARD THE CALL AND ANSWERED! HE SEES WITH MANY-FACETED EYES...AND HE UNDERSTANDS! HIS ANTENNAE QUIVER AS HE SENDS A CALL FOR HELP!

AND SO THEY COME... *THE ANTS*, SWARMING TO KORR'S SIGNAL...

AND THEY CARRY THE HELPLESS ANT-SIZE HUMANS AWAY!

WHILE TRAGO PLAYS...

AND, THROUGHOUT THE CITY, PEOPLE ARE FROZEN IN A HYPNOTIC TRANCE!

BUT TRAGO HAS NOT FORGOTTEN THE TWO TINY HUMANS HE ONCE SAW, WHO FOILED HIS EARLIER ATTEMPT AT ROBBERY...AND HIS HORN SENDS A MESSAGE TO THE REPTILES IN THE GARDENS AND FIELDS..."*FIND ANTMAN, CAPTURE HIM!*"

THEN TRAGO'S EYES SEND THEIR MESSAGE TO HIS HYPNOTIZED MUSICIANS!

HEAR ME! HEAR MY MENTAL COMMANDS! FIND THOSE *BANKS* IN THE CITY WHERE MY MUSIC HAS REACHED...AND *LOOT THEM!!* NOW GO!

9.

MEANWHILE, KORR CARRIES HIS ANT-SIZE HUMAN FRIENDS DEEP INTO THE MIDDLE OF A HUGE ANT-HILL, WHERE THE HYPNOTIC BLARE OF TRAGO'S TRUMPET CANNOT REACH!

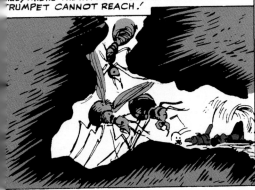

THEN, ANTMAN STIRS, FREE FROM THE MAD SYMPHONY, BUT STILL NUMBED BY THE TERRIBLE MENTAL PRESSURE! SUDDENLY, THE ANTS BEGIN TO SWAY, TO MOVE BACKWARDS!

WASP, WAKE UP! I...I REMEMBER SOMETHING... SOMETHING NEHRADU ONCE SAID...

SILENTLY, A FORM SLITHERS TOWARDS THEM! ONLY A SMALL GARDEN SNAKE, BUT A GIGANTIC MENACE TO THE TINY HUMANS! ANTMAN AND THE WASP TRY TO RISE TO FIGHT THE DEADLY DANGER, BUT THEY ARE STILL TOO WEAK!

THE ARMY OF ANTS FORM FOR BATTLE! BUT THEY WILL BE TOO LATE TO SAVE ANTMAN AND THE WASP! THIS KORR KNOWS, AS HE ATTACKS FIRST!

I..FORGOT MY GAS CONTAINERS! THE REDUCING GAS...USE IT, WASP!!

THE HISSING SNAKE STRIKES AT KORR, AND IN THAT SECOND THE WASP AIMS AND RELEASES A STREAM OF REDUCING GAS...BUT TOO LATE TO SAVE THE FAITHFUL ANT!

THAT DANGER IS OVER! IT WILL BECOME SMALL AS A WORM AND THE ANTS WILL TAKE CARE OF IT! BUT...POOR KORR...HE IS BEYOND HELP! WELL, COME ON! TIGHTEN YOUR EAR DISCS TO BLOT OUT TRAGO'S NOTES! ONLY USE YOUR ANTENNAE...

YOU SAID SOMETHING ABOUT NEHRADU..!

ASTRIDE THE FLYING ANT, FOSS, BROTHER OF THE FAITHFUL KORR, ANTMAN DEPARTS WITH THE WASP!

WEARING MY CYBERNETIC HELMET CUTS OFF THE EFFECT OF TRAGO'S MUSIC! WHAT STATION WAS THAT YOU TUNED IN ON, JAN? BECAUSE, THAT'S WHERE WE'RE HEADED!

BUT... WHAT WILL WE DO NOW?

10.

 REMEMBER, TRAGO WENT TO INDIA?! AND NEHRADU TOLD US ABOUT AN INDIAN MYSTIC WHO COULD HYPNOTIZE *MEN*, AS WELL AS SNAKES WITH HIS MUSIC! TRAGO MUST HAVE LEARNED THE ART FROM *HIM*!

LOOK AT THE PEOPLE ...FROZEN, HYPNOTIZED, AND THEIR FACES MIRRORING THEIR SHOCK!

 HERE'S THE BROADCASTING STATION! THOSE THREE MEN EMERGING *AREN'T* HYPNOTIZED! THAT MEANS... *WAIT!!* I'M GETTING A MESSAGE FROM THE ANTS IN THE STUDIO... ABOUT *TRAGO*...

 THOSE THREE ARE *TRAGO'S MUSICIANS!* HE HAS THEM UNDER HIS SPELL, AND HAS SENT THEM OUT TO ROB AND LOOT! WASP, *STOP THEM!* DRIVE THEM BACK INTO THE STUDIO!

 THE WASP BUZZES RAPIDLY FROM ONE OF THE HYPNOTIZED MUSICIANS TO THE OTHER, STINGING THEM AND, WITH HER STING, HERDING THEM LIKE SHEEP!

YEEOWW!

HALP!

 AS ANTMAN ENTERS THE STUDIO...

NOW I'LL USE MY ENLARGING GAS AGAIN! ONCE I GET MY HANDS ON TRAGO, HE'LL NEVER PLAY ANOTHER HYPNOTIC NOTE!

 I-I *FORGOT!* I DON'T *HAVE* MY GAS TUBES! I'LL HAVE TO BATTLE TRAGO WHILE I'M *ANT-SIZED* SOMEHOW!

 AND, AT THAT INSTANT, TRAGO *SEES* ANT-MAN!

11.

HE *SAW* ME! HE'S TRYING TO *GET* ME! HAVE TO MOVE *FAST*!!

PLINK PLINK PL

I'VE BEEN LUCKY SO FAR...BUT I CAN'T EVADE HIM MUCH LONGER!

WAIT! I *REMEMBER* NOW WHAT IT WAS NEHRANDU SAID!...IF THE INDIAN MYSTIC PLAYED THE *WRONG* NOTES, HE *HIMSELF* WOULD BE AFFECTED! IT MUST BE THE SAME WITH *TRAGO!* I'VE *GOT* TO GET *INSIDE HIS TRUMPET!!*

CLANG

TRAGO MUST HAVE CHANGED OR ALTERED THE PLAYING MECHANISM OF THE TRUMPET TO PRODUCE HIS HYPNOTIC MUSIC! IF I CAN SOMEHOW *ALTER* THE TONE...

BOOM! BOOM!

INSIDE THE TRUMPET, WIND AND MUSIC BEAT AT ANTMAN LIKE A TORNADO AS HE STRUGGLES TO HOLD HIS BALANCE ON THE SHINY, SLIPPERY BRASS!

THEN, HENRY PYM'S ARMY OF ANTS ATTACK----CRAWLING UP THE LEGS OF THE MAD TRUMPETER, ADVANCING UNTIL THEY REACH HIS *FACE*...

FOR A MOMENT HE STOPS BLOWING, SWIPES AT THE CRAWLING, ITCHING HORDE OF INSECTS ON HIS FACE AND, IN THAT INSTANT, ANTMAN RUSHES UP THE INSIDE OF THE TRUMPET...

LASSOING THE PLUNGER, AND PULLING BACK WITH ALL HIS MIGHT...

LUCKILY, MY REDUCING GAS DOESN'T REDUCE MY FULL-GROWN STRENGTH AS WELL AS MY SIZE! AH, IT'S *BENDING!*

12.

SUDDENLY, TRAGO CAN NO LONGER PLAY THE HYPNOTIC NOTES! DISCORD BLARES FROM THE HORN AS TRAGO, IN PANIC, PLAYS A SERIES OF NOTES HE HAS NEVER PLAYED BEFORE...

I HERDED THOSE THREE INTO THE AUDITION BOOTH AND LOCKED THE DOOR!

GOOD WORK, JAN! NOW, KEEP YOUR EYES ON TRAGO!

THOSE NOTES HE HIT BY CHANCE WERE THE ONES GHAZANDI HAD WARNED HIM ABOUT... NOTES THAT AFFECTED THE PLAYER, CHANGING HIS CHARACTER, HIS MENTALITY, STEALING AWAY HIS POWER...

WH...WHAT AM I DOING HERE? I...I FEEL AS THOUGH I'VE BEEN ASLEEP FOR AGES! AND NOW I'VE BEEN REBORN! DON'T REMEMBER ANYTHING SINCE I GOT MY FIRST JOB PLAYING THE HORN!

THROUGHOUT THE CITY PEOPLE STIR, MOVE, CONTINUE ON THEIR VARIOUS WAYS, NOT REMEMBERING THE HYPNOSIS, THE NIGHTMARE THAT HAD DESCENDED ON NEW YORK!

THAT WRAPS THE TRAGO CAPER UP! WE STOPPED HIM BEFORE HE ACTUALLY COMMITTED ANY CRIME! ...AND NO ONE, INCLUDING TRAGO, WILL REMEMBER WHAT HAPPENED! NO ONE, BUT JAN AND I, AND THE ANTS!!

SEVERAL WEEKS LATER, AT A LOCAL BISTRO...

TRAGO'S HAPPY NOW! HE DOESN'T REMEMBER THE PAST, BUT HE'S DOING WHAT HE LOVES BEST... PLAYING THE TRUMPET!

YES, HE'S JUST ANOTHER JAZZ TRUMPETER! YOU HEAR THEM EVERY DAY AND NEVER QUITE REMEMBER THEM!

LEAVING SO SOON? BUT I THOUGHT YOU WERE GETTING TO LIKE JAZZ!

I AM, JAN, BUT I'D LIKE TO GO SOMEPLACE WHERE IT'S QUIET...

I SUPPOSE YOU'LL THINK I'M CORNY... JUST A SENTIMENTAL FOOL, BUT... I'M THINKING OF KORR! HE WAS ONLY AN ANT, BUT...

I KNOW, HENRY! I KNOW HOW YOU FEEL!

"GREATER LOVE HATH NO ONE THAN THIS, THAT HE LAY DOWN HIS LIFE FOR HIS FRIENDS!"

The End

13.

TALES TO ASTONISH

MARVEL COMICS GROUP 12¢

APPROVED BY THE COMICS CODE AUTHORITY

IND.

48 OCT.

ANT-MAN and The WASP BATTLE: THE PORCUPINE

ANT-MAN IS DROWNING, AND I'M POWERLESS TO SAVE HIM!

NO ONE THAT LIVES IS MIGHTY ENOUGH TO RESIST ME!

THE DREADED PORCUPINE A SUPER-VILLAIN YOU'LL NEVER FORGET!

ANT-MAN and THE WASP DEFY THE PORCUPINE!

STORY PLOT: **STAN LEE**
SCRIPT: **H.E. HUNTLEY**

ART: **DON HECK**
LETTERING: **S. ROSEN**

THAT'S AN **ARMY ORDNANCE PLANT** BELOW US, JAN! SOME OF THE FINEST INVENTIVE BRAINS IN THE COUNTRY WORK THERE, CONSTANTLY STRIVING TO CREATE NEWER AND BETTER WEAPONS FOR OUR DEFENSE!

YOU WORRY ABOUT THE WEAPONS, ANT-MAN! **I'D** RATHER THINK ABOUT ALL THE GLAMOROUS, ELIGIBLE **MALES** WHO MUST BE WORKING THERE! =SIGH!= I WISH WE HAD SOMETHING TO INVESTIGATE DOWN THERE!

A LIGHT BANTERING CONVERSATION OCCURS AS **ANT-MAN** AND THE **WASP** WING THEIR WAY OVER THE ARMY ORDNANCE CENTER! YET, HOW CAN THEY KNOW THAT WITHIN THOSE WALLS A THREAT IS BEING SPAWNED, A PERIL WITH WHICH THEY WILL SOON COME TO GRIPS...THAT THE MOST DANGEROUS AND DEADLY MENACE THEY HAVE EVER FACED IS EVEN AT THAT MOMENT TAKING SHAPE...

X-387

BUT, JUST AS ANT-MAN AND THE WASP ARE UNAWARE OF WHAT IS HAPPENING BELOW, SO ALEX GENTRY, IN THE LAB AT THE ORDNANCE CENTER, IS UNAWARE OF THEIR FLIGHT **ABOVE** HIM AS HE HOLDS A PICTURE IN HIS HAND AND STUDIES IT...

YES, THE **PORCUPINE** IS NATURE'S PERFECT FIGHTING MACHINE FOR ATTACK OR DEFENSE...A CREATURE THAT **WEARS** ITS WEAPONS, AND THEN SHOOTS THEM AT HIS ENEMY! SO SIMPLE, SO DIRECT...SO FOOLPROOF!

1

USING THE PORCUPINE AS A MODEL, I THINK MY COMBAT SUIT IS THE ULTIMATE IN WEAPONRY! EVERY SOLDIER WEARING IT WILL BECOME A ONE-MAN REGIMENT!

I PERSONALLY SHALL MAKE THE FINAL TEST... BUT WITHOUT LOADING THE QUILL-LIKE TUBES!

AND I MUSTN'T FORGET THE GAS MASK SO THAT THE WEARER WILL NOT BE AFFECTED BY FUMES FROM THE GAS TUBES!

YES, EACH BUTTON CONTROLS A SPECIAL GROUP OF TUBES! ONCE THE QUILLS ARE LOADED... SOME WITH GAS, SOME WITH STUN-PELLETS, AMMONIA, LIQUID FIRE, DETECTOR MINE TUBES AND ALL THE REST... THE MAN WHO WEARS THIS SUIT COULD DEFEAT *ANY* FOE!

A MAN COULD BECOME *ALL-POWERFUL* BY WEARING MY MARVELOUS PORCUPINE SUIT!

AND WHAT WILL BE *MY* REWARD FOR TURNING IT OVER TO THE GOVERNMENT? WILL I BECOME RICH, POWERFUL? NO, THEY'LL SAY, "GOOD JOB, GENTRY! NOW WHIP US UP SOMETHING *ELSE* AND MAYBE IF YOU'RE REALLY SUCCESSFUL IN THE NEXT YEAR OR TWO, WE'LL GIVE YOU A TEN DOLLAR RAISE, IF THE DEFENSE DEPARTMENT *OKAYS* IT!"

NO! *NOT THIS TIME!* THIS IS MY ONE BIG CHANCE! I COULD BECOME A *KING* USING THIS SUIT... YES.. A KING OF CRIMINALS! ME! ALEX GENTRY! NO, NOT ALEX GENTRY... *THE PORCUPINE* ... I SHALL BECOME THE GREATEST CRIMINAL THE WORLD HAS EVER KNOWN!

SLAM!

2

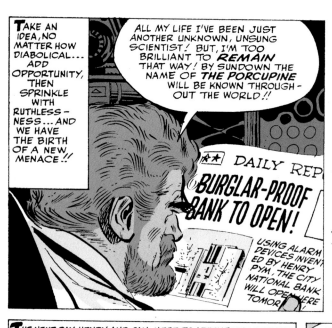

TAKE AN IDEA, NO MATTER HOW DIABOLICAL... ADD OPPORTUNITY, THEN SPRINKLE WITH RUTHLESS-NESS... AND WE HAVE THE BIRTH OF A NEW MENACE!!

ALL MY LIFE I'VE BEEN JUST ANOTHER UNKNOWN, UNSUNG SCIENTIST! BUT, I'M TOO BRILLIANT TO REMAIN THAT WAY! BY SUNDOWN THE NAME OF THE PORCUPINE WILL BE KNOWN THROUGH-OUT THE WORLD!!

DAILY REP
BURGLAR-PROOF BANK TO OPEN!

USING ALARM DEVICES INVENTED BY HENRY PYM, THE CITY NATIONAL BANK WILL OPEN HERE TOMOR

...AND I'LL BE AS RICH AS MIDAS! NOW TO SELECT THE ITEMS FOR MY QUILL TUBES! I'LL USE THIS LAB AS MY HEADQUARTERS! WHO WOULD EVER THINK OF LOOKING FOR A MASTER-CRIMINAL AT AN ARMY ORDNANCE CENTER !!?

...NOW, LET'S SEE... ATOMIC PELLETS, LIQUID FIRE, GAS PELLETS, FOG PELLETS, LIQUID CEMENT...

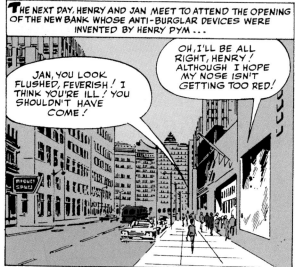

THE NEXT DAY, HENRY AND JAN MEET TO ATTEND THE OPENING OF THE NEW BANK WHOSE ANTI-BURGLAR DEVICES WERE INVENTED BY HENRY PYM...

JAN, YOU LOOK FLUSHED, FEVERISH! I THINK YOU'RE ILL! YOU SHOULDN'T HAVE COME!

OH, I'LL BE ALL RIGHT, HENRY! ALTHOUGH I HOPE MY NOSE ISN'T GETTING TOO RED!

CAN'T YOU EVER THINK OF ANYTHING BUT THE WAY YOU LOOK? I'M TAKING YOU RIGHT HOME AND...

OH, SHUSH, YOU SILLY WORRY-WART! I'M ALL RIGHT! STOP SOUNDING SO MUCH LIKE A...A HUSBAND!

ATTENTION, FOLKS...

I WANT TO TELL YOU A LITTLE ABOUT OUR NEW BANK BEFORE IT IS OFFICIAL-LY OPENED! WE HAVE THE LARGEST VAULT IN THE WORLD! IT CAN ONLY BE OPENED BY TWO PEOPLE WHOSE FINGERPRINTS WERE PREVIOUSLY RECORDED! SENSITIVE MECHANISMS WITHIN THE COMBINATION DIAL READ THE PRINTS!

GRAND OPE

HMM... I THOUGHT YOU WERE GOING TO HOLD MY HAND, BUT I SEE YOU ONLY WANTED TO FEEL MY PULSE!

SHH! BE QUIET A MOMENT...

AS THE BANK PRESIDENT CONTINUES HIS SPEECH, A STRANGE BULKY FIGURE ENTERS UNNOTICED IN THE CROWD...

3.

...AND THE STEEL COMPOUND OF THE VAULT CANNOT BE AFFECTED BY ANYTHING LESS THAN FLAME SO HOT THAT IT WOULD MELT DIAMONDS! GOOD THING, TOO! FOR INSIDE THAT VAULT, FIVE MILLION DOLLARS ARE SAFELY STORED AWAY!

THE BURGLAR ALARMS THROUGHOUT THE BUILDING ARE A NEW, AND DARINGLY DIFFERENT, DESIGN! AS ADVERTISED, THIS BANK IS ABSOLUTELY BURGLAR-PROOF...

...AND CONTAINS EVERY POSSIBLE SAFEGUARD AGAINST ROBBERY! NOW, I WOULD LIKE TO INTRODUCE YOU TO THE MAN WHO *DESIGNED* OUR BANK'S PROTECTIVE SYSTEM, THE EMINENT SCIENTIST, MR. HENRY...

SUDDENLY, A STRANGE MURMUR RUNS THROUGH THE CROWD... A SHIFTING, AN UNEASY STIRRING...

SOMEBODY BETTER CALL THE ZOO!

WHAT ON EARTH CAN THAT BE?

LOOK, HENRY... THAT FIGURE! WHAT A STRANGE COSTUME! YOU DIDN'T TELL ME THEY WERE GOING TO PULL A GAG LIKE THIS!

I HAVE A SNEAKING SUSPICION THAT THIS *ISN'T* A GAG, JAN!

EEEE!!

SIR, I DON'T KNOW WHO YOU ARE, BUT THIS IS IN VERY POOR TASTE! I'M SURE YOU DON'T *BELONG* HERE! GUARDS! THROW *THAT*... THAT *CREATURE* OUT!

BUT *OF COURSE, I, THE PORCUPINE,* BELONG HERE! WHERE *ELSE* DOES A BANK ROBBER BELONG BUT IN A *BANK?*

AS THE GUARDS RUSH FORWARD, THE PORCUPINE PRESSES A STUD IN HIS BELT...

TEAR GAS TO BLIND THEM TEMPORARILY... LIQUID CEMENT TO CLOG THEIR WEAPONS, MAKING THEM USELESS!

4.

AND THEN, PANDEMONIUM BREAKS LOOSE...

HELP!! LET US OUT!

NOT WITHOUT A WHIFF OF *SLEEPING GAS* FIRST!

PEOPLE JAM AGAINST EACH OTHER, LOOKING FOR ESCAPE! BUT THE DOORS OPEN INWARD AND THE PRESSURE OF THE PANICKY CROWD KEEPS THEM CLOSED, LOCKING EVERYONE IN!

SOME KIND OF SLEEPING GAS! TRY TO BLOCK OUT AS MUCH AS YOU CAN WITH YOUR HANDKERCHIEF...

HENRY, WE'VE GOT TO *DO* SOMETHING...

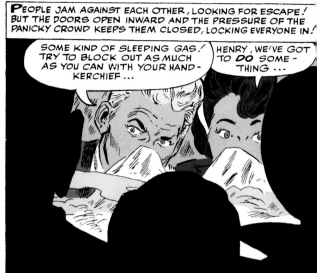

WE CAN'T DO ANYTHING IN THIS CROWD! WE CAN SCARCELY MOVE...

I..I'M BEGINNING TO FEEL DROWSY... THE GAS...

NOW, A *SMOKE SCREEN* TO HIDE MY MOVEMENTS, THEN ACETYLENE FLAME, AS HOT AS ANY YET DEVISED BY MAN TO BURN THROUGH THE VAULT LOCK!

JAN! LIE DOWN FLAT ON YOUR FACE! PUT YOUR NOSE CLOSE TO THE DOOR! THE GAS *RISES*...JAN, DO YOU *HEAR* ME? JAN??

5.

WITH THE SLEEPING GAS FUMES SLOWLY DRAINING HIS STRENGTH, HENRY PYM DRAGS THE INERT FORM OF THE LOVELY JAN OVER THE SLEEPING FIGURES ON THE FLOOR...

IF I CAN REACH THE OFFICE... SHUT DOOR... KEEP OUT FUMES... I'VE **GOT** TO MAKE IT!!

PRESIDENT

JUST ANOTHER FEW INCHES...

THE WINDOW! M-MUST GET *AIR*!!

CRASH

MEANWHILE, IN THE MAIN HALL OF THE BANK...

HA, IT WAS EASY... EASIER THAN I ANTICIPATED! AND NOW...

A *FORTUNE*!... MINE!... ALL MINE! AND THIS IS JUST THE BEGINNING! *THE PORCUPINE* WILL LOOT THE TREASURE TROVES OF THE WORLD!

LADEN WITH HIS LOOT, THE PORCUPINE PRESSES ANOTHER BUTTON ON HIS BELT, ACTIVATING A GROUP OF POWER JETS THAT LIFT HIM HIGH OVER THE CITY!

BY THE TIME THEY AWAKE, I'LL BE SAFELY HOME!

CRASH!

WOOSH!

6.

A FEW MINUTES LATER...

JAN! WAKE UP! WAKE UP!

OH, HENRY, I WAS HAVING THE NICEST DREAM! I MET THE MOST ROMANTIC BOY AND...

WAIT!! NOW I REMEMBER! THE BANK! THAT PORCUPINE CREATURE... WHAT DO WE DO NOW?

WE DO NOTHING! BUT ANT-MAN AND WASP HAVE A JOB TO DO! CAN'T LET THE PORCUPINE GET AWAY WITH THIS! I GUARANTEED THAT MY DEVICES WOULD MAKE THIS BANK BURGLAR-PROOF...

AND AGAIN GAS SWIRLS! BUT THIS TIME IT IS THE ASTONISHING REDUCING GAS, AND IN SECONDS, HENRY PYM AND JANET VAN DYNE BECOME... ANT-MAN AND THE WASP!

WE'LL JUST WALK UNDER THE DOOR AND...

TOO LATE! HE'S ALREADY LOOTED THE BANK AND DISAPPEARED!

HENRY, MY HEAD IS SPINNING! I ...I FEEL FAINT!

I'D BETTER GET YOU HOME RIGHT AWAY! I KNEW YOU WERE FEELING ILL! HERE COME THE POLICE! NOTHING WE CAN DO HERE NOW, ANYWAY!

ANT-MAN SENDS OUT A CALL TO HIS ANTS THROUGH HIS CYBERNETIC HELMET, AND WITHIN SECONDS, TORNE ARRIVES...

MMM...IT'S WORTH BEING ILL TO HAVE YOU HOLD ME IN YOUR ARMS LIKE THIS, HANK...

POOR KID...THE FEVER'S MADE YOU DELIRIOUS!

7.

I'M NOT THE ONE WHO'S SICK, SICK, SICK! WHAT ARE YOU MADE OF... STONE?

STOP TALKING LIKE A CHILD! THIS IS NO TIME FOR SWEET NOTHINGS...NOT WITH THE PORCUPINE AT LARGE!

LATER, IN THE GUEST ROOM, BEHIND THE LAB...

I'VE SENT FOR THE DOCTOR, DEAR! JUST TAKE IT EASY, LITTLE PARTNER...THE ASPIRIN I GAVE YOU SHOULD REDUCE YOUR FEVER SOON!

FINE THING, WHEN THIS IS THE ONLY WAY I CAN GET YOU TO CALL ME "DEAR"!

REMEMBER, STAY PUT UNTIL YOUR FEVER BREAKS! I'VE GOT TO GO AND CONTACT THE ANTS NOW!

YOU AND YOUR OLD ANTS! I'LL BET IF I HAD SIX LEGS, YOU'D LIKE ME BETTER!

The NEXT MORNING...

SHE'S STILL ASLEEP! IT WILL DO HER GOOD! I'LL TURN ON THE RADIO AND SEE IF THERE'S ANY MORE NEWS OF THE PORCUPINE!

MEANWHILE, AS A BANK IN THE DOWNTOWN DISTRICT OPENS AND THE DEPOSITORS START FILING IN...

LOOK! IT'S THE PORCUPINE!

PARALYZING PELLETS AND HYPNOTIC WHEELS SHOULD KEEP EVERYBODY UNDER CONTROL!

THE FEARFUL EYES OF EVERYONE IN THE BANK FOLLOW THE WHIRLING WHEELS AND IN SECONDS, ARE TRAPPED IN A HYPNOTIC TRANCE!

ONE THING IS CERTAIN...ANT-MAN AND THE WASP WILL BE ON MY TRAIL BEFORE VERY LONG...SO I MUST PREPARE FOR THEM AFTER THIS JOB!

BLAM!

8.

BUT, UNBLINKING EYES, MANY-FACETED ANT EYES, WATCH THE PORCUPINE'S EVERY MOVE, AS HE LEAVES THROUGH AN ALLEY AFTER HIS SECOND BRAZEN THEFT...

EACH STEP OF THE WAY AN ARMY OF ANTS WATCH...AS HE DIVESTS HIMSELF OF HIS PORCUPINE IDENTITY TO ENTER THE ORDNANCE BUILDING...

SOON, MESSAGES ARE RELAYED TO ANT-MAN'S ELECTRONIC COMMUNICATIONS MACHINE...

ARMY ORDNANCE CENTER? TOP FLOOR LAB? IT..IT DOESN'T SEEM POSSIBLE THAT THE PORCUPINE SHOULD COME FROM *THERE!* BUT MY ANTS ARE NEVER WRONG!

IN SECONDS, THROUGH THE USE OF HIS REDUCING GAS, HENRY PYM BECOMES *ANT-MAN* AGAIN...

I'LL LET JAN SLEEP... SHE NEEDS IT! I'LL HANDLE THIS *MYSELF!*

DOWN A TINY ELEVATOR TO HIS SMALL BUT HIGHLY EFFICIENT CATAPULT, ANT-MAN GOES! HE PRESSES A LEVER AND THE CATAPULT EJECTS HIM HIGH IN THE AIR...

PWWAM

LATER, INSIDE THE CHARGED WIRE THAT SURROUNDS THE ARMY ORDNANCE BUILDING...

OH OH! THE *GUARD* WOULDN'T HAVE SEEN ME! BUT THE *DOG...*

GRRRR!

COME ON, ALF, YOU'RE *SEEING* THINGS! THERE ISN'T ANYTHING THERE!

WHEW!

9.

THEN, WITHOUT FURTHER INCIDENT, ANT-MAN CRAWLS UNDER THE DOOR OF THE TOP FLOOR LAB, AND EMERGES IN STYGIAN DARKNESS!

WELCOME, ANT-MAN! I'VE BEEN EXPECTING YOU!

YOUR TINY SIZE WON'T SAVE YOU THIS TIME, ANT-MAN! THESE PHOSPHORESCENT PELLETS ARE ATTRACTED TO THE METAL OF YOUR HELMET AND WILL SPOT-LIGHT YOU NO MATTER WHERE YOU TRY TO HIDE, WHILE I REMAIN IN THE DARK!

THE PORCUPINE CHUCKLES AS HE PRESSES ANOTHER BUTTON ON HIS BELT... AND TINY NETS FLY OUT, ATTRACTED BY A MAGNETIC FIELD SET UP BY THE GLOWING PELLETS!

DON'T STRUGGLE, ANT-MAN! IT'S ALL SO FUTILE!

CAN'T GET LOOSE IN TIME!

NOW, I MERELY REMOVE THE NET, AND THEN I CARE-FULLY TAKE YOUR HELMET, LASSO, AND BELT WITH ITS TINY TUBES! I'M NOT GOING TO LEAVE YOU ANY MEANS OF ESCAPE, MY ANT-SIZED FOE!

I'VE GOT TO CONTACT MY ANTS... FAST!

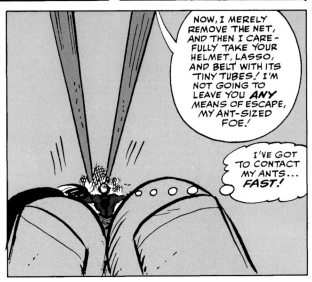

BUT, BEFORE ANT-MAN CAN SUMMON HIS INSECT FRIENDS, HIS HELMET IS PLUCKED FROM HIS HEAD AND...

COME ALONG, ANT-MAN, YOU'RE GOING FOR A SWIM! BY THE TIME I GET BACK, WE'LL SEE IF YOU WERE ABLE TO REMAIN ABOVE WATER LONG ENOUGH TO SURVIVE!

TREADING WATER FRANTICALLY, ANT-MAN HEARS THE PORCUPINE'S DEPARTING FOOTSTEPS, AND THEN... SILENCE! MOMENTS PASS... HIS ARMS AND LEGS GROW WEARY, AS HE DESPERATELY SEEKS A WAY OUT OF THE SLIPPERY TUB...

10.

MEANWHILE, BACK AT THE LAB, *THE WASP,* HER FEVER NORMAL AGAIN, BEGINS TO WORRY ABOUT ANT-MAN'S PROLONGED ABSENCE...

ONLY *ONE* THING COULD HAVE TAKEN HIM AWAY...HE'S TRACKED DOWN THE PORCUPINE! I'LL CHECK WITH THE *ANTS!* *THEY'LL* KNOW WHERE HE IS!

THE ELECTRONIC COMMUNICATIONS MACHINE, CHANGING THE ANTENNA IMPULSES OF THE ANTS INTO HUMAN LANGUAGE, BRINGS AN OMINOUS MESSAGE TO THE WASP...

ANT-MAN ENTERED THE ARMY ORDNANCE BUILDING, TOP FLOOR LABORATORY, TRAILING THE PORCUPINE! HE'S BEEN GONE OVERLONG, BUT WE CANNOT GO TO HIM UNLESS HE COMMANDS US TO!

YOU MUST *MEET* ME AT THE LAB! I FEAR ANT-MAN IS IN DANGER AND NEEDS OUR HELP!

IN SECONDS, THE NOW FRANTIC GIRL REDUCES HER SIZE AND PREPARES FOR ACTION...

MAYBE IT'S MY WOMEN'S INTUITION, BUT I'M SURE HENRY'S IN TROUBLE! ALTHOUGH HE *WOULDN'T* BE IF HE HADN'T TREATED ME LIKE AN *INVALID*... AND HAD TAKEN ME *WITH* HIM!

LATER...

HENRY, WHERE *ARE* YOU? *HENRY!*

IN *HERE!* HURRY!

I...I CAN'T HOLD OUT MUCH LONGER! ...NEVER BEEN SO GLAD TO SEE ANYONE IN MY *LIFE!*

SOME COMPLIMENT. WHEN YOU'RE *DROWNING* YOU'RE GLAD TO SEE ME!

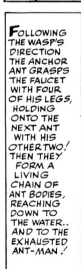

FOLLOWING THE WASP'S DIRECTION THE ANCHOR ANT GRASPS THE FAUCET WITH FOUR OF HIS LEGS, HOLDING ONTO THE NEXT ANT WITH HIS OTHER TWO! THEN THEY FORM A LIVING CHAIN OF ANT BODIES, REACHING DOWN TO THE WATER.. AND TO THE EXHAUSTED ANT-MAN!

CAREFUL... CAREFUL...

GOT YOU, JAN... YOU *DID* IT!

BUT THE *PORCUPINE* WILL BE BACK ANY MINUTE AND WE MUST BE *READY* FOR HIM! JUST LET ME CATCH MY BREATH...MEANWHILE, JAN, GET ME MY BELT AND HELMET THERE ON THE SINK!

JUST LIKE A MAN...THE MINUTE YOU'RE SAFE, YOU START GIVING ORDERS!

WE'VE GOT TO FIND SOME WAY TO PLUG HIS QUILL TUBES! AH, I KNOW! YOU REMEMBER HOW THAT LIQUID CEMENT HE SQUIRTED OUT PLUGGED THE BANK GUARD'S GUNS? WE'LL USE HIS OWN WEAPONS TO DEFEAT HIM!

LIQUID CEMENT

PULL! *PULL!* GOOD! IT'S TIPPING...

I'VE FOUND SOME PLASTIC BAGS! WILL *THEY* BE OF ANY HELP?

JUST WHAT WE NEED! I'LL PRY THE STOPPER OFF THIS CAN IN A SECOND!

AS WE FILL THEM, WE'LL TWIST THE ENDS CLOSED AND YOU ANTS CARRY THEM UP ON TOP OF THE TABLE! HURRY! THE PORCUPINE WILL BE BACK ANY MINUTE!

FINALLY, ANT-MAN AND HIS TINY INSECT WARRIORS CLIMB TO THE TABLE TOP...

IF THIS WAS AN ADVENTURE STORY, IT WOULD SAY "THE TENSION MOUNTS" AT THIS POINT!

QUIET, JAN! I HEAR FOOTSTEPS!

AND THEN...

HA! I *SEE* YOU, *ANT-MAN!* YOU'RE CLEVERER THAN I THOUGHT! BUT *THIS* TIME YOU WILL *NOT* ESCAPE! NEITHER WILL THE *WASP..* OR YOUR HELPLESS ANTS!

THE PORCUPINE'S FINGERS FLY TO HIS BUTTON-STUDDED BELT! BUT, BEFORE HE CAN PRESS THE BUTTON THAT WILL RELEASE A LETHAL RADIATION GAS, *THE WASP STRIKES!*

OW!

GOOD WORK, WASP! NOW QUICKLY, JUMP ATOP ONE OF THE SACKS WITH ME... *HURRY!*

12

BLIPPFT!

His dreaded weapon tubes clogged with cement, the porcupine presses his control buttons in vain!

I'M *STILL* NOT BEATEN! YOU FORGET...

...MY BACK QUILLS ARE STILL WORKABLE!

BLIPPFFT!

OHHH! I FORGOT ABOUT THOSE ACCURSED *ANTS* BEHIND ME!

Meanwhile, Ant-Man lassos Porcupine's arm and...

CRASH!

But, as the porcupine plunges toward the ground, he frantically pushes two more studs on his belt...and two tiny jet tubes, untouched by the liquid cement, manage to break his fall!

ANT-MAN WON THE FIRST ROUND... BUT I'LL MAKE MY SUIT MORE PERFECT, AND THEN... I'LL BE *BACK*!!

OH, HENRY... IF..IF I HADN'T GOTTEN HERE IN TIME... IF ANYTHING HAD *HAPPENED* TO YOU...

THERE, THERE! TAKE IT EASY, JAN! LISTEN, LET'S GET BACK TO THE LAB! I'VE *GOT* SOMETHING FOR YOU...

Later, as Jan eagerly waits...

WHAT CAN IT *BE?* FURS? JEWELRY? OR PERHAPS... A *RING??*

HERE, JAN, I GOT THIS FOR YOU! *AUREOMYCIN!* I WANT YOU TO GO BACK HOME AND TAKE THIS ANTIBIOTIC! I DON'T WANT YOU TO HAVE A RELAPSE OF THE FLU!

HENRY PYM... I *HATE* YOU!

LIKE I ALWAYS SAY...

...YOU CAN'T PLEASE A FEMALE!

13.

THE END

Character Sketches by Tim Seeley

Character Sketches by Tim Seeley

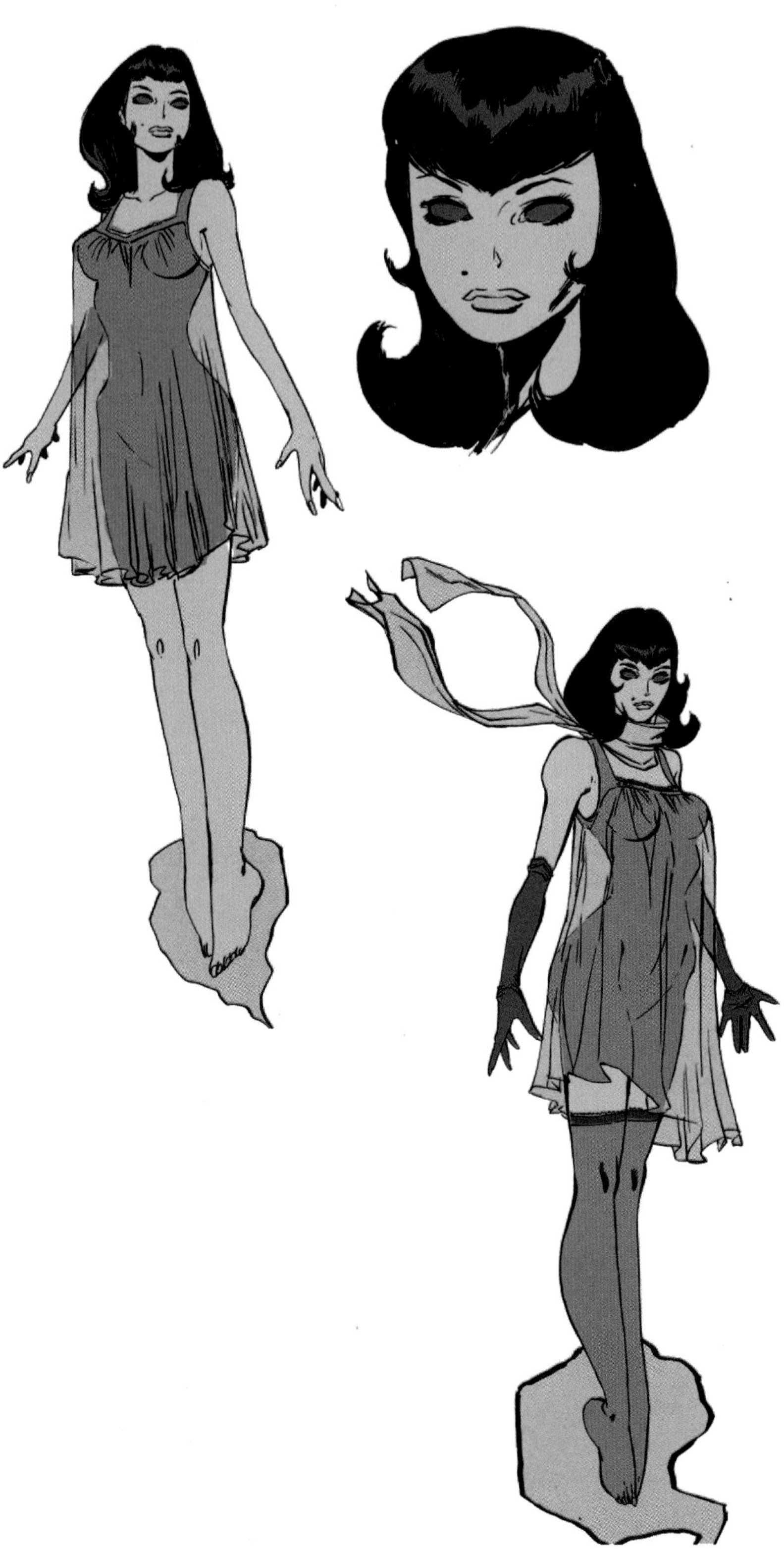

ISSUE #1 Cover Sketches by Salva Espin

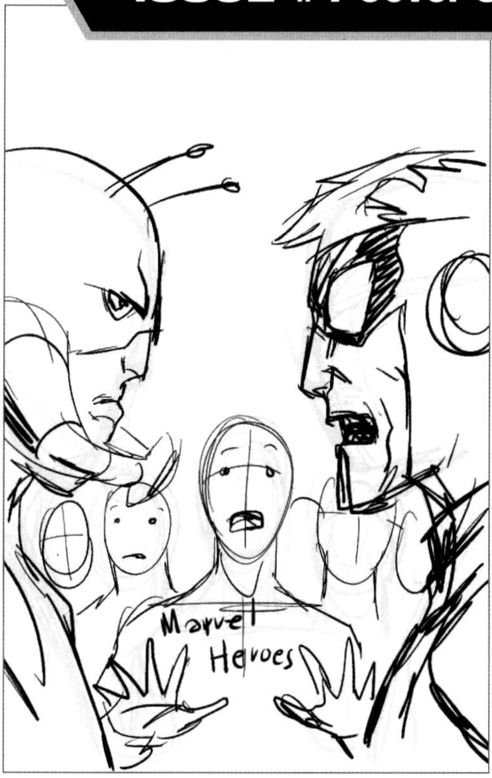
Marvel
Heroes

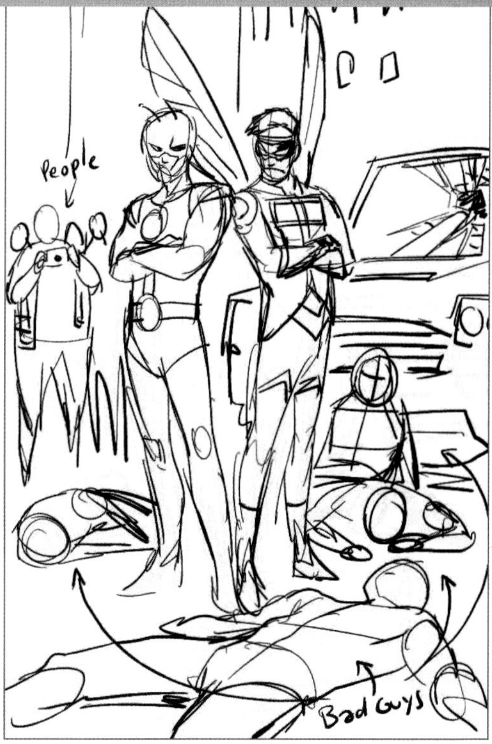
People
Bad Guys

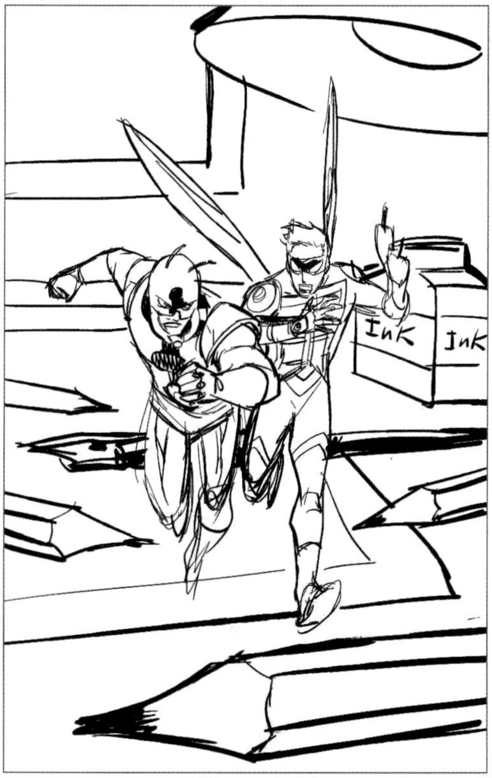
Ink
Ink

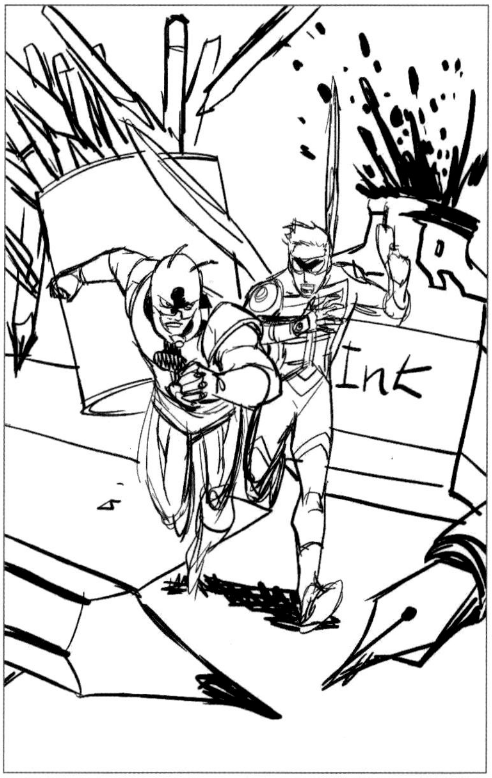
Ink

ISSUE #2 Cover Sketches by Salva Espin

ISSUE #3 Cover Sketches by Salva Espin

GUARDIANS OF THE GALAXY

WAR OF KINGS

S0-ARB-180

GUARDIANS OF THE GALAXY

WAR OF KINGS

WRITERS: **DAN ABNETT & ANDY LANNING**

PENCILERS: **PAUL PELLETIER, BRAD WALKER, CARLOS MAGNO & WES CRAIG**

INKERS: **RICK MAGYAR, VICTOR OLAZABA, JACK PURCELL, LIVESAY, RODNEY RAMOS & WES CRAIG**

COLORIST: **WIL QUINTANA WITH BRUNO HANG (ISSUE #9)**

LETTERER: **VIRTUAL CALLIGRAPHY'S JOE CARAMAGNA**

COVER ARTISTS: **CLINT LANGLEY, DAVID YARDIN & PAUL RENAUD**

ASSISTANT EDITOR: **MICHAEL HORWITZ WITH LAUREN HENRY**

EDITOR: **BILL ROSEMANN**

COLLECTION EDITOR: **CORY LEVINE**

EDITORIAL ASSISTANT: **ALEX STARBUCK**

ASSISTANT EDITOR: **JOHN DENNING**

EDITORS, SPECIAL PROJECTS: **JENNIFER GRÜNWALD & MARK D. BEAZLEY**

SENIOR EDITOR, SPECIAL PROJECTS: **JEFF YOUNGQUIST**

SENIOR VICE PRESIDENT OF SALES: **DAVID GABRIEL**

PRODUCTION: **JERRON QUALITY COLOR & JERRY KALINOWSKI**

EDITOR IN CHIEF: **JOE QUESADA**

PUBLISHER: **DAN BUCKLEY**

EXECUTIVE PRODUCER: **ALAN FINE**

GUARDIANS OF THE GALAXY VOL. 2: WAR OF KINGS BOOK 1. Contains material originally published in magazine form as GUARDIANS OF THE GALAXY #7-12. First printing 2009. Hardcover ISBN# 978-0-7851-3982-9. Softcover ISBN# 978-0-7851-3339-1. Published by MARVEL PUBLISHING, INC., a subsidiary of MARVEL ENTERTAINMENT, INC. OFFICE OF PUBLICATION: 417 5th Avenue, New York, NY 10016. Copyright © 2009 Marvel Characters, Inc. All rights reserved. Hardcover: $24.99 per copy in the U.S. (GST #R127032852). Softcover: $19.99 per copy in the U.S. (GST #R127032852). Canadian Agreement #40668537. All characters featured in this issue and the distinctive names and likenesses thereof, and all related indicia are trademarks of Marvel Characters, Inc. No similarity between any of the names, characters, persons, and/or institutions in this magazine with those of any living or dead person or institution is intended, and any such similarity which may exist is purely coincidental. **Printed in the U.S.A.** ALAN FINE, CEO Marvel Publishing Division and EVP & CMO Marvel Characters B.V.; DAN BUCKLEY, President of Publishing - Print & Digital Media; JIM SOKOLOWSKI, Chief Operating Officer; DAVID GABRIEL, SVP of Publishing Sales & Circulation; DAVID BOGART, SVP of Business Affairs & Talent Management; MICHAEL PASCIULLO, VP Merchandising & Communications; JIM O'KEEFE, VP of Operations & Logistics; DAN CARR, Executive Director of Publishing Technology; JUSTIN F. GABRIE, Director of Publishing & Editorial Operations; SUSAN CRESPI, Editorial Operations Manager; ALEX MORALES, Publishing Operations Manager; STAN LEE, Chairman Emeritus. For information regarding advertising in Marvel Comics or on Marvel.com, please contact Mitch Dane, Advertising Director, at mdane@marvel.com. For Marvel subscription inquiries, please call 800-217-9158.

10 9 8 7 6 5 4 3 2 1

In the wake of two catastrophic Annihilation events, the Universe is in a fragile and weakened state. With the fabric of space itself damaged, anomalous fissures are beginning to appear, fissures that could crack and spread, collapsing reality and letting in things that should not exist in our dimension.

Guided by the mystical insight of the newly returned Adam Warlock, the gun-slinging Star-Lord has forged a proactive team of proven cosmic champions ready to protect the vulnerable universe and prevent any large-scale disasters from ever happening again. Together, Star-Lord, Warlock, Quasar, Gamora, Drax, Mantis and Rocket Raccoon are the Guardians of the Galaxy!

During an infiltration of Knowhere by the shape-shifting alien Skrulls, the mysterious time-hopping being known as Starhawk -- now in the form of a female -- has been captured. But the infiltration itself has had shocking and unforeseen consequences. The team learned that in order to form the Guardians as quickly as possible, Star-Lord had Mantis influence their minds to make them more cooperative.

Appalled by Star-Lord's actions, and feeling unable to trust him further, the team has collapsed, and several of the members have left Knowhere to pursue their own destinies.

In the aftermath, two questions remain.
Who will guard the Galaxy now?
And what the d'ast has happened to Star-Lord?

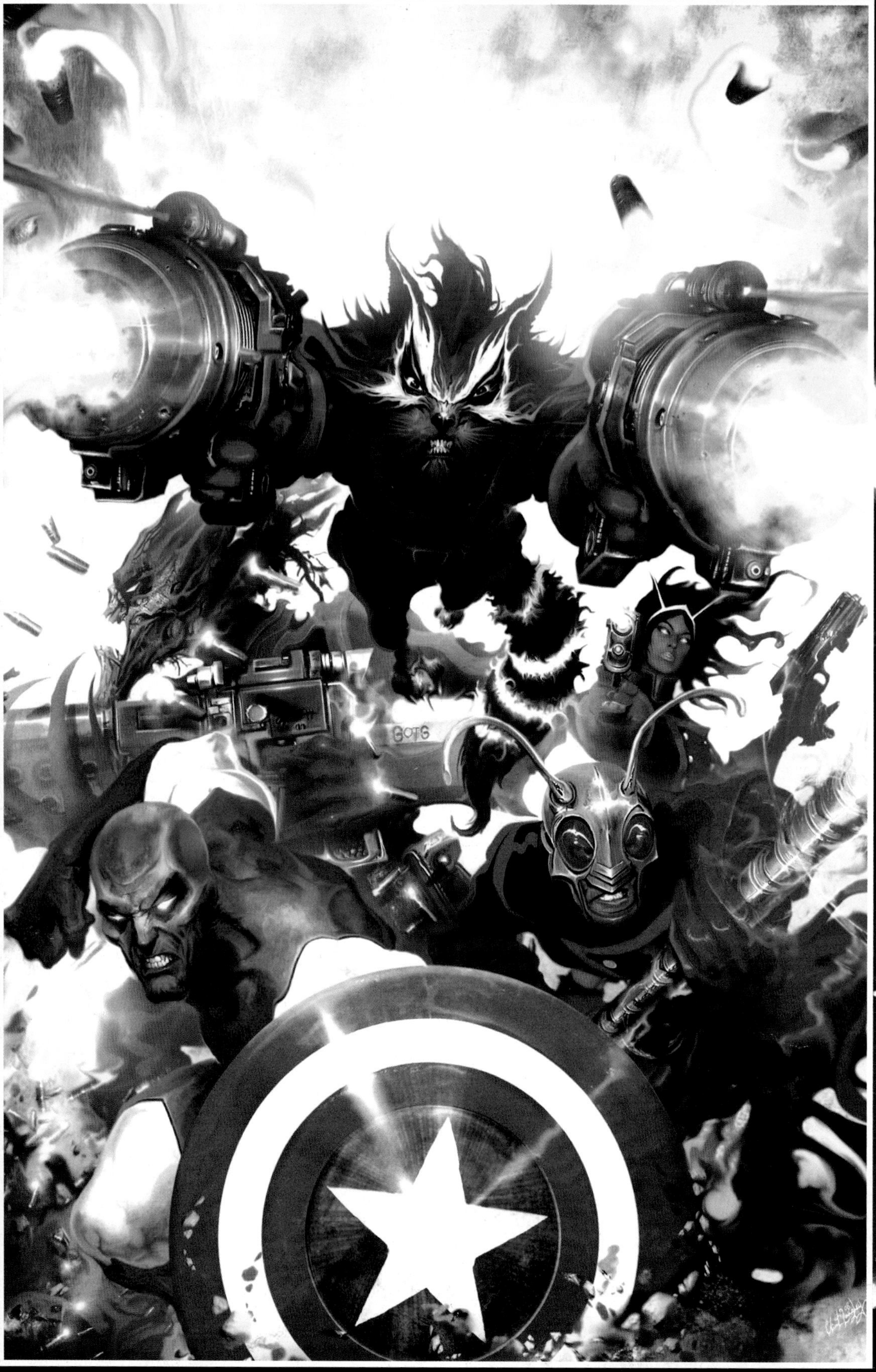
GOTG

7

"IN THE FUTURE, A *THOUSAND* YEARS FROM NOW, THERE WILL BE A STATE OF WAR.

KEEP RUNNING! KEEP RUNNING! THEY'RE COMING FOR US!

I CAN HEAR THEIR FLYING DISKS!

"EARTH AND ITS COLONIES WILL HAVE BEEN BROUGHT TO THE BRINK OF EXTINCTION BY THE ALIEN *BADOON*.

DOWN THERE! MORE MANLING SURVIVORS. SHALL I CALL DOWN AN ORBITAL BOMBARDMENT TO LEVEL THIS ZONE?

NO NEED. THE *FINAL CULL* HAS BEEN INITIATED...

...THE *ZOM BRIGADES* WILL STERILIZE *ANY* REMAINING MANLING ACTIVITY.

"ONLY ONE BAND OF FREEDOM FIGHTERS WILL DARE TO OPPOSE THEM...

"...AND WE WILL CALL OURSELVES THE *GUARDIANS OF THE GALAXY.*

"SOME OF US WILL BE *HUMAN HYBRIDS.* A THOUSAND YEARS FROM NOW, HUMANITY WILL HAVE RESHAPED ITSELF IN *ASTONISHING* WAYS.

"*CHARLIE-27,* FOR EXAMPLE, WILL HAVE THE ENHANCED BONE AND MUSCLE MASS OF A MAN BIOENGINEERED TO WITHSTAND THE PUNISHING GRAVITY OF JUPITER.

LET'S GO, GUARDIANS! EARTH SHALL OVERCOME!

NO FUTURE

DAN ABNETT and ANDY LANNING
WRITERS

PAUL PELLETIER
PENCILER

RICK MAGYAR
INKER

WIL QUINTANA
COLORIST

VC'S JOE CARAMAGNA
LETTERER

CLINT LANGLEY
COVER ARTIST

LAUREN HENRY
ASST. EDITOR

BILL ROSEMANN
EDITOR

JOE QUESADA
EDITOR IN CHIEF

DAN BUCKLEY
PUBLISHER

"MARTINEX WILL BE A SILICON BEING, HIS BIOLOGY ALTERED TO ENDURE PLUTO'S EXTREMES OF TEMPERATURE.

"HIS CRYSTALINE STRUCTURE WILL EFFORTLESSLY CHANNEL THERMAL RADIATION.

YOUR RALLYING CRY IS HEARD AND ANSWERED.

"VANCE ASTRO, A SURVIVOR OF THE TWENTIETH CENTURY, WILL BE A MAN OUT OF HIS OWN TIME. VANCE COULD PERISH OF OLD AGE WITHOUT THE HERMETICALLY SEALED PROTECTION OF HIS BODY SUIT.

"YET HIS PHYSICAL INFIRMITY WILL BE MORE THAN COMPENSATED BY HIS FORMIDABLE PSYCHOKINETIC POWERS.

YEAH, WHAT FACET-FACE SAID, CHUCK!

WE'RE WITH YOU ALL THE WAY!

"YONDU FROM CENTAURI WILL APPEAR TO BE A BOWHUNTER FROM A SIMPLER, MORE PRIMITIVE ERA.

"BUT THE SONIC-RESONANT METAL OF HIS ARROWS WILL MAKE HIM AN ELITE WARRIOR.

"SIDE BY SIDE, A THOUSAND YEARS FROM NOW, WE WILL FIGHT TO SAVE MANKIND.

"AND WE WILL FAIL.

"IT WILL NOT BE THE BADOON THAT DEFEATS US.

"NO... THEIR M... THRAL... ROBOTS B... THE CADA... THEIR ENE...

"WE WILL SIMPLY RUN OUT OF TIME."

STARHAWK? WHAT'S HAPPENING?

FTSSSSHHH

NOT AGAIN. PLEASE, NOT AGAIN.

AHKKKK--

STARHAWK! DO SOMETHING BEFORE--

"AS A CONSEQUENCE, TIME HAS UNRAVELED, AND OBLITERATED EVERYTHING THAT WILL BE.

"THE FUTURE TENSE IS DOOMED. AN ERROR HAS OCCURRED IN THE COADUNATE PATTERN OF TIME.

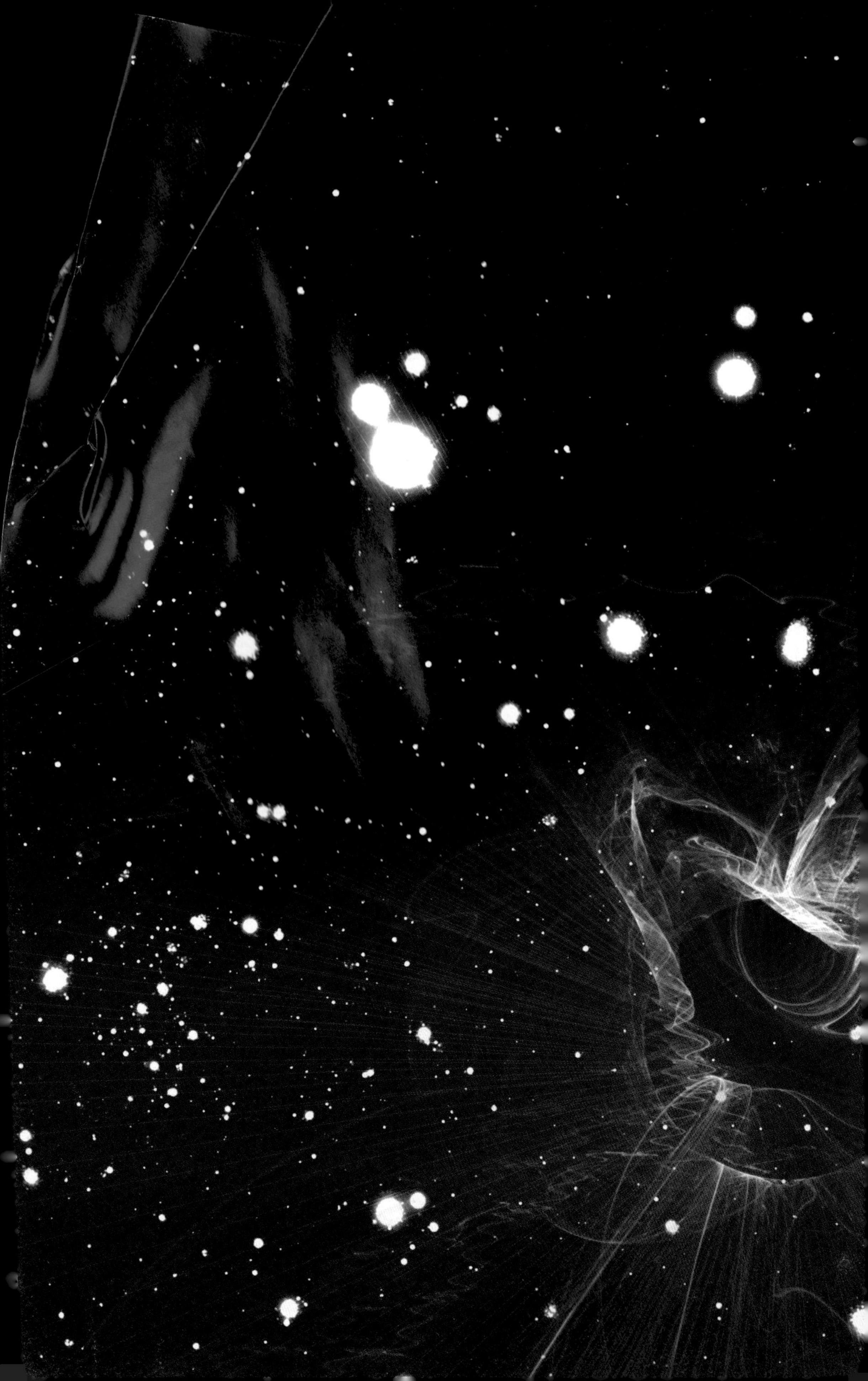

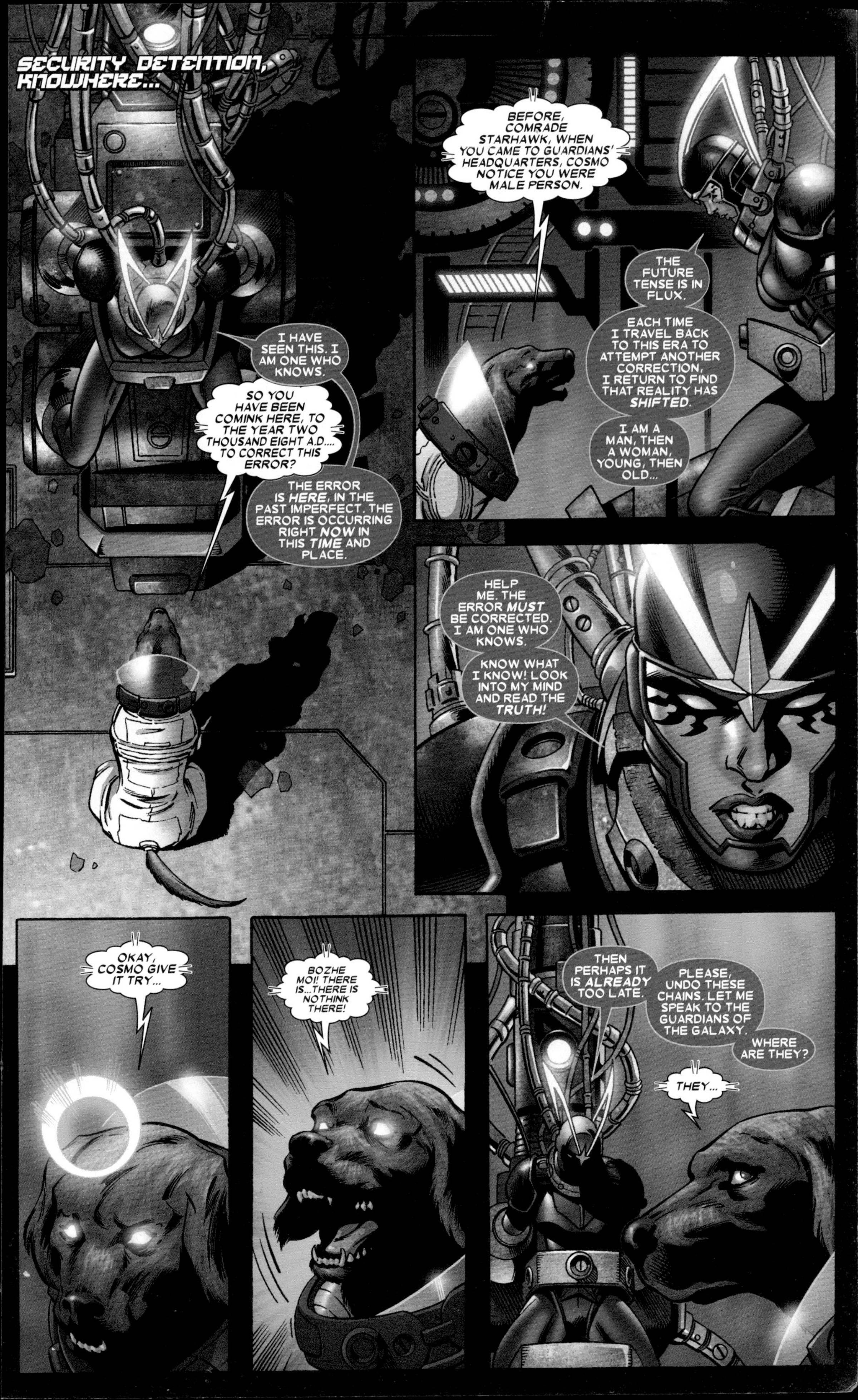
SECURITY DETENTION, KNOWHERE...
BEFORE, COMRADE STARHAWK, WHEN YOU CAME TO GUARDIANS' HEADQUARTERS, COSMO NOTICE YOU WERE MALE PERSON.
THE FUTURE TENSE IS IN FLUX.
EACH TIME I TRAVEL BACK TO THIS ERA TO ATTEMPT ANOTHER CORRECTION, I RETURN TO FIND THAT REALITY HAS SHIFTED.
I AM A MAN, THEN A WOMAN, YOUNG, THEN OLD...
I HAVE SEEN THIS. I AM ONE WHO KNOWS.
SO YOU HAVE BEEN COMINK HERE, TO THE YEAR TWO THOUSAND EIGHT A.D.... TO CORRECT THIS ERROR?
THE ERROR IS HERE, IN THE PAST IMPERFECT. THE ERROR IS OCCURRING RIGHT NOW IN THIS TIME AND PLACE.
HELP ME. THE ERROR MUST BE CORRECTED. I AM ONE WHO KNOWS.
KNOW WHAT I KNOW! LOOK INTO MY MIND AND READ THE TRUTH!
OKAY, COSMO GIVE IT TRY...
BOZHE MOI! THERE IS...THERE IS NOTHINK THERE!
THEN PERHAPS IT IS ALREADY TOO LATE.
PLEASE, UNDO THESE CHAINS. LET ME SPEAK TO THE GUARDIANS OF THE GALAXY.
WHERE ARE THEY?
THEY...

"...THEY ARE VERY BUSY ON IMPORTANT MISSION."

"SO, BENTHUS COLONY IS A SPARTOI DEPENDENCY IN THE CALLISTO SECTOR.

"MANTIS WAS WOKEN IN THE MIDDLE OF THE NIGHT BY... WELL, A SCREAM, REALLY. A PSYCHIC SCREAM OF PAIN AND HORROR.

"THAT'S THE KIND OF SCROD THAT HAPPENS TO YOU WHEN YOU'RE A MENTAT. ANYWAY, BENTHUS WAS IN TROUBLE, AND I HAD A CHOICE TO MAKE...

"DO I SIT AROUND FEELING SORRY FOR MYSELF BECAUSE THE GUARDIANS OF THE GALAXY JUST SPLIT UP IN THE MOST ACRIMONIOUS CIRCUMSTANCES?

"OR DO I TRY AND THROW A NEW TEAM TOGETHER AND DO SOMETHING ABOUT IT?

"(HINT--THIS IS US ON BENTHUS COLONY DOING SOMETHING ABOUT IT.)"

GANG? GANG? BEFORE WE GET TOTALLY IMPRESSED BY OUR OWN HEROISM, ANYBODY GOT A CLUE WHAT THESE THINGS ARE?

APART FROM ‡TIK!‡ REVOLTING, YOU MEAN?

I AM GROOT!

CAN'T HELP YOU, I'M AFRAID.

YEAH, YEAH...WE KNOW WHO *YOU* ARE, BIG BUDDY.

I WAS HOPING FOR A POSITIVE MAKE ON THESE *FREAKAZOIDS.*

THEY ARE *DEAD FLESH,* ROCKET RACCOON.

THEY ARE THE WASTE MEAT OF THE SLAIN *REENGINEERED* INTO IMPLEMENTS OF WAR.

THEIR MINDS ARE *EXTINCT,* EXCEPT THE DEEP ROOTS... OH, *HORROR!*

ROCKET, THE ATAVISTIC BRAINSTEMS...THE OLDEST AND MOST *PRIMITIVE* PARTS OF THEIR CEREBRAL ANATOMY...

...THEY ARE BEING AGITATED BY *REPTILIAN* THOUGHT-COMMANDS!

RR-CHKK

OOO-KAY.

THAT'S *THAT* CLEARED UP, THEN.

DEBRIEF LOG: ROCKET RACCOON (EVOLVED MAMMAL, TACTICAL AND DEMOLITIONS EXPERTISE)

RIGHT FROM THE GET-GO, *DESPITE* MY TEASING, I THOUGHT THE GUARDIANS OF THE GALAXY WAS A GOOD IDEA.

A *FINE* IDEA.

LET'S BE HONEST HERE, THE GALAXY CAN'T BE TRUSTED TO LOOK AFTER *ITSELF.*

THEN PETE GOES AND SCREWS IT ALL UP.

IT COMES OUT THAT HE GOT MANTIS TO *BRAINWASH* US ALL INTO THE JOINING.

OH, THERE ARE MITIGATING REASONS, BUT STILL...

HOW DID HE *THINK* WE'D TAKE THAT BOMBSHELL?

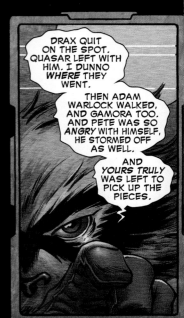

DRAX QUIT ON THE SPOT. QUASAR LEFT WITH HIM. I DUNNO *WHERE* THEY WENT.

THEN ADAM WARLOCK WALKED, AND GAMORA TOO. AND PETE WAS SO *ANGRY* WITH HIMSELF, HE STORMED OFF AS WELL.

AND *YOURS TRULY* WAS LEFT TO PICK UP THE PIECES.

"SO, FOR THE DURATION, OUR MARTIAL ARTISTE SLASH MENTAT *MANTIS* GETS A PROMOTION TO ACTIVE STATUS.

GROOT! ATTENTION! TO YOUR *LEFT!*

--I AM GROOT!

"*GROOT'S* GROWN BACK ENOUGH BIOMASS TO HANDLE SOME HEAVY LIFTING.

"AND BUG...WELL, I GAVE THE OL' LOVERBUG A CALL AND HE SAID HE'D HELP US OUT.

HEY, THIS IS-- --TIK!---JUST LIKE OLD TIMES.

MAN, OLD TIMES *SUCKED.*

DEBRIEF LOG: BUG (KALIKLAK ENTOMOLOGICAL BIOFORM, WARRIOR-ACROBAT)

SURE, I SAID. *FINE,* I SAID. *NOW* YOU-- --TIK!---WANT ME, I SAID.

SO I WASN'T *GOOD* ENOUGH TO MAKE THE FIRST CUT, HUH?

"'COURSE, I'M CHANCING MY PAW WITH *MAJOR VICTORY*.

"WE DON'T KNOW WHAT HE IS YET. D'AST, *HE DON'T* KNOW WHAT HE IS.

"BUT HE'S HANDY IN A SCRUM, AND RIGHT NOW WE NEED ALL THE *PECS APPEAL* WE CAN GET."

MR. RACCOON!

JUST ROCKET'LL DO. WHAT'S UP, MAJOR?

ZOMS.

SAY AGAIN?

ZOMS. I DON'T KNOW WHERE THAT WORD COMES FROM. IT'S JUST *SUDDENLY* IN MY HEAD.

THESE ARE *ZOMS.* THESE ARE ZOM *SLAVE* TROOPS.

THAT MEANS THE *BADOON* ARE HERE...

BADOON? THEY'RE LIKE *LIZARD* DUDES, RIGHT?

COME *OFF* IT, MAJE...BADOONS ARE A *MINOR* RACE. THEY'RE NOT CAPABLE OF... *THIS.*

WHEN YOU SAY *"CONQUERED THE GALAXY"* WHAT EXACTLY DO YOU MEAN?

HEY! *WAIT UP!*

I'VE NO IDEA WHAT KIND OF BADOON YOU HAVE *HERE.*

WHERE I COME FROM, THEY CONQUERED THE GALAXY AND *EXTERMINATED* THE HUMAN RACE.

THEY'LL BE CLOSE BY SOMEWHERE! THEY'LL BE *CLOAKED!*

OI! LITTLE-- --TIK!-- HELP! WE GOT FRANKENSTEIN TANKS NOW!

BE CALM, BUG. GROOT IS C--

I AM GROOT! I AM HELP!

SEE GROOT HELP!

CAN YOU SMELL THAT? THAT SWEET STENCH, LIKE OILED LEATHER?

THAT'S BADOON. I TOLD YOU THIS WAS THEIR WORK.

I TOLD YOU THEY WERE HERE.

YEAH, BUT WH--

OH MAN...

...I REALLY WISH THE OTHERS WERE HERE.

THE OTHER SIDE OF THE GALAXY...

YOU REALLY DIDN'T HAVE TO COME WITH ME, YOU KNOW.

I KNOW.

THUK

SHUK

I DIDN'T HAVE ANYTHING BETTER TO DO.

IT'S NOT LIKE I WAS GOING TO STAY WITH QUILL AND HIS LOSERS.

KHUD

AND YOU SAID YOU HAD STUFF TO DO. I THOUGHT I COULD HELP.

WHHKK

AND I APPRECIATE IT. I SEE YOU'RE FIT, GAMORA. ALMOST HEALED.

'CEPT THE HAIR.

SO COME ON, ADAM WARLOCK. WHAT ARE WE DOING?

APART FROM HAVING FUN AND WORKING UP A SWEAT?

THE UNIVERSAL CHURCH OF TRUTH. I HAVE DECIDED I NEED TO KNOW ALL ABOUT IT.

ORIGINALLY, I BELIEVED THAT THE CHURCH HAD BEEN *ACCIDENTALLY* ENTANGLED IN THE FISSURE CRISIS I SEEK TO PREVENT.

BUT THE SPECULATIONS OF MY META-TALENTS--

YOU MEAN YOUR *MAGIC?*

MY *NEW GIFTS*, YES. THEY HAVE HINTED AT *DARKER* TRUTHS AND *FATAL* PURPOSES.

THE CHURCH MAY BE MORE *DEEPLY* INVOLVED IN THE FISSURE CRISIS THAN I FIRST SUSPECTED.

SO I INTEND TO DISCOVER WHAT THEIR *"TRUTH"* REALLY IS.

OKAY. BUT THERE ARE *BILLIONS* OF THEM AND ONLY *TWO* OF US. YOU KEEP GOING AT THEM, THEY *WILL* KILL YOU.

WHAT I'M SAYING, ADAM, IS YOU CAN'T FIGHT YOUR WAY THROUGH *ALL* OF THEM.

I DON'T *PLAN* TO...

...I PLAN ON *LEADING* THEM.

ON THE OTHER OTHER SIDE OF THE GALAXY...

I DON'T KNOW! I DON'T KNOW! I SWEAR! DON'T HURT ME!

I DON'T KNOW ANY CAMMI, AND I DON'T KNOW WHERE SHE IS!

PLEASE!

HE REALLY DOESN'T KNOW, DRAX.

HE COULD BE BLUFFING.

DRAX, YOU CAN SMELL HE ISN'T.

LOOK, I SAID I'D HELP YOU FIND CAMMI, IF THAT'S GOING TO GIVE YOU SOME PEACE OF MIND.

BUT I'M NOT GOING TO HELP YOU TERRORIZE PEOPLE.

I'M QUASAR, I'M THE PROTECTOR OF THE UNIVERSE. I'M NOT A DEMANDER-WITH-MENACES.

SOME PLANET OF SOOTHSAYERS THIS TURNED OUT TO BE.

WELL, I COULD HAVE PREDICTED IT WASN'T GOING TO BE MUCH MORE THAN A TOURIST TRAP, AND I DON'T CLAIM TO BE ABLE TO SEE THE FUTURE.

THAT MUST BE THE TENTH JOINT YOU'VE WRECKED THIS MORNING.

HNN. USELESS PLACE.

IS IT ABOUT THE WAR?

WHAT?

THE *WAR*? IS IT ABOUT THE WAR BETWEEN THE KINGS? THE *ERROR*? THE DOOM OF THE *FUTURE TENSE*?

IS *THAT* WHAT YOU WANT TO KNOW ABOUT?

NO.

OH, MY MISTAKE.

WE WANT TO KNOW ABOUT THE GIRL.

THE GIRL? OH, YES. RIGHT. OF *COURSE.* I CAN *SEE* THAT NOW. THE GIRL.

WELL... SHE'S *LOST.* IT WILL BE *HARD* TO FIND HER. A *PAINFUL* QUEST.

BUT *NOT* IMPOSSIBLE.

WAIT, YOU'RE SAYING YOU CAN TELL US WHERE CAMMI IS?

CAMMI? WHO'S *CAMMI?*

I'M TALKING ABOUT A GIRL CALLED *HEATHER.*

BENTHUS COLONY...

HOSTILE ORGANISMS HAVE BEEN DETECTED. THEY ARE ASSAULTING THE WAR FACTORIES.

SHOULD WE SUSPEND TESTING?

THE HINDBRAIN RESPONSES OF THE ZOM UNITS HAVE NOT YET BEEN EXHAUSTIVELY TESTED. WE WILL CONTINUE.

HAVE THE ORGANISMS BEEN IDENTIFIED?

THEY HAVE PROCLAIMED THEMSELVES TO BE THE GUARDIANS OF THE GALAXY.

THEN I PITY THE GALAXY.

RELEASE A MONSTER TO CULL THEM.

Zz-ZZZMM

WHO-WHOA-WHOA!

WE GOT A ‡TIK!‡ BIG PROBLEM COMING OUR WAY!

A MONSTER.

HUH? OH, GIVE ME A BREAK.

A MONSTER. THAT'S WHAT THE BADOON CALL THEM.

A SUPER-HEAVYWEIGHT BATTLEFIELD BIO-CONSTRUCT.

I REALLY WISH THE OTHERS WERE HERE.

ESPECIALLY PETER. HE'D KNOW WHAT TO DO...

"...I WONDER WHAT THE HELL HAPPENED TO HIM?"

EEAAAAARRRGHHHH!

UGHNN!

OWWW... OW...WHERE THE *HECK*...

PETER QUILL. AS I LIVE AND BREATHE.

W-WHO'S THERE?

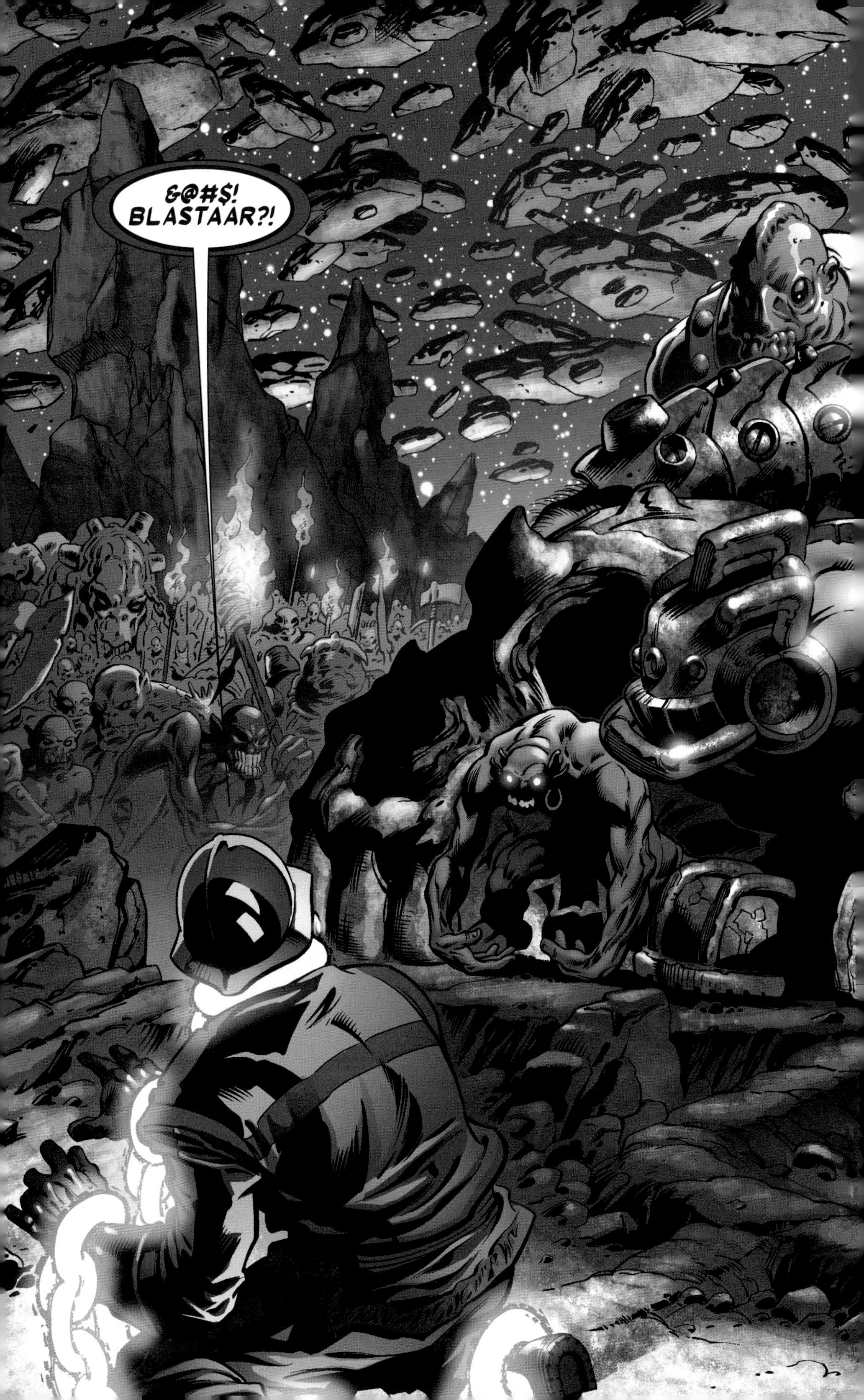
&@#$! BLASTAAR?!

KING BLASTAAR, IF YOU PLEASE.

WELCOME TO THE NEGATIVE ZONE.

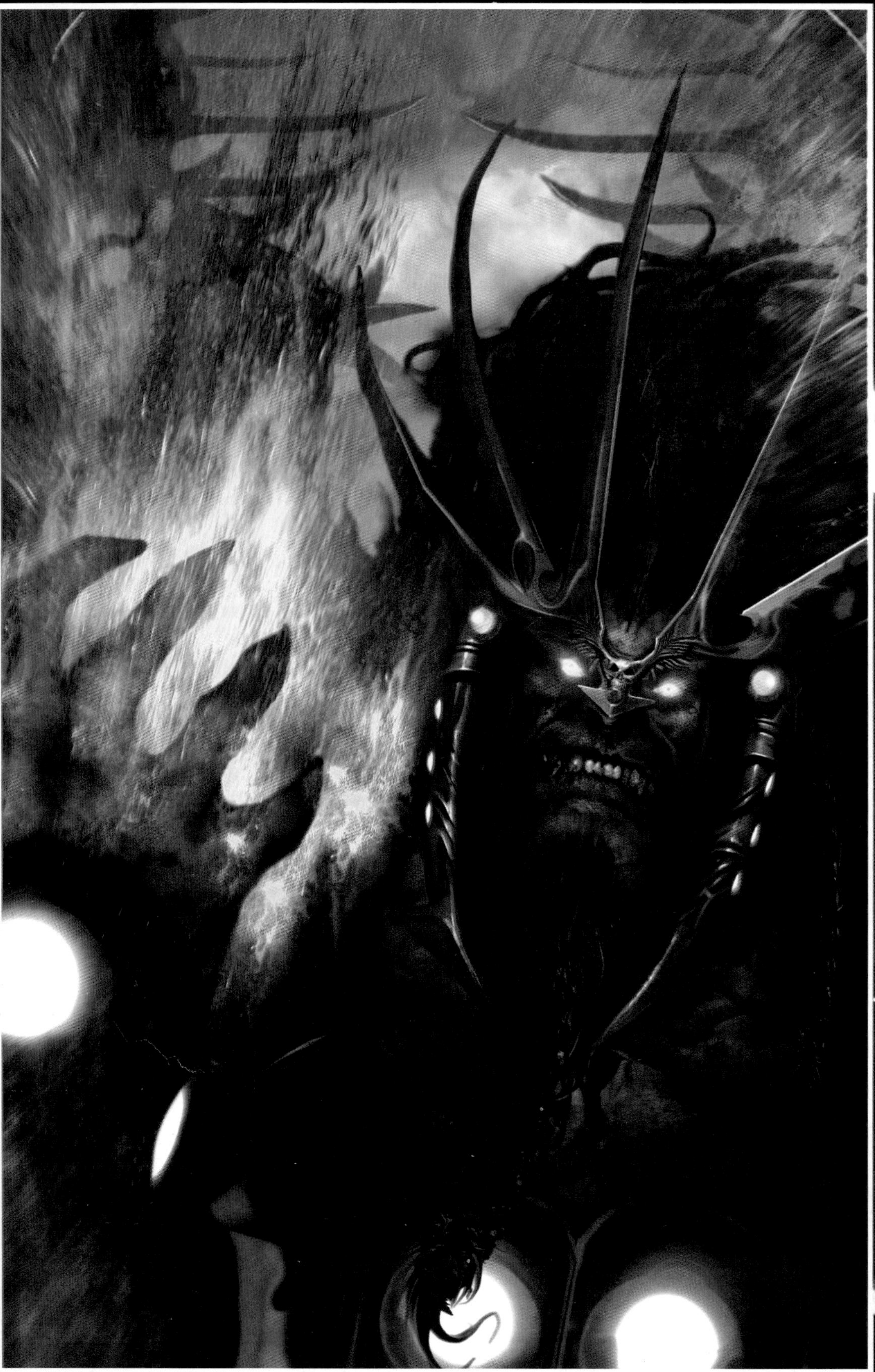

HALA, CAPITAL WORLD OF THE KREE EMPIRE. 24 HOURS AGO...

CHZZZMM

YOU LIVE A LIFE LIKE MINE, YOU END UP WITH A POCKETFUL OF REGRETS.

A GOOD REGRET GIVES A MAN CHARACTER, IF YOU ASK ME. I DIDN'T GET TO BE THIS HANDSOME AND LACONIC THROUGH CLEAN LIVING.

OF ALL MY BIG, UGLY REGRETS, MY BIGGEST AND UGLIEST IS THAT, THANKS TO ME, THE KREE EMPIRE FELL TO THE PHALANX.

I WAS THE IDIOT THAT LET THEM IN. I WAS THE JOKER THAT CONVINCED THE KREE TO LOWER THEIR GUARD AND LET THE PHALANX SUCKER-PUNCH THEM.

THAT GUILT HAS KINDA FESTERED. IT'S WHAT DROVE ME TO CREATE THE GUARDIANS.

NOW I'M MAD AS *HELL*. THE GUARDIANS CONCEPT HAS BLOWN UP ON THE LAUNCH PAD, BUT BEFORE I CAN PICK UP *THOSE* PIECES...

...MY CONSCIENCE HAS BROUGHT ME BACK TO HALA.

THE SKRULLS ARE MAKING A PLAY. THEY DEEP-INFILTRATED KNOWHERE. LORD KNOWS WHAT *ELSE* THEY'RE TRYING, BUT THE KREE ARE THEIR *OLDEST* ENEMIES.

I SENT A WARNING TO THE KREE WARNET AND GOT NO ANSWER.

I COULDN'T SAVE THEM FROM THE PHALANX, BUT I'LL BE *DAMNED* IF I LET THE KREE GET SPANKED BY THE SKRULLS *TOO*.

SO THIS IS WHAT I LOOK LIKE WHEN I'M BEING NOBLE AND HEROIC.

AND *THIS* IS WHAT I LOOK LIKE WHEN I REALIZE I'VE GOT IT ALL WRONG.

OH ✳✳✳✳✳!

THERE'S ANOTHER REASON THE KREE HAVE GONE QUIET.

DAN ABNETT and ANDY LANNING
WRITERS

BRAD WALKER
PENCILER

VICTOR OLAZABA
INKER

WIL QUINTANA
COLORIST

VC'S JOE CARAMAGNA
LETTERER

CLINT LANGLEY
COVER ARTIST

MICHAEL HORWITZ
ASST. EDITOR

BILL ROSEMANN
EDITOR

JOE QUESADA
EDITOR IN CHIEF

DAN BUCKLEY
PUBLISHER

PAST MISTAKES

THE BABEL SPIRE. YOU MANIACS WENT AND REBUILT IT.

WE RECEIVED YOUR WARNING.

AND YOU CHOSE TO IGNORE IT?

IT IS EXTRAORDINARILY ARROGANT OF YOU TO ASSUME THAT THE KREE WOULD NEED YOUR HELP TO DEAL WITH A FEW SKRULLS.

EARTH WAS THEIR PRINCIPAL TARGET. THEY DEPLOYED AGENTS ON HALA TO PREVENT US FROM INTERVENING ON THE TERRANS' SIDE.

WE FOUND THEM AND WE EXECUTED THEM.

AND A SIMPLE MESSAGE WOULD HAVE KILLED YOU?

"DEAR STAR-LORD, THANKS FOR THE WARNING, BUT EVERYTHING'S COOL, SINCERELY, RONAN THE ACCUSER"?

I DON'T OWE YOU ANYTHING. YOU LET THE PHALANX IN.

THE KREE PEOPLE MAY REGARD YOU AS A HERO FOR THE WAY YOU FOUGHT DURING THE PHALANX WAR, BUT I HAVE NOT FORGOTTEN WHAT YOU DID.

OH YEAH, BRING THAT UP.

WHATEVER. YOU WANT TO EXPLAIN THAT TO ME?

SINCE THE CONQUEST, WE HAVE BEEN *WEAK*. PHALANX SPIRE SHIELD TECHNOLOGY OFFERS US *PROTECTION*.

WE CAN ISOLATE OURSELVES FROM THE REST OF THE GALAXY WHILE WE *REBUILD*.

THE FACT THAT WE CAN POWER THE SPIRE WITH THE BODIES OF OUR ENEMIES IS MERELY A *BONUS*.

SPIRE TECHNOLOGY IS TOO *DANGEROUS* TO USE, RONAN. THE FABRIC OF SPACE IS UNSTABLE. YOU COULD RIP IT RIGHT OPEN.

DO I *LOOK* LIKE I CARE?

SHUT THE SPIRE DOWN, ACCUSER. SHUT IT DOWN, OR THE GUARDIANS WILL SHUT IT DOWN *FOR YOU.*

THE GUARDIANS? YOUR GUARDIANS OF THE GALAXY?

I'VE HEARD *SO* MUCH ABOUT THEM. WHERE *ARE* THEY?

THEY-- I DECIDED I COULD HANDLE THIS *ALONE.*

BAD DECISION.

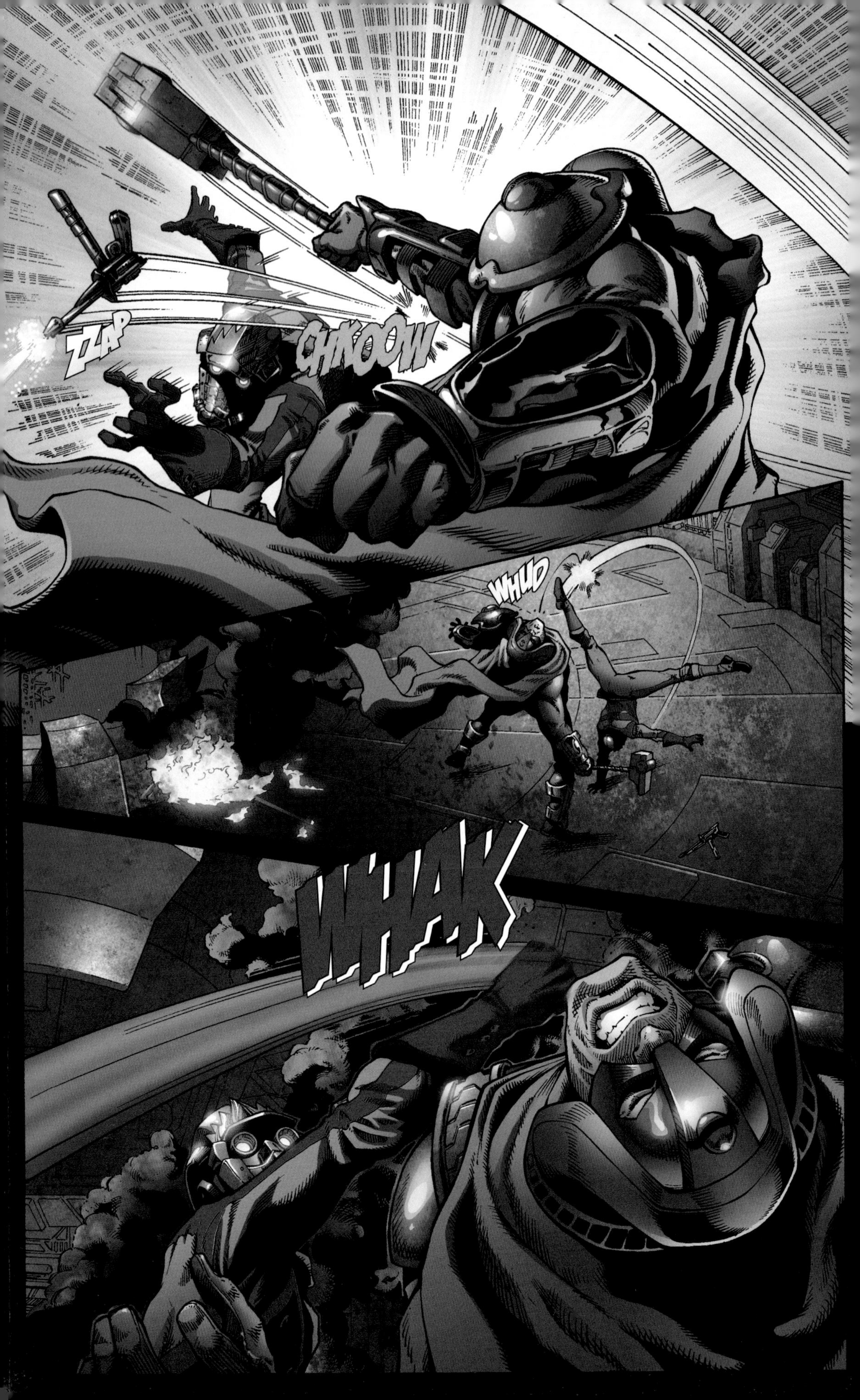

ZZAP
CHKOOM
WHUD
WHAK

I AM AN *ACCUSER*. AND *YOU*...THE KREE SCIENTISTS STRIPPED YOU OF ALL YOUR POWERS AND IMPLANTS WHEN THEY PREPARED YOU TO INFILTRATE THE PHALANX.

DO YOU HAVE *ANY* COMPREHENSION OF HOW OUTCLASSED YOU ARE?

GHHK! Y-YEAH. B-BUT I MADE YOU BREAK A *SWEAT*.

GUUHHH!

PETER JASON QUILL...

...I ACCUSE YOU OF CRIMES AGAINST THE KREE EMPIRE. I ACCUSE YOU OF AIDING AND ABETTING THE *ENEMIES* OF THE KREE EMPIRE.

THE SENTENCE IS *BANISHMENT.*

CAST HIM INTO THE ZONE.

ACCUSER, COULD WE NOT JUST FEED HIM TO THE SPIRE?

HE HAS TOO MANY ADMIRERS. I WILL NOT HAVE HIM BECOMING A *RALLYING* FIGURE FOR UNREST.

NOT *NOW*, WHILE THE DRUMS OF WAR BUILD.

BESIDES, IF ANY OF HIS *"GUARDIANS"* COME LOOKING FOR HIM...

"... I WANT HIM TO HAVE *VANISHED* WITHOUT A TRACE."

EEAAAARRRGHHHH!

UGHNN!

OWWW... OW...WHERE THE *HECK*...

PETER QUILL. AS I LIVE AND BREATHE.

W-WHO'S THERE?

※☠※☠! BLASTAAR?!

KING BLASTAAR, IF YOU PLEASE.

WELCOME TO THE NEGATIVE ZONE.

BENTHUS COLONY, CALISTO SECTOR... now...

THE NAME'S RACCOON. ROCKET RACCOON.

THIS IS ME AND THE GUARDIANS OF THE GALAXY GETTING OUR FACES PUSHED IN IT BY SOMETHING CALLED THE MONSTER OF THE BADOON, TOGETHER WITH A BUNCH OF MEAT-TROOPS CALLED ZOMS.

(BTW--I'M THE *HOT* ONE WITH THE BUTTON NOSE AND THE WHISKERS TO DIE FOR.)

YOU KNOW WHAT *I'M* THINKING?

YES. YOU'RE THINKING "WHAT WOULD STAR-LORD DO"?

I'M THINKING, "WHAT WOULD STAR-LORD DO"?

GO IN WITH-- ‡TIK!‡--A PLAN? HAVE THE FIRST CLUE? BE ABLE TO LOCATE HIS OWN *BACKSIDE* WITH BOTH HANDS, A FLASHLIGHT AND A--‡TIK!‡--SET OF WRITTEN INSTRUCTIONS?

OH, COME *ON*, BUG, I THOUGHT YOU'D *MET* STAR-LORD.

HA HA. SO WHERE *IS*--‡TIK!‡--QUILL, ANYWAY?

I THINK HE QUIT ALONG WITH THE OTHERS.

HE *WHAT? WHAT?* YOU--‡TIK!‡--NEVER TOLD ME THAT WHEN YOU ASKED ME TO JOIN, ROCKET!

MEMBERSHIP ISSUES, YOU SAID!

WELL THANK YOU *SO* MUCH, MAJOR VICTORY!

WE WERE KINDA KEEPING THE "*EVERYONE ELSE QUIT*" VIBE ON THE Q.T. UNTIL BUG WAS FULLY TEAM-INTEGRATED.

SORRY. I JUST ASSUMED YOU WANTED TO AVOID ANY MORE *DECEPTION* LIKE THE MANTIS-BRAINWASHING-EVERYONE THING.

THE--‡TIK!‡--WHAT?

NEVER MIND THAT! *PAY ATTENTION!*

WHAT HAVE YOU GOT, MANTIS?

IN FIVE POINT TWO SECONDS, A *POSITIVE* SWING IN OUR FORTUNES WILL BE SIGNALED BY THREE WORDS.

WHAT THREE WORDS? *"WE ARE LEAVING"?* *"HERE COMES PETER?"*

NO...

I AM GROOT!

YOU KNOW, FOR A TREE, HE'S GOT A *BEAUTIFUL* RIGHT HOOK.

ATTENTION! WHY HAVE YOU INTERFERED WITH OUR ACTIVITIES?

THE BADOON WANT TO TALK.

YEAH, NOW THAT WE'VE---*TIK!*--- BROKEN THEIR *MONSTER.*

BADOON! SHOW YOURSELVES!

WE CHOOSE NOT TO. YOU ARE NOT FIT TO GAZE UPON THE BEAUTY OF THE BADOON.

WHY HAVE YOU RUINED OUR WEAPONS TEST?

WEAPONS TEST? THIS WAS A *TEST?*

A LEGITIMATE AND SCHEDULED EVALUATION OF MILITARY TECHNOLOGIES.

AGAINST *LIVE TARGETS?* AGAINST A *PEACEFUL COLONY WORLD?*

HOW ELSE SHOULD WEAPONS BE TESTED EXCEPT AGAINST LIVE TARGETS?

YOU PEOPLE ARE *MONSTERS.*

I *TOLD* YOU.

UNLESS YOU WANT A *REAL* FIGHT, BADOON, YOU'D BETTER LEAVE. *NOW.*

WHY?

BECAUSE THIS WORLD IS NOW UNDER THE PROTECTION OF THE *GUARDIANS OF THE GALAXY.*

RR-CHAK

DEBRIEF LOG: MAJOR VICTORY (VANCE ASTRO, TIME-DISPLACED HUMAN, COMBAT GENIUS)

THE BADOON REMOVED THEIR WAR FACTORIES FROM BENTHUS WITHOUT ANOTHER WORD.

I WANTED TO *PURSUE* THEM, BUT THERE WERE TOO MANY LOCAL CASUALTIES *DESPERATE* FOR OUR HELP.

I DON'T KNOW WHAT KIND OF TIME I'VE ENDED UP IN, BUT YOU'VE GOT TO START TAKING THE BADOON *SERIOUSLY*.

ANOTHER FEW YEARS, A DECADE *TOPS*, AND THEY'RE GOING TO MAKE *EVERY* OTHER THREAT YOU'VE EVER FACED LOOK LIKE *KIDS STUFF*.

THE NEGATIVE ZONE...

BLASTAAR. HE'S ALL *KINDS* OF BAD NEWS.

GNNR!

RAAGH!

NUTJOB. BERSERKER. VIRTUALLY *INDESTRUCTIBLE* PSYCHO.

LIKE *BAD* OLD ANNIHILUS, BLASTAAR IS A NEGATIVE ZONE POTENTATE WHO LIKES TO INCLUDE "CONQUEROR!" AND "COSMIC PAIN IN THE ASS" ON HIS RESUME.

WE'VE NEVER BEEN WHAT YOU'D CALL *CLOSE*.

FROM WHERE I'M STANDING, THE FRYING PAN'S LOOKING *AWFULLY* INVITING.

SHRAKK

AIGHHH!

OH, DID I MENTION HE CAN BLAST KINETIC FORCE FROM HIS HANDS LIKE A LIVING *BOMB*?

IF THAT'S NOT HOW HE GOT HIS NAME, I DON'T KNOW *WHAT* HIS FOLKS WERE THINKING.

AND *THAT*, MY SUBJECTS, IS WHY I AM *FIT* TO BE KING AND PRINCE GRONCH HERE IS A WITLESS *FOOL* TO CHALLENGE ME.

THAT CONCLUDES TODAY'S COUNCIL AGENDA.

ANY OTHER BUSINESS?

WE'VE GOT A REAL *MESSY* HISTORY, YOU AND ME.

YOU SHOULD JUST *KILL* ME, BECAUSE IF I GET FREE, I AIN'T GONNA *HESITATE* TO KILL YOU, BLASTAAR.

KING BLASTAAR, IF YOU PLEASE.

THIS IS THE *NEGATIVE ZONE.* YOU COULD PAINT YOUR BUTT *PURPLE* AND DECLARE YOURSELF *GOD OF THE UNIVERSE*, AND NO ONE WOULD CARE.

BUT I AM KING. I BEAR *FULL* SOVEREIGNTY, AS GRANTED TO ME BY THE *KREE EMPIRE*, TO *RULE* THE NEGATIVE ZONE AT ITS BEHEST.

WHAT? WAIT! *WHAT?*

THE ACCUSER MADE YOU A *CLIENT KING?* YOU'RE HIS *MUSCLE* HERE? HIS *LOCAL ENFORCER?*

KING, IF YOU PLEASE. THE KREE NEEDED *SOMEONE* TO KEEP THE NEGATIVE ZONE IN LINE. I WAS THE *OBVIOUS* CHOICE TO REPLACE ANNIHILUS.

THEY *ASSISTED* WITH MY ASCENDANCY, AND THEY SPONSOR MY REGIME *WELL* ENOUGH TO KEEP THE MOST *TROUBLESOME* UNDER-KIN QUIET.

EXCEPT FOOLS LIKE GRONCH HERE.

RONAN'S THE *FOOL.* YOU MAKE A SKRULL LAWYER LOOK TRUST-WORTHY.

YOU'LL *TURN* ON HIM.

OF *COURSE.* IN TIME. I KNOW THAT. *HE* KNOWS IT.

FOR NOW, THE ARRANGEMENT WORKS.

GREAT. THE NEGATIVE ZONE HAS *MILITARIZED* AGAIN. THAT'S *ALL* WE NEED.

YOU WERE A *SPECIALIST ADVISOR* TO THE KREE, QUILL. YOU HAVE *SKILLS* I NEED.

I'M NOT LOOKING FOR WORK.

I'M NOT *ASKING* YOU, I'M *TELLING* YOU.

DYATOM SHRINE, OUTPOST OF THE UNIVERSAL CHURCH OF TRUTH...

KREESH

K-TOOM

I BELIEVE! YOUR WITCHCRAFT WILL NOT HARM ME, PAGAN!

YOU REALLY HAVE NO IDEA WHO YOU'RE UP AGAINST.

UGHN!

IS HE BEATEN?

HE'S BEATEN, GAMORA.

IS HE *STAYING* BEATEN, OR SHOULD I CROP SOME OF HIS LIMBS AS AN *INDUCEMENT*?

HE'S *STAYING* BEATEN.

AREN'T YOU?

P-PLEASE...

WHAT'S YOUR NAME?

AROKINE.

WELL, CARDINAL AROKINE, I WANT YOU TO *DO* SOMETHING FOR ME.

I WANT YOU TO CONVEY A *MESSAGE* FROM ME DIRECTLY TO THE *HOLY MATRIARCH*.

TELL HER, IT IS TIME SHE AND *ADAM WARLOCK* MET FACE-TO-FACE.

THE NEGATIVE ZONE...

THERE, QUILL. GET ME IN THERE.

WHAT THE D'AST IS THAT?

MY SPIES TELL ME IT'S CALLED 42.

AN INTERDIMENSIONAL JAIL THAT THE EARTHMEN BUILT TO *CAGE* THEIR SUPER-POWERED MISFITS.

MY GOD! I HEARD RUMORS OF A PLACE LIKE THAT.

IT IS ALSO A POTENTIAL *GATEWAY*.

YOU WILL *OPEN* IT FOR ME.

I *WHAT*?

OH, YEAH, *SURE*, BLASTAAR! LIKE I'M GOING TO HELP *YOU*.

KING, IF YOU PLEASE. AND *YES*, YOU *ARE* GOING TO HELP ME.

WE'RE GOING TO INVADE EARTH.

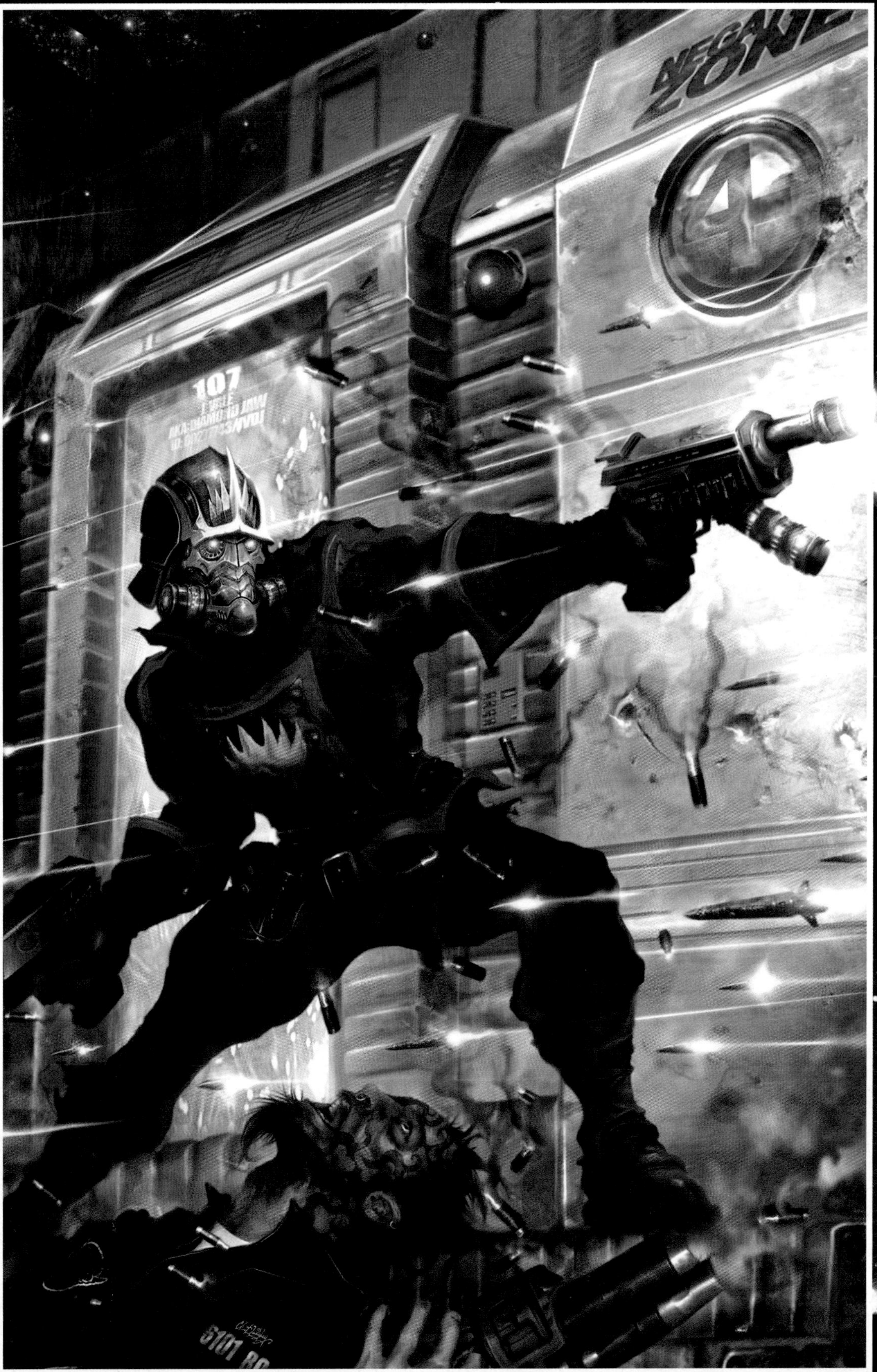
ZONE
107

DEBRIEF LOG: JACK FLAG (JACK HARRISON, VIGILANTE, ENHANCED STRENGTH AND CONSTITUTION)

I HATE COSMIC STUFF.

I MEAN I ✕✕✕✕ING HATE COSMIC STUFF. I JUST DON'T GET IT.

"LOOK AT THIS. WHO ARE THESE GUYS? WHAT ARE THEY DOING? ARE THEY EVEN GUYS?"

"I MEAN, CAPTAIN AMERICA. I GET CAP. I GET THE FALCON. I EVEN GET IRON MAN."

"THEY BELONG TO THE REGULAR WORLD. A REGULAR WORLD I UNDERSTAND.

"BUT COSMIC STUFF? CAPTAIN ✕✕✕✕ING MARVEL AND THAT GIANT GALACTUS FREAK? PLEASE."

"DOES IT EVEN MEAN ANYTHING?"

"I'M JUST A GUY FROM SANDHAVEN, ARIZONA.

"I DON'T DO COSMIC STUFF.

"BUT *SUDDENLY* I'M SLAP-BANG IN THE *MIDDLE* OF SOME."

PUSH THOSE SCALING LADDERS BACK! GET THEM OFF THE ✱✱✱✱✱ WALLS!

"FOR WHAT WE'LL CALL '*VIOLATIONS OF THE SUPERHUMAN REGISTRATION ACT*', ME AND 100 OTHER UNLUCKY MASKS WOUND UP SERVING TIME IN THE *INITIATIVE PRISON 42*, THE SO-CALLED '*FANTASY ISLAND.*'

"42 WAS BUILT IN THE *NEGATIVE ZONE*, WHICH MEANS IT'S IN A *PARALLEL DIMENSION* TO EARTH. ✱✱✱✱✱. LET'S NOT EVEN GO THERE, RIGHT?

"ANYWAY, LAST WEEK, SOME COSMIC JOKER CALLED *BLASTAAR* AND HIS HAIRY DRONES LAID SIEGE TO 42.

"SO THIS IS HOW MY LIFE IS, RIGHT NOW.

"THE WARDEN AND THE PRISON BULLS FLED THE MOMENT EVERYTHING WENT *MEDIEVAL.*

"THEY BUGGED BACK *EARTHSIDE* AND THEY CLOSED THE NEGATIVE ZONE PORTAL BEHIND THEM, *TRAPPING* US HERE.

"THEY HAD THE *DECENCY* TO LEAVE OUR CELLS OPEN, AND TO SHUT DOWN THE DAMPENING FIELDS THAT KEEP OUR *POWERS* IN CHECK.

"JUST ABOUT *EVERYONE* IN THE PRISON POPULATION HAS A SPECIAL POWER OF SOME KIND.

NYAAH!

"MINE'S *SUPER-STRENGTH.*

"AND WE'VE BEEN FIGHTING THE INVADERS OFF EVER SINCE. THEY COME AT THE WALLS, WE DRIVE THEM BACK.

"AN HOUR OR TWO PASSES, THEY TRY SOMETHING *ELSE.* IT'S BEEN LIKE THIS FOR *SIX DAYS.*

OKAY! THEY'RE FALLING BACK!

REFILL THE OIL DRUMS! GET THAT SECTION OF WIRE PATCHED UP!

"I DON'T HONESTLY KNOW HOW MUCH LONGER WE'RE GOING TO HOLD."

HEY, JACK! LOOK!

WHAT THE ☒☒☒☒ IS THIS NOW?

UH... HEY IN THERE.

PRISON BREAK

DAN ABNETT and ANDY LANNING
WRITERS

BRAD WALKER and CARLOS MAGNO
PENCILERS

VICTOR OLAZABA and JACK PURCELL
INKERS

WIL QUINTANA and BRUNO HANG
COLORISTS

VC'S JOE CARAMAGNA
LETTERER

CLINT LANGLEY
COVER ARTIST

MICHAEL HORWITZ
ASST. EDITOR

BILL ROSEMANN
EDITOR

JOE QUESADA
EDITOR IN CHIEF

DAN BUCKLEY
PUBLISHER

MORNING.

JACK FLAG.

STAR-LORD.

FORGIVE ME IF I DON'T GET UP.

HAVE THEY REDESIGNED YOUR COSTUME *AGAIN?*

BLASTAAR SENT ME IN HERE TO TALK TERMS. YOU IN CHARGE?

NO ONE'S IN CHARGE.

BUT A FEW OF THE STRONGEST *PERSONALITIES* HAVE FLOATED TO THE TOP?

IT'S LIKE *LIVING DEMOCRACY.* IT'S A *BEAUTIFUL* THING.

STAR-LORD, HUH?

YEAH. BLASTAAR TOOK MY SUIT IN CASE I DID ANYTHING FUNNY.

IT'S *STILL* PRETTY FUNNY.

YOU'RE ONE OF THE COSMIC TYPES, RIGHT?

I GUESS. AND YOU?

STRICTLY *BLUE COLLAR* SUPERHEROICS. I *HATE* COSMIC STUFF. NO OFFENSE.

NONE TAKEN. WHAT HAPPENED TO YOU?

BULLSEYE GOUGED OUT MY SPINE. I DON'T DO *WALKING* ANY MORE.

HOW ABOUT *TALKING?* BLASTAAR'S GIVEN ME AN HOUR.

TELL CONDOR, KI, G-MAN AND BISON TO MEET ME IN THE MESS HALL!

AND SOMEONE GET STAR-LORD SOME *SWEATS* FOR ✗✗✗✗ SAKE!

"I CALL THE TOP DOGS TOGETHER TO HEAR WHAT THIS STAR-LORD FELLA HAS TO SAY.

CLOSE THE DOOR. WE CAN TALK IN HERE.

WHAT THE ✖✖✖✖ IS THIS *ABOUT*, FLAG? WHO THE ✖✖✖✖ IS *THIS*?

I'M *STAR-LORD*. BLASTAAR SENT ME IN HERE TO TALK YOU INTO SURRENDERING.

SHOULD WE CONSIDER DOING THIS?

"CONDOR'S YOUR BASIC *GENIUS CRIMINAL INVENTOR WITH WINGS*. HE'S TOO *SMART* TO BE TRUSTWORTHY.

ABSOLUTELY *NOT*. HE'LL *KILL* YOU.

WE JUST STICK TO OUR ORIGINAL PLAN.

THIS IS HOW YOU *NEGOTIATE*, STAR-LORD?

KI *SWORE* HE COULD GET THE PORTAL OPEN.

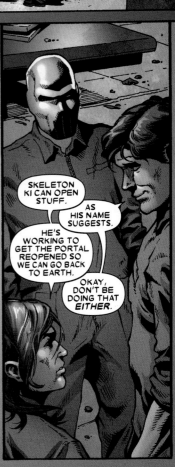

SKELETON KI CAN OPEN STUFF.

AS HIS NAME SUGGESTS.

HE'S WORKING TO GET THE PORTAL REOPENED SO WE CAN GO BACK TO EARTH.

OKAY, DON'T BE DOING THAT *EITHER*.

"GORILLA MAN IS AN OLD-SCHOOL *FREAK VILLAIN*. NOT MY PLACE TO SAY, OF COURSE, BUT I THINK HE TOOK THE WHOLE TRANSPLANT OPERATION THING *WAY* TOO FAR.

YOU GOING TO TELL US WHAT WE CAN AND CAN'T DO, SPACE-LORD?

STAR-LORD.

I'M GOING TO ADVISE YOU *AGAINST* OPENING A DIMENSIONAL GATEWAY THAT WOULD GIVE BLASTAAR AND HIS ARMIES DIRECT ACCESS TO EARTH.

WHY?

I CAN'T BELIEVE I *NEED* TO EXPLAIN WHY IT'S A *BAD* IDEA, BUT THEN AGAIN I CAN'T BELIEVE *YOU* THOUGHT SEWING YOUR HEAD ONTO A MONKEY'S ASS WAS A *GOOD* ONE.

WE DON'T *CARE* ABOUT EARTH.

"BISON. WHAT CAN I SAY? YOU DON'T ※※※※ WITH SOMEBODY WHO LOOKS LIKE *THAT*."

EARTH *DITCHED* US HERE. EARTH DOESN'T CARE *WHAT* HAPPENS TO US.

I SAY WE OPEN THE GATE. LET THEM *SUFFER*.

YEAH, *THAT'LL* LEARN 'EM.

HERE'S THE *SMART* OPTION. HELP ME CONTACT MY TEAM. I GET THEM TO BEAM IN HERE AND TURN THIS SITUATION AROUND.

TEAM? *WHAT* TEAM?

THE GUARDIANS OF THE GALAXY.

WHO?

THE GUARDIANS OF THE--

WHO?

WHAT THE ※※※※? I THOUGHT YOU MEANT THE *AVENGERS* OR SOMETHING!

YOU JUST MADE THAT NAME UP.

THE GUARDIANS ARE--

THAT'S NOT A *REAL* TEAM!

WE'RE COSMIC-BASED--

COSMIC? ※※※※! SO WE WOULDN'T HAVE HEARD OF THEM BECAUSE THEY'RE ALL *COSMIC* AND *COMPLICATED*?

YEAH, *RIGHT*. YOU'RE MAKING THIS UP!

I MEAN, WHO'D *ACTUALLY* BE CALLED *SPACE-LORD*?

IT'S STAR-LORD...

THIS IS A *TRICK!* A TRICK TO *BREAK* US!

I SAY WE OPEN THE FRONT GATES AND LET THEM IN!

WHAT? *WHOA!*

YOU THINK THIS STAR-LORD GUY IS TRYING TO *TRICK* US, SO THE WAY TO *OUTFOX* HIM IS TO *OPEN* THE GATES?

WHEN THEY GRAFTED YOUR HEAD ONTO THAT GORILLA, DID ANYTHING *FALL OUT* BEFORE THEY STITCHED IT IN PLACE?

WE'RE OPENING THE GATES.

SHUT UP, YOU LITTLE--

YEAH, I *REALLY* CAN'T LET YOU DO THAT--

UHN!

WHO'S GOING TO STOP US, *SPACE-LORD?*

IT'S STAR-LORD.

WHAM!

OOOK!

WHNNNCH

JUST STAY DOWN!

SHHKOW

GUUHHHK!

WHA--

I MAY HATE COSMIC ✖✖✖✖, BUT I DO DIG THESE BLASTERS.

YOU TREACHEROUS ✖✖✖✖✖!

SHHKOW

I GOT THIS OFF A ZONE WARRIOR WHO CAME OVER THE WALL THIS MORNING.

YOU MUST KNOW ALL ABOUT RAY GUNS, BEING THE COSMIC GUY. I HAD THIS SET ON *STUN*, RIGHT?

I DIDN'T JUST *KILL* THEM, DID I?

SADLY NO.

KI?

HEY, I JUST DO *DOORS* AND *LOCKS!* I GOT NO ARGUMENT WITH *YOU*, JACK!

GOOD.

SO YOU WANT TO CONTACT THIS *TEAM* OF YOURS?

YOU GOT COMS?

THEY'RE *FRIED*. THE GUARDS BURNED THEM OUT BEFORE THEY LEFT.

THEN HOW ABOUT A *TELEPATH?* YOU GOT A *TELEPATH?*

THIS IS *42*, PAL. WE'VE PRETTY MUCH GOT ONE OF *EVERYTHING*.

COME ON.

KI. STAY *HERE.*

SURE THING, JACK.

"OF COURSE, IN HINDSIGHT, I REALIZE I SHOULD HAVE SHOT KI TOO."

HEY! HEY! WE SURRENDER!

SATURN'S MOON TITAN, HOME OF THE TITANIAN ETERNALS...

IT'S JUST THAT HEATHER HAS...WELL...*SURVIVED* DEATH BEFORE.

...SO YOU'LL FORGIVE US FOR COMING TO YOU WITH SUCH AN *OUTLANDISH* TALE, FATHER MENTOR.

INDEED SHE *HAS*, PHYLA-VELL QUASAR.

MOONDRAGON'S SOUL IS QUITE REMARKABLY *RESILIENT*. THE OUTER VOIDS HAVE GREAT DIFFICULTY HOLDING ON TO HER.

I DON'T KNOW WHAT TO SAY. THERE'S BEEN NO EVIDENCE, UNLIKE *PREVIOUS* OCCASIONS, OF HEATHER ATTEMPTING TO PIERCE THE VEIL AND REACH ME.

I FEAR HER DEATH WAS NOT A *DEATH* AT ALL. I FEAR IT WAS SOME *METAPHYSICAL TRANSFORMATION* INITIATED BY THE DRAGON.

IT'S USING HER? FOR *WHAT?*

IMPOSSIBLE TO KNOW.

ISAAC, HAVE WE OR THE SHAO LOM MONKS DETECTED ANY UNUSUAL OR RESIDUAL *PSIONIC* ACTIVITY IN THE LAST FEW DAYS?

WE HAVE *NOT*, FATHER MENTOR.

BUT THEN, I AM MERELY THE MAN WHO *RAISED* HER. I AM NOT HER *LOVER* OR HER *BIOLOGICAL* FATHER.

IT MAKES *MORE* SENSE THAT SHE WOULD TRY TO REACH OUT TO EITHER OF YOU.

KNOWHERE, THE GUARDIANS' HQ....

SO HOW OFTEN ARE YOU PLANNING TO DO THIS? JUST COME IN HERE AND SIT THERE *STARING* AT ME?

AS OFTEN AS IT TAKES.

WE COULD USE THE TIME TO *CONVERSE*, MAJOR VICTORY. WE COULD *TALK*, AND PERHAPS THAT MIGHT--

TO WHAT?

TO *REMEMBER*.

I DON'T WANT YOU TO *TALK*, STARHAWK. I DON'T WANT YOU *PUTTING* THINGS IN MY HEAD.

I JUST WANT TO LOOK AT YOU IN THE HOPE THAT IT WILL *TRIGGER* SOMETHING.

I JUST WANT TO LOOK AT YOU UNTIL I REMEMBER FOR *MYSELF*.

AND DO YOU *LIKE* WHAT YOU SEE?

MAJOR? THEY'RE BACK.

ON MY WAY, MANTIS.

DON'T GO.

DON'T LEAVE ME.

I'LL BE BACK WHEN I CAN.

HOW DID MR. RACCOON AND GROOT DO ON LOCATING STAR-LORD?

THEY WERE JUST FILLING ME IN, MAJOR.

NOTHING TO FILL. ME AND GROOT MET WITH THE KREE AMBASSADOR.

HE MAINTAINED THAT THE KREE HAVE NO KNOWLEDGE OF PETE'S WHERE-ABOUTS, EVEN WHEN GROOT SAID--

I AM GROOT!

NOT EVEN THEN.

THIS IS MOST DISTRESSING.

THE CONTINUUM CORTEX LOGS SHOW HALA AS THE LAST DESTINATION CODED INTO STAR-LORD'S PASSPORT.

WHY ARE THE KREE LYING TO US?

SEEMS TO ⸗TIK!⸗ME THAT EITHER STAR-LORD'S GONE TO GREAT LENGTHS TO DISAPPEAR...

...OR ⸗TIK!⸗ SOMEONE ELSE HAS DISAPPEARED HIM BIG TIME.

ROBOT MODELS

THAT'S ALL VERY WELL TO SAY, BUG, BUT--

OOOHH!

MANTIS?! WHAT'S WRONG?!

A TEEP SIGNAL...VERY WEAK...OH, GOD, I SMELL DEATH AND DECAY... PAIN...

IT'S PETER! I CAN HEAR HIM!

OH, THERE IS PAIN! HE'S IN TERRIBLE TROUBLE!

DON'T HIT ME! STOP HITTING ME! STOP!

STOP IT! WHY ARE YOU *DOING* THIS?

STOP *HITTING* ME!

WE WANT TO BE SURE YOU'VE SENT THE *MESSAGE,* CARRION.

WHY ME, FLAG? WHY *ME?*

BECAUSE *YOU'VE* GOT BASIC TELEPATHIC ABILITIES.

HAVE YOU SENT THE MESSAGE?

YES, I *SENT* IT! I DON'T KNOW *WHO'LL* GET IT!

HE COULD BE *LYING.*

HE'S ONE OF SPIDER-MAN'S FOES. HE'S A *LOWLIFE.*

OF *COURSE* HE COULD BE LYING.

JUST AS LONG AS YOU SENT IT.

I *DID!* NOW STOP *HITTING* ME!

WE'D BETTER MAKE SURE.

NOOO--

--NO! AHHH! STOP HITTING ME!

MANTIS?

IT WAS *PETER*. HE'S IN SUCH *AWFUL* DANGER. I FELT *FISTS*, HORRIBLE *RUTHLESS* FISTS.

WE *MUST* HELP HIM!

DID YOUR *TIK!* MENTAT FLASH GIVE YOU ANY CLUES, MANTIS? ANY AT *ALL*?

YES. THREE WORDS. "THE NEGATIVE ZONE."

KNOWHERE'S CONTINUUM CORTEX, TWO MINUTES LATER...

NEGATIVE ZONE, EH? THIS IS MAKINK MUCH MORE SENSE TO COSMO.

NO WONDER WE COULD NOT DETECT PASSPORT BEINK WORN BY STAR-LORD.

NEGATIVE ZONE IS NOT IN REAL UNIVERSE.

YOU SEE WHAT COSMO IS SAYINK?

YOU WERE LOOKING IN THE WRONG PLACE.

GIVE CHEWY TREAT TO MAN WITH BIG FRISBEE! YES, COSMO WAS LOOKINK IN WRONG PLACE!

BUT CAN YOU *FIND* HIM?

HURRY, COSMO!

COSMO HAS *ALREADY* FOUND HIM. EASY WHEN YOU KNOW WHERE TO LOOK.

I HAVE STRONG LOCATOR SIGNAL FROM HIS PASSPORT, RIGHT IN MIDDLE OF NEGATIVE ZONE.

I CAN TRANSPORT YOU TO WITHIN *FOUR METERS* OF IT.

FOUR METERS?

YUP! LENGTH OF A DECENT DOG LEAD.

YOU CAN *BE* THAT ACCURATE?

OF COURSE. IS EASE-OF-PEASEY. WOULD COSMO LET HIS VERY GOOD FRIENDS DOWN?

THEN *LET'S DO IT.*

RRCHHAK

YES, INDEED! HOW YOU SAY "ROCK AND LOAD"!

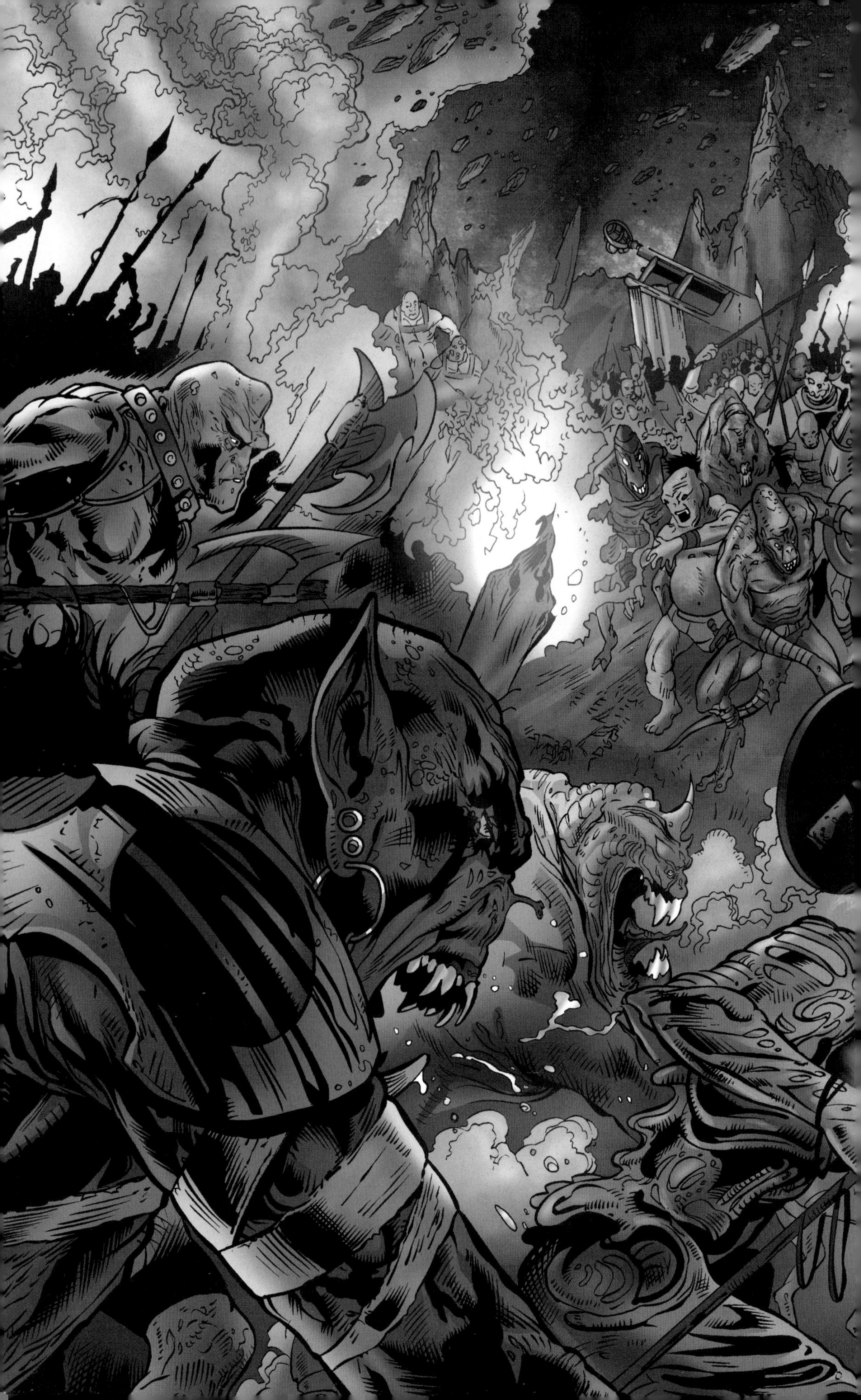

I AM GOING TO *KILL* THAT DOG.

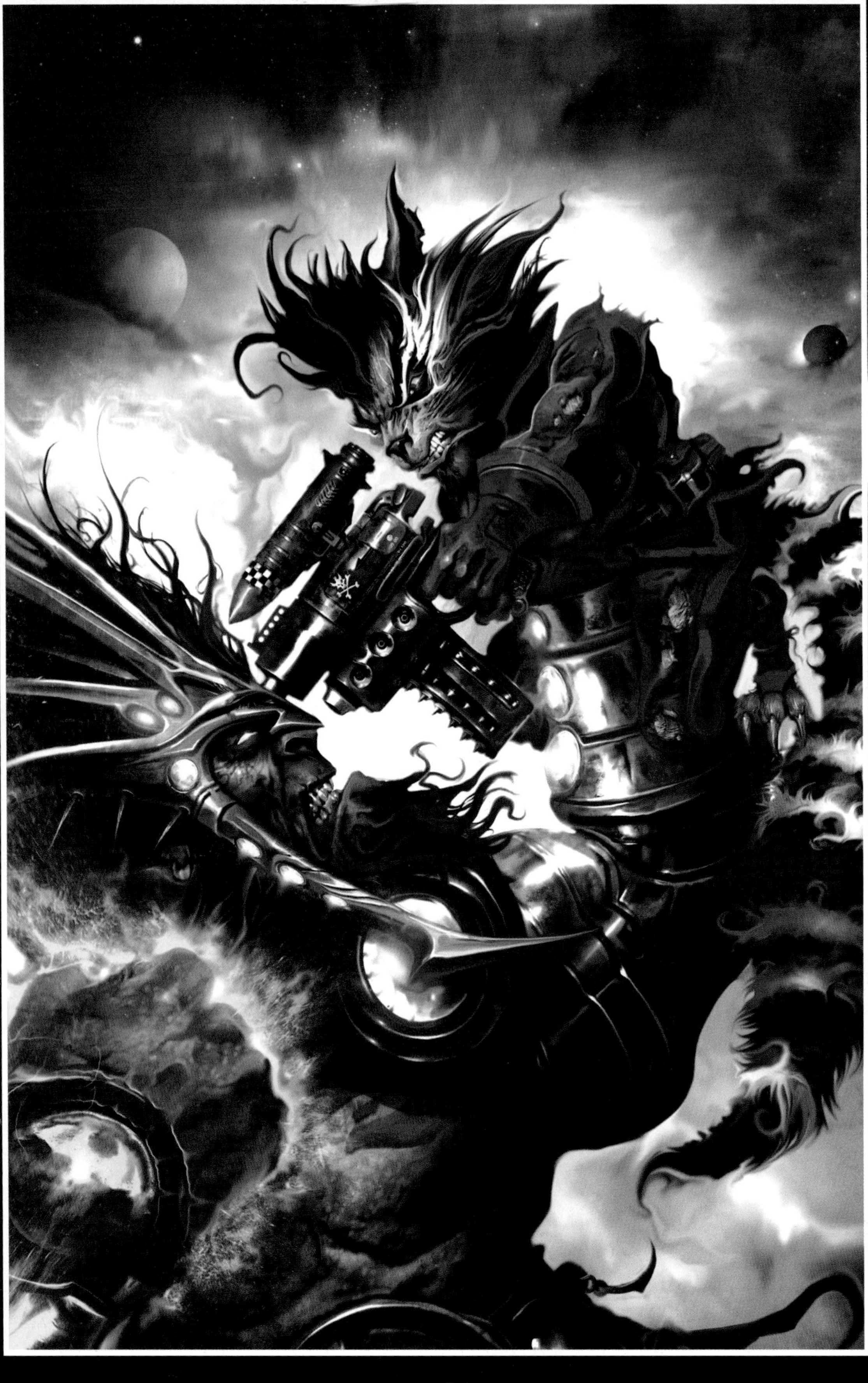

10

NEGATIVE ZONE. INITIATIVE PRISON, MAIN GATE.

ONWARDS, MY WARRIORS!

AND SO WE ARRIVE AT THAT SOLEMN MOMENT OF CONJUNCTION BETWEEN THE *FAN* AND THE *FECAL MATTER*, BLASTAAR'S BROKEN THROUGH THE GATES.

WE'RE TRAPPED HERE IN THE NEGATIVE ZONE, LITERALLY AND METAPHORICALLY *OUT OF TIME*.

BLASTAARED!

DAN ABNETT and ANDY LANNING
WRITERS

BRAD WALKER
PENCILER

OLAZABA, RAMOS and LIVESAY
INKERS

WIL QUINTANA
COLORIST

VC'S JOE CARAMAGNA
LETTERER

CLINT LANGLEY
COVER ARTIST

MICHAEL HORWITZ
ASST. EDITOR

BILL ROSEMANN
EDITOR

JOE QUESADA
EDITOR IN CHIEF

DAN BUCKLEY
PUBLISHER

I'M THINKING THAT THE LIFE EXPECTANCY FOR ME AND JACK FLAG IS SOMEWHERE BETWEEN *SIXTY SECONDS* AND THE DURATION OF THE *LAST* AMMO CLIPS.

I HATE TO PUT THIS SO BLUNTLY, BUT WE ARE *SO DEAD.*

WHAT KIND OF *IDIOT* OPENED THE GATES?

I DON'T KNOW, STAR-LORD, I'M GOING TO SAY THE *BAD* KIND?

YOUR *MAJESTY!* YOUR *MAGNIFICENCE!*

PLEASE DON'T KILL ME!

I'M *SKELETON KI!* I'M THE ONE WHO OPENED THE *GATES* FOR YOU!

YOU *DID?*

WELL DONE.

URK!

THIS ONE GETS TO KEEP HIS LIFE!

EVERYONE ELSE....

...SURRENDER OR DIE!

IF YOU THINK WE'RE GOING TO GIVE UP TO SOME MONKEY FACED--

GRRRRRR

RRRAAAAA!

KIDDING! SURRENDER IT IS!

YEAH, WE'LL GO WITH SURRENDER! DO YOU WANT IT IN WRITING, OR WILL A SYMBOLIC TOSSING ASIDE OF OUR WEAPONS BE OKAY?

OKAY, THAT'S NOT A GREAT DEVELOPMENT.

NO, FLAG, IT'S REALLY NOT.

THIS IS NOT GOING TO END WELL FOR US.

QUILL! I SEE YOU, YOU TREACHEROUS DOG!

STILL YOU RESIST ME!

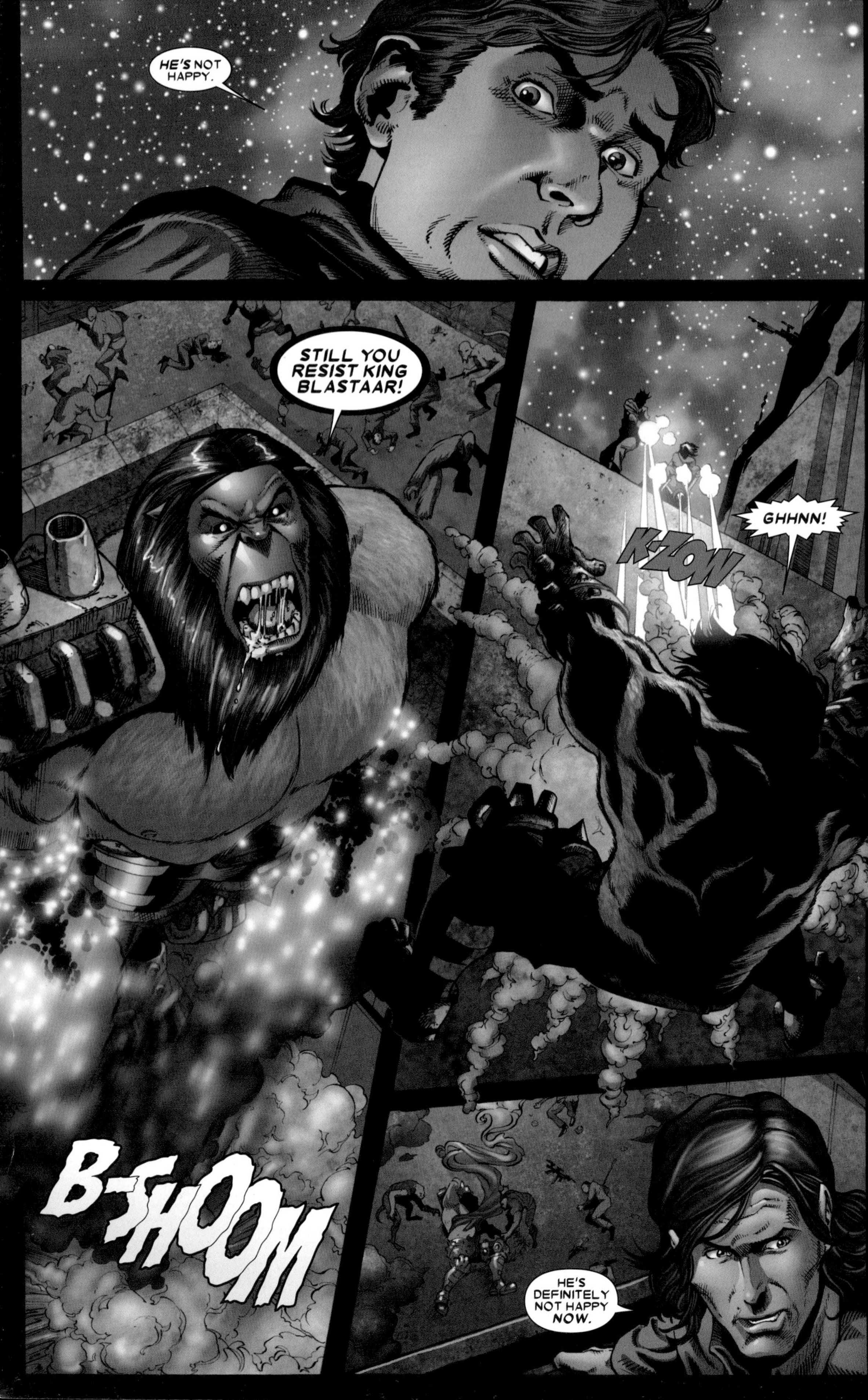
HE'S NOT HAPPY.
STILL YOU RESIST KING BLASTAAR!
GHHNN!
K-ZOW
B-FHOOM
HE'S DEFINITELY NOT HAPPY NOW.

KILL THEM!

RETREAT?

WE'RE OUT OF AMMO SO I VOTE YES.

TROUBLE IS, THERE'S NO-WHERE LEFT TO RETREAT TO!

WE'VE JUST GOT TO HOLD THEM OFF UNTIL THE GUARDIANS ARRIVE TO RESCUE US! THAT'S OUR ONLY CHANCE!

AND IF THEY DON'T?

I HAVE TOTAL FAITH.

AND IF YOUR FAITH IS MISPLACED?

EVERYTHING'S GOING TO BE FINE, FLAG!

UM.

IN THE LONG RUN, I MEAN.

NOT RIGHT NOW, OBVIOUSLY.

OH, ✳✳✳✳.

OUTSIDE THE PRISON WALLS...

HOW COME WE'VE MATERIALIZED RIGHT IN THE HEART OF A RAVENING HORDE?!

HOW IS THIS POSSIBLE?!

IT'S THAT DOG, ISN'T IT? THAT SMELLY COSMO SENT US HERE ON PURPOSE!

HE REALLY DOESN'T LIKE ME, DOES HE?!

GROOOT!

YEOW! THIS HELMET IS STAR-LORD'S!

URG! AND IT'S NOT EMPTY!

DEBRIEF LOG: ROCKET RACCOON (EVOLVED MAMMAL, TACTICAL AND DEMOLITIONS EXPERTISE)

THEN I REALIZED THAT BLASTAAR'S FREAKAZOIDS MUST HAVE TAKEN PETE'S BODY ARMOR OFF HIM AS SPOILS OF WAR.

WE'D LOCKED ONTO PETE'S TELEPORTATION PASSPORT, BUT PETE WASN'T WEARING IT ANYMORE.

SO I SAID TO MANTIS, I SAID--

I SUGGEST YOU CHANNEL ALL THAT AGGRESSION INTO CLOSE-QUARTER FIGHTING, ROCKET, OR WE ARE DONE FOR!

MANTIS! TEEP PETER! HE'S GOT TO BE CLOSE BY!

TEEP HIM SO WE CAN FIX HIS POSITION!

I'LL TRY!

PETER! PETER QUILL!

PETER, THIS IS MANTIS. CAN YOU READ MY MIND?

MANTIS! MANTIS, YOU *SWEET GREEN THING!* AM I HAPPY TO HEAR YOU TEEPING OR WHAT?

YOUR HAPPINESS IS *EVIDENT* FROM THE UNGUARDED AND, MAY I SAY, RATHER *GRAPHIC* THOUGHT-CLUTTER ACCOMPANYING YOUR RESPONSE.

I HAVE LOCATED PETER. HE IS IN *DEEP* TROUBLE.

SO *TIK!* NEAR *HERE,* THEN?

CONTINUUM CORTEX, KNOWHERE...

MANTIS TO KNOWHERE! COSMO?

WE NEED *IMMEDIATE* TRANSPOSITION TO STAR-LORD'S *ACTUAL* LOCATION!

COSMO IS RECEIVINK ADJUSTED COORDINATES NOW.

COSMO LIKE GETTINK TEEP FROM NICE CELESTIAL MADONNA LADY. HER MIND, IT SMELL OF FLOWERS.

STAND BY FOR TRANSFER!

FZZMMM--

WHAT'S--

--MMMM

GOOD TO SEE YOU ALIVE, STAR-LORD.

MAJOR VICTORY? YOU'RE ON THE TEAM?

MAN, HOW LONG HAVE I BEEN HERE?

K-TANG

LONG ENOUGH TO MISLAY YOUR UNIFORM, APPARENTLY.

GUHKK!

I AM GROOT!

UGHHNNN!

I GOT THE -TIK!- LAST OF THEM!

NO NO NO! HE'S WITH ME!

MY BAD.

EVERYONE, THIS IS JACK FLAG.

HIYA, JACK.

I AM GROOT.

HI.

HEY, MISTER.

THIS IS YOUR TEAM?

YEAH. GREAT, AREN'T THEY?

IS ONE OF THEM A TREE?

UH-UH.

I HATE COSMIC STUFF.

WE GOT NO TIME FOR CHIT-CHAT!

MAJOR! YOU AND GROOT WATCH THE EXITS!

MANTIS! RESET OUR PASSPORT FIELDS TO COVER PETER AND HIS PAL! THEN TEEP THE DOG AND TELL HIM TO PULL US OUT OF HERE PRONTO!

PETE, I FOUND YOUR HAT.

UH... THANKS, ROCKY.

YOU MAY WANT TO WASH IT.

EWW.

HEADS UP!

WE'VE GOT COMPANY...

...AND IT DOESN'T LOOK FRIENDLY.

WHERE IS HE? WHERE IS HE?!

FZZMMM

BYE-BYE, BLASTAAR.

NRRRRAAHHH!

QUILL....

SACROSANCT HOMEWORLD OF THE UNIVERSAL CHURCH OF TRUTH...

WILL WE BE ABLE TO DETECT HIS APPROACH, CARDINAL RAKER?

WE WILL SENSE HIS MAGIC WITH OUR BELIEF FIELDS, MATRIARCH.

ACTUALLY...

...I DON'T BELIEVE YOU WILL.

MATRIARCH, I AM ADAM WARLOCK. THIS IS MY COMPANION, GAMORA.

I UNDERSTAND YOU'VE BEEN TOLD TO EXPECT US.

THE PAGAN DEVIL IS HERE *ALREADY!*

STAND *DOWN,* CARDINALS! THIS MEETING IS INTENDED TO BE *PEACEFUL!*

A WISE MOVE. DO NOT TEST ME.

I HAVE COME TO SAY *THIS:* I AM YOUR *MESSIAH.* I AM THE *TRUTH* YOU WORSHIP.

AND YOU *KNOW* IT.

IT IS *FORETOLD* THAT A WARLOCK WILL COME. I DO NOT *DENY* IT.

BUT THERE HAVE BEEN *FALSE* PROPHETS, *FALSE* MAGI, AND THEIR TRICKERY HAS BEEN *CAST DOWN* BY THE CHURCH.

WE MUST BE *SURE* THAT YOU ARE NOT FALSE. WE MUST BE *SURE* THAT YOU ARE NOT A *TRICK.*

IN THE LAST FEW DAYS, I HAVE BEEN TORMENTED BY *DREAMS* AND VISIONS.

A *WAR* IS COMING. A WAR OF *KINGS.* UNLESS IT IS *STOPPED,* IT WILL DESTROY US *ALL.*

I WILL STOP THE WAR. I WILL *PROVE* MYSELF BY *SAVING CREATION.*

THEN YOU WILL BELIEVE IN ME.

ZZZKKSHHHH

WE *MUST* KNOW! WE *MUST* KNOW FOR *CERTAIN!*

BUT THERE IS STILL *THIS* *COCCOON!*

AND ITS VERY *EXISTENCE* PROCLAIMS ADAM WARLOCK A *FALSE MESSIAH!*

ALL THE SIGNS AND PORTENTS INDICATE THAT THE *TRUE* WARLOCK HAS BEEN BORN TO US!

AND IF THAT IS SO, THEN THE CHURCH MUST *REJOICE* AND *EMBRACE* HIM WITH OPEN ARMS!

ATTENDANTS! HOW MUCH *LONGER* BEFORE YOUR FAITH ENERGIES *OPEN* IT AND REVEAL ITS CONTENTS?

PERHAPS, EXCELLENCY, A *MONTH*...OR *TWO*?

TOO SLOW! WE MUST *KNOW!* WE MUST--

DO NOT TEST ME!

AHHNN...

MATRIARCH!

OPEN IT. OPEN THAT THING *NOW*.

INITIATIVE PRISON, NEGATIVE ZONE...

THE PRISON IS NOW UNDER *YOUR* CONTROL, KING BLASTAAR.

THIS PLEASES ME.

AND...?

THE INMATES WERE TOLD TO JOIN YOUR ARMY OR *DIE.*

MOST OF THEM JOINED, GREAT ONE.

WHAT DID THE *REST* DO?

THEY *DIED.*

AHA! THE ONE WHO OPENED THE *GATES* FOR ME! *SKELETON KI,* WASN'T IT?

COME WITH ME!

Y-YES, KING BLASTAAR, YOUR HIGHNESS!

Y-YES, KING BLASTAAR!

I'M TOLD YOU CAN OPEN *ANY* LOCK OR ANY DOOR, MISTER KI?

TH-THAT'S *WHY* I CALL MYSELF *"SKELETON KI"*, YOUR HIGHNESS.

AH, YES. I'VE *JUST* GOT THAT. VERY GOOD.

DO YOU KNOW WHAT *THAT* IS?

IT'S THE *DIMENSIONAL PORTAL* THAT LINKS THIS PLACE TO *EARTH*, YOUR HIGHNESS.

IT'S *SEALED* SHUT, OF COURSE.

YOU *KNOW* WHAT I'M GOING TO ASK YOU, DON'T YOU?

Y-YOU WANT ME TO *OPEN* IT FOR YOU.

I WANT YOU TO *OPEN* IT FOR ME.

AND FOR THE SAKE OF ARGUMENT, MISTER KI, LET'S *ASSUME* YOUR LIFE DEPENDS ON IT.

JUST DON'T *EVER* OPEN IT. *EVER.*

EARTHSIDE OF THE PORTAL, CAMP HAMMOND, CONNECTICUT...

I'M *NOT* FOOLING. THAT PORTAL STAYS *SHUT* OR YOU ANSWER TO *ME.*

AND IF YOU *EVER* SEE IT STARTING TO OPEN, YOU HIT *EVERY* PANIC BUTTON YOU'VE GOT.

ARE WE *CRYSTAL?*

ABSOLUTELY.

BLASTAAR'S ON THE OTHER SIDE WITH A GIGANTIC ARMY OF NEGATIVE ZONE...I BELIEVE YOU USED THE TERM... *"WHACK-JOBS".*

SO...DON'T OPEN THE PORTAL. GOT IT.

GREAT. THANKS, DR. RICHARDS.

OKAY, JOB DONE. WE'RE *OUT* OF HERE.

ONE QUESTION, THOUGH... WHO ARE YOU AGAIN?

HAVEN'T YOU HEARD? WE'RE THE GUARDIANS OF THE GALAXY.

RIIIIIGHT.

KNOWHERE...

YOU'RE BACK, HUH? HOW DID IT GO?

WELL, I THINK THE FABULOUS FOUR TOOK OUR WARNING SERIOUSLY.

FANTASTIC. FANTASTIC FOUR.

WELL, I'M A WANTED MAN ON EARTH, SO I CAN'T GO HOME.

SURE, BUT ANYWHERE THAT ISN'T EARTH IS KIND OF "COSMIC" AND I KNOW HOW YOU HATE THAT.

LISTEN, PETER. THE DOCTORS HERE FIXED MY BACK IN TWO MINUTES BY WAVING A WAND AT IT.

I GET ALL THOSE EARTH HEROES CONFUSED.

SO CAN I GET THE CORTEX TO DROP YOU OFF ANYWHERE?

YOU NAME IT. ANYWHERE IN TIME AND/OR SPACE.

YUP, NOTICED THE WALKING.

WHAT I'M SAYING IS, MAYBE THIS COSMIC STUFF ISN'T SO BAD. MAYBE I'LL HANG FOR A WHILE, IF THAT'S OKAY.

HEY, GREAT. LET ME BUY YOU A COSMIC DRINK.

LET'S BE CLEAR, I MAY NOT HATE THE COSMIC STUFF SO MUCH, BUT I STILL DON'T LOVE IT.

OH, TELL ME ABOUT IT. TODAY, RIGHT? BLASTAAR? ALL OF THAT STUFF?

"THAT, JACK, WAS A QUIET DAY."

KNOWHERE, SECURITY DETENTION...

COME BACK TO STARE AT ME, HAVE YOU?

SOMETHING LIKE THAT.

SO...CAN *YOU* FEEL IT CHANGING?

WHAT?

TIME. EVEN IN THE FEW *SHORT* DAYS I HAVE BEEN HELD HERE, I HAVE FELT THE FUTURE TENSE SHUDDER AND WRITHE.

IN *PAIN.* CHANGING *AGAIN* AND *AGAIN.*

YOU'VE *FELT* IT?

I AM ONE WHO KNOWS.

THE ERROR IS *HERE.* HERE IN THE PAST IMPERFECT. IT WILL OCCUR JUST DAYS OR HOURS OR *MINUTES* FROM NOW.

THIS IS THE ERROR THAT *YOU* CLAIM WILL SPLINTER TIME AND OBLITERATE THE FUTURE YOU COME FROM?

IS *THAT* WHAT YOU MEAN, STARHAWK?

CAN'T YOU *FEEL* IT? CAN'T YOU *HEAR* IT?

THE KING WITH NO WORDS HAS *SCREAMED* IN DEFIANCE, AND HIS CRY HAS SPLIT THE *UNIVERSE* IN HALF.

IT'S *STARTING...*

...THE WAR THAT ENDS *EVERYTHING.*

7 Variant by Jim Valentino

YARDIN HANG

MMNNNNNHHG...

OH, HOLY PAMA, MY HEAD...

NHHH....

WELCOME TO OBLIVION

...WAITAMINUTE.

WHERE THE HELL..?

DAN ABNETT and **ANDY LANNING**
WRITERS

WES CRAIG
ARTIST

WIL QUINTANA
COLORIST

VC'S JOE CARAMAGNA
LETTERER

DAVID YARDIN
COVER ARTIST

MICHAEL HORWITZ
ASST. EDITOR

BILL ROSEMANN
EDITOR

JOE QUESADA
EDITOR IN CHIEF

DAN BUCKLEY
PUBLISHER

HOW-- HOW DID I GET HERE? WHERE IS HERE? HOW--

NO! THE QUANTUM BANDS!

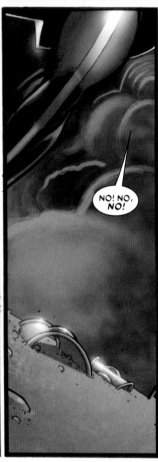

NO! NO, NO!

COME BACK, PLEASE!

COME BACK! COME BACK!

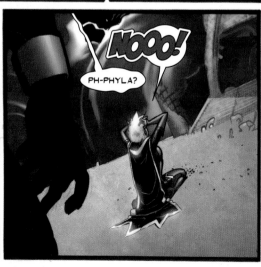

NOOO!

PH-PHYLA?

HUH?! WHO'S THERE? DRAX, IS THAT--

OH, HALA. THAT'S NOT *POSSIBLE*. THAT'S NOT EVEN *SLIGHTLY* POSSIBLE...

FATHER? FATHER, IS THAT *YOU*?

HOW *CAN* IT BE YOU?

FATHER? CAPTAIN MAR-VELL?

G-KKHHHHHHH!

AAAAH!

GAAAAHHHHHGGGG!

NO! NOOOOO!

G-KHHHKKK!

GGHH-KKKTTT!

GHH-KKKK!

GENIS? NOT YOU TOO!

PLEASE! LEAVE ME ALONE!

AAAAAAAHHH!

NO!

PHYLA!

HANG ON!

DRAX?

I THOUGHT I WAS DONE WITH BUGS.

KTOOM

GHHH-KKKKK!

I'M A DESTROYER. I WAS *MADE* TO DESTROY DEATH.

THEY CAN *SMELL* THAT ON ME. THEY DON'T LIKE IT.

WH-WHAT *ARE* THEY?

GHOSTS.

YOU OKAY?

DRAX?

S'ALL RIGHT. THEY'RE BACKING OFF.

GHOSTS?

THEY'RE YOUR DOUBTS AND FEARS, YOUR REGRETS AND YOUR LIES.

YOU CAN'T FIGHT YOUR *OWN* DEMONS, PHY. YOU NEED SOMEONE'S HELP TO DO IT.

SO WHERE ARE *YOUR* GHOSTS? WHERE ARE *YOUR* DOUBTS AND REGRETS?

I DON'T HAVE ANY.

I LEARNED TO LET GO OF REMORSE *YEARS* AGO. S'PART OF BEING A DESTROYER.

DRAX, WHAT THE *HELL* HAS HAPPENED TO US?

DON'T YOU REMEMBER?

MENTOR *KILLED* US.

SO THIS IS THE *AFTERLIFE?*

NO, PHYLA. *WELL...*

HEAVEN? THE UNDERWORLD? *LIMBO?*

IT *FEELS* LIKE LIMBO. VERY GREY. VERY DRY.

YOU EVER *BEEN* TO LIMBO? *THIS* AIN'T LIMBO.

YOU'VE BEEN TO LIMBO?

I THINK... NAH, ON REFLECTION, MAYBE IT WAS RENO.

DRAX, WILL YOU TAKE THIS *SERIOUSLY?*

RIGHT. THIS FROM SOMEONE WHO HASN'T DONE MUCH SINCE SHE GOT HERE 'CEPT *SCREAM* LIKE A LITTLE GIRL.

WELL, EXCUSE *ME* FOR BEING SPOOKED! I WAKE UP TO FIND I'M SUDDENLY IN THE *REALM OF DEATH--*

YEAH, IT AIN'T THE REALM OF DEATH *EITHER.* TRUST ME.

REALM OF DEATH, YOU'D HAVE *MORE* TO WORRY ABOUT THAN A FEW GHOSTS THAT LOOK VAGUELY LIKE PEOPLE YOU ONCE KNEW.

BUT THIS AIN'T NO *DREAM-SCAPE.* YOU GET YOURSELF KILLED HERE, YOU'RE DEAD IN A VERY REAL AND *LEGALLY BINDING* SENSE. THIS--

HMM.

WHAT?

HAD A SENSE THERE WERE *EYES* ON US JUST THEN.

IT'S NOTHING.

LIKE I WAS SAYIN', THIS *AIN'T* THE REALM OF DEATH.

THOUGH IT'S *CLOSE* TO IT.

LIKE LIMBO?

WILL YOU *FORGET* ABOUT LIMBO?

THIS IS ONE OF THE *HALF-WAY* PLACES. THE BORDERLANDS. THERE ARE *LOADS* OF 'EM.

THEY'RE LIMINAL ZONES THAT EXIST ON THE FRINGES OF THE MAJOR REALITIES.

THEY'VE GOT NAMES LIKE DECAY AND ENNUI. OBLIVION. DESPAIR. ANGST. I DUNNO. *VAGUE DISAPPOINTMENT.*

DON'T ASK *ME.* IT'S ALL *SYMBOLIC.*

SYMBOLIC?

YEAH. EVEN THE BIGGIES LIKE DEATH AND--YES--*LIMBO,* THEY'RE JUST SYMBOLIC TOO.

THE UNIVERSE WE LIVE IN IS WILD AND RAW, BUT SOMETIMES IT GIVES ITSELF A LITTLE *MEANING* AND *STRUCTURE.*

SOMETIMES IT *SIMPLIFIES* ITSELF SO WE CAN *UNDERSTAND* IT.

I'VE BEEN IN ROOMS WHERE THERE'S BEEN *ENTROPY* SITTING ON ONE SIDE OF THE TABLE AND *DEATH* ON THE OTHER, AND BETWEEN THEM, *ETERNITY* AND *CHAOS.*

THEY WEREN'T *REAL* PEOPLE. THEY WERE *CONCEPTS. AVATARS.* JUST LIKE *THIS* PLACE.

THE UNIVERSE HAS SIMPLIFIED ITSELF SO THAT WE CAN GRASP ITS *MEANING* FOR A MOMENT.

WHY?

IT WANTS US TO DO SOMETHING.

UH-HUH. THE *UNIVERSE* WANTS *US* TO DO IT A FAVOR?

OH HALA.

WHAT?

DON'T *DO* THIS! IT FREAKS ME OUT EVERY TIME YOU GO EXISTENTIAL ON ME!

ALSO, YOU USED "*LIMINAL*" IN A SENTENCE!

HEY...

...HEY! WHAT HAPPENED TO YOUR BANDS, PHY? WHAT HAPPENED TO YOUR *QUANTUM BANDS?*

I *LOST* THEM. THEY FELL OFF ME WHEN I WOKE UP HERE. THEY'RE *GONE.*

OH, *DAS'T.*

THEN THIS *AIN'T* WHAT I THOUGHT IT WAS.

WHAT? WHAT DID YOU *THINK* IT WAS?

I THOUGHT IT WAS ONE OF MENTOR'S *TRICKS.* A LITTLE MIND GAME TO TEST THE LIKELIHOOD OF MOONDRAGON'S SURVIVAL.

BUT IT *AIN'T.*

THE SON OF A SHLAG *REALLY* KILLED US.

THE BANDS ONLY COME OFF YOU IF YOU *DIE*. THEY GO TO FIND A *NEW* OWNER.

⚔☠✖! WE'RE IN TROUBLE.

MENTOR MUST BE *UNBELIEVABLY* DESPERATE TO GET HIS STEPDAUGHTER BACK.

HE ACTUALLY *KILLED* US SO WE COULD CROSS OVER INTO LIMBO, OR WHEREVER THE *HELL* THIS IS, TO FIND HER.

NO, IT'S OBLIVION. HE'S MY BOSS.

HI.

I SEE FROM YOUR FACES YOU RECOGNIZE ME.

MAELSTR-- NGHHHG!

UGHHNK!

SHA-DOOM

I'VE BEEN STRANDED HERE IN THIS...THIS NOTHINGNESS...FOR SO LONG WITHOUT COMPANY. WITHOUT POWER.

WITHOUT A WAY OUT.

YOU STILL HAVE A SPARK OF LIFE ABOUT YOU! YOU'LL BE MY WAY OUT!

GKK--KK--KK

THAT'S RIGHT. MAELSTROM.

COSMIC MANIPULATOR AND SERVANT OF OBLIVION.

I'M SO VERY PLEASED TO SEE YOU.

UHNNN...

OOOFF!

OR YOU, DRAX. YOU'LL DO JUST AS WELL.

DO YOU REMEMBER THE *OLD DAYS?* WE WERE *BOTH* CONCEPTUAL ENTITIES.

ME, THE INSTRUMENT OF COSMIC *FINALITY.*

YOU, THE AGENT OF *LIFE,* ENTRUSTED TO LIMIT DEATH BY *DESTROYING* ITS CHAMPION.

HOW DID *THAT* GO?

I KILLED THANOS.

BRAVO! WE CONCEPTUALS VERY *SELDOM* FULFILL OUR GIVEN ROLES.

TAKE *ME,* FOR EXAMPLE.

THE UNIVERSE IS *STILL* ALIVE.

A STATE OF AFFAIRS I WILL RECTIFY JUST AS *SOON* AS I GET MYSELF OUT OF HERE.

YOU DID THIS? YOU LURED US HERE TO GET YOU OUT?

I NEEDED A LIFELINE TO *HAUL* MYSELF BACK INTO REALITY. BUT IT HAD TO BE THROWN *CLOSE*, SO I COULD GRAB IT.

I HAD TO GET YOU TO *CROSS THE LINE* AND COME HERE. YOU TOOK THE BAIT.

KREESH

KREESH

MOONDRAGON?

YES, YOUR DEAR DAUGHTER *MOONDRAGON*. A *HINT* HERE, A SOOTHSAYER THERE, JUST ENOUGH TO KEEP YOU *INTERESTED*.

JUST ENOUGH TO--

GNUUUGGH!

SHTOKKK

I THOUGHT SHE WAS *ALIVE!*

I THOUGHT I COULD STILL *SAVE* HER, YOU 🕱🕱🕱🕱!

WHKK
WHKK

WHKK

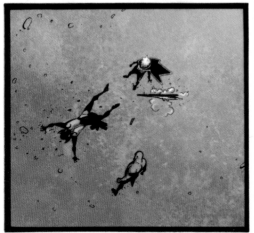

OKAY, WE'RE DONE HERE. LET'S FIND A WAY OUT.

IT WAS A *TRICK.*

YEAH, I'M SORRY. IT WAS *HIS* TRICK. THERE WASN'T *EVER* A HEATHER WE COULD RESCUE.

COME *ON...* OF *COURSE* THERE WAS. I COULDN'T FOOL *YOU.* THE BAIT HAD TO *SMELL* RIGHT.

I CAN TAKE YOU TO HER, IF YOU LIKE.

THE UNIVERSE *NEEDS* ME, IT REALLY *DOES*.

IT'S ALL BENT OUT OF SHAPE. DEATH IS DEAD. LIFE IS RUNNING *WILD*.

SHUT UP.

LOOK, WE REPRESENT CONCEPTUAL *OPPOSITES*. LIFE AND DEATH. ETERNITY AND OBLIVION.

WE WERE NEVER GOING TO BE *FRIENDS*, I ACCEPT THAT.

BUT IT DOESN'T MAKE *ME* EVIL AND *YOU* GOOD.

YET IT CLEARLY MAKES YOU *LOUD* AND ME *QUIET*.

LIFE AND DEATH, THEY'RE JUST TWO HALVES OF NATURE. NEITHER ONE IS *RIGHT*, NEITHER ONE IS *WRONG*.

THEY FIGHT EACH OTHER, LIKE ALL GREAT COSMIC CONCEPTS DO, AND EVERY NOW AND THEN, ONE GETS THE UPPER HAND.

DOES HE *EVER* SHUT UP?

LET'S JUST KILL HIM AND FIND OUT.

THE TRUTH IS, IT DOESN'T *MATTER*, SO LONG AS THEY STAY *BALANCED*.

CHECKS AND BALANCES, YOU SEE. CHECKS AND BALANCES.

THAT'S THE WAY THE GREAT UNIVERSAL GAME PLAYS. AND IF THE BALANCE SWINGS... *LOOK OUT!*

YOU SAY YOU OFFED THANOS?

WHAT *ABOUT* IT?

WELL, DEATH'S CHAMPION IS *GONE*. THE BALANCE IS *SHOT*. THE FORCE OF *LIFE* IS STRONGER NOW THAN IT'S BEEN IN *EONS*.

WE DON'T CARE.

BUT YOU *WILL*. THIS IS MY POINT. IF LIFE WINS, IT'LL BE JUST AS *BAD* AS IF DEATH WAS VICTORIOUS.

DIFFERENT BAD, THAT'S ALL.

ANYWAY, YOU'RE NOT LISTENING TO ME, SO I'LL SHUT UP. JUST DON'T SAY I DIDN'T TRY TO *WARN* YOU.

BY THE WAY, WE'VE *ARRIVED*.

AH. YOU'D *REALIZED* THAT, HADN'T YOU?

MAY I PRESENT...

...THE DRAGON OF THE MOON.

I ALWAYS THOUGHT THAT SHOULD BE THE NAME OF A *PRETTY MOTH* OR A *FABULOUS ORCHID.*

NOT ONE OF THE MOST *SICK-HEARTED* DEMONS *EVER* TO SLITHER IN FROM THE OUTER DARK.

STILL, I DIDN'T NAME IT.

HEATHER WAS...I MEAN, IT WAS *PART* OF HER...SHE WAS *BECOMING* IT...

I NEVER REALIZED IT WAS SO *HIDEOUS.*

HEATHER DOUGLAS HAS *ALWAYS* BEEN THE DRAGON'S CONDUIT TO THE REAL WORLD.

IT HAD BEEN GROWING THROUGH HER, GETTING *STRONGER.* IT HAD EVEN CHANGED HER INTO *DRACONIAN* FORM.

IT WAS JUST *WEEKS* AWAY FROM FULL MANIFESTATION, WHEN ULTRON *KILLED* HER.

IT WAS CAST INTO OBLIVION, TO SLEEP AND REGAIN ITS STRENGTH.

IN ANOTHER *MILLION* YEARS, IT'LL WAKE AND FIND *ANOTHER* HEATHER DOUGLAS AND TRY *AGAIN.*

IF IT EVER GETS OUT INTO THE REAL WORLD, IT WILL WREAK COSMIC *ARMAGEDDON.*

WHERE'S HEATHER? *WHERE IS* SHE?!

YOU TOLD US SHE WAS *HERE!*

I DON'T WANT THE DRAGON!

I'M GUESSING SHE'S SOME-WHERE *INSIDE* IT.

SO GOOD LUCK WITH THAT.

BASTARD!

UGHNN!

PATHETIC.

WE FIND THAT EXIT AND--

WHAT DO WE DO NOW?

THEY REMEMBER ME...

WHAT DID HE SAY?

THE QUANTUM BANDS. THEY *REMEMBER* ME. *LOOK.*

OH MY GOD! GRAB HIM BEFORE--

AAAGH!

NNNHHH!

NOW *THAT'S* POWER!

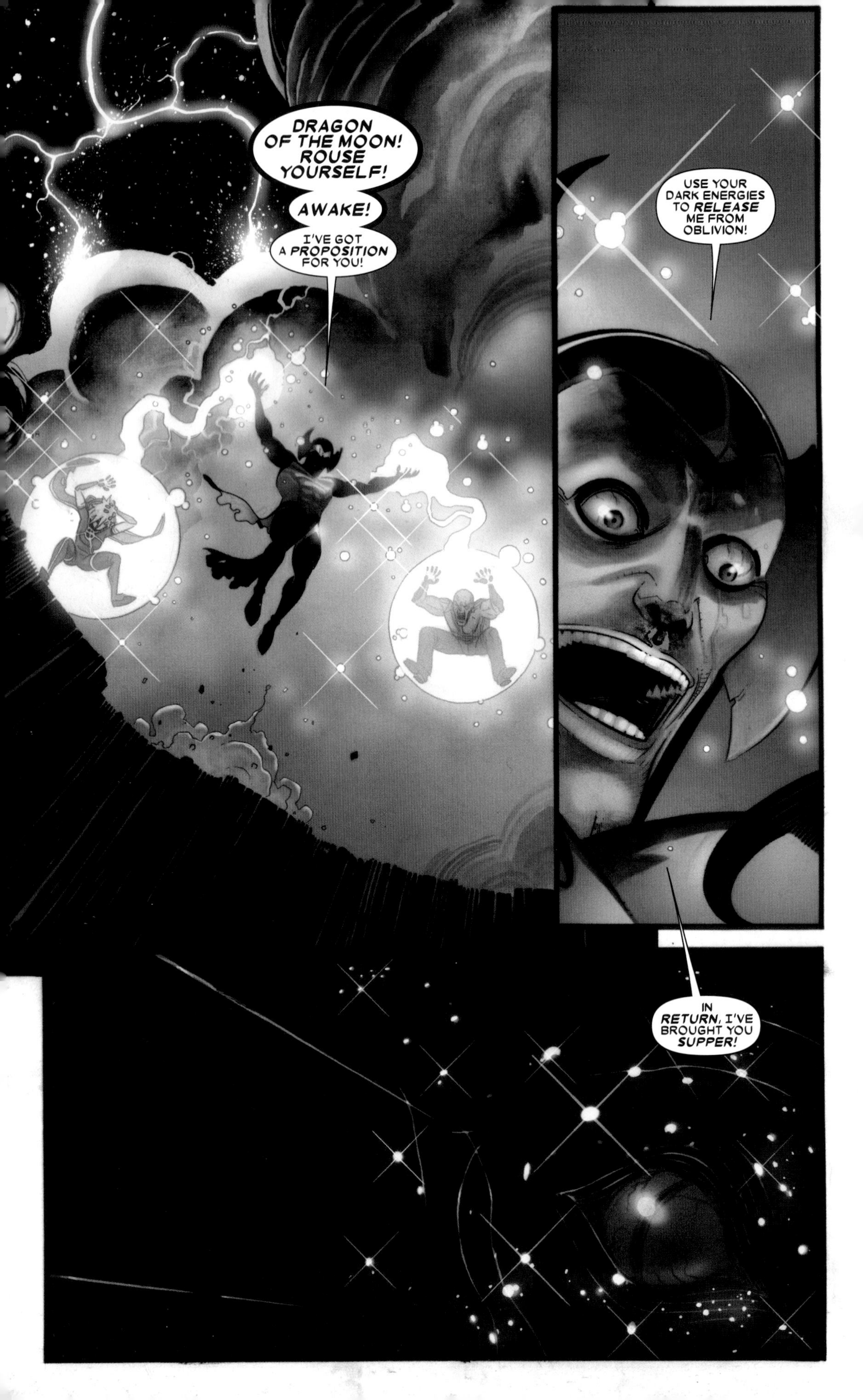
DRAGON OF THE MOON! ROUSE YOURSELF!
AWAKE!
I'VE GOT A PROPOSITION FOR YOU!
USE YOUR DARK ENERGIES TO RELEASE ME FROM OBLIVION!
IN RETURN, I'VE BROUGHT YOU SUPPER!

8 Variant by Brandon Peterson

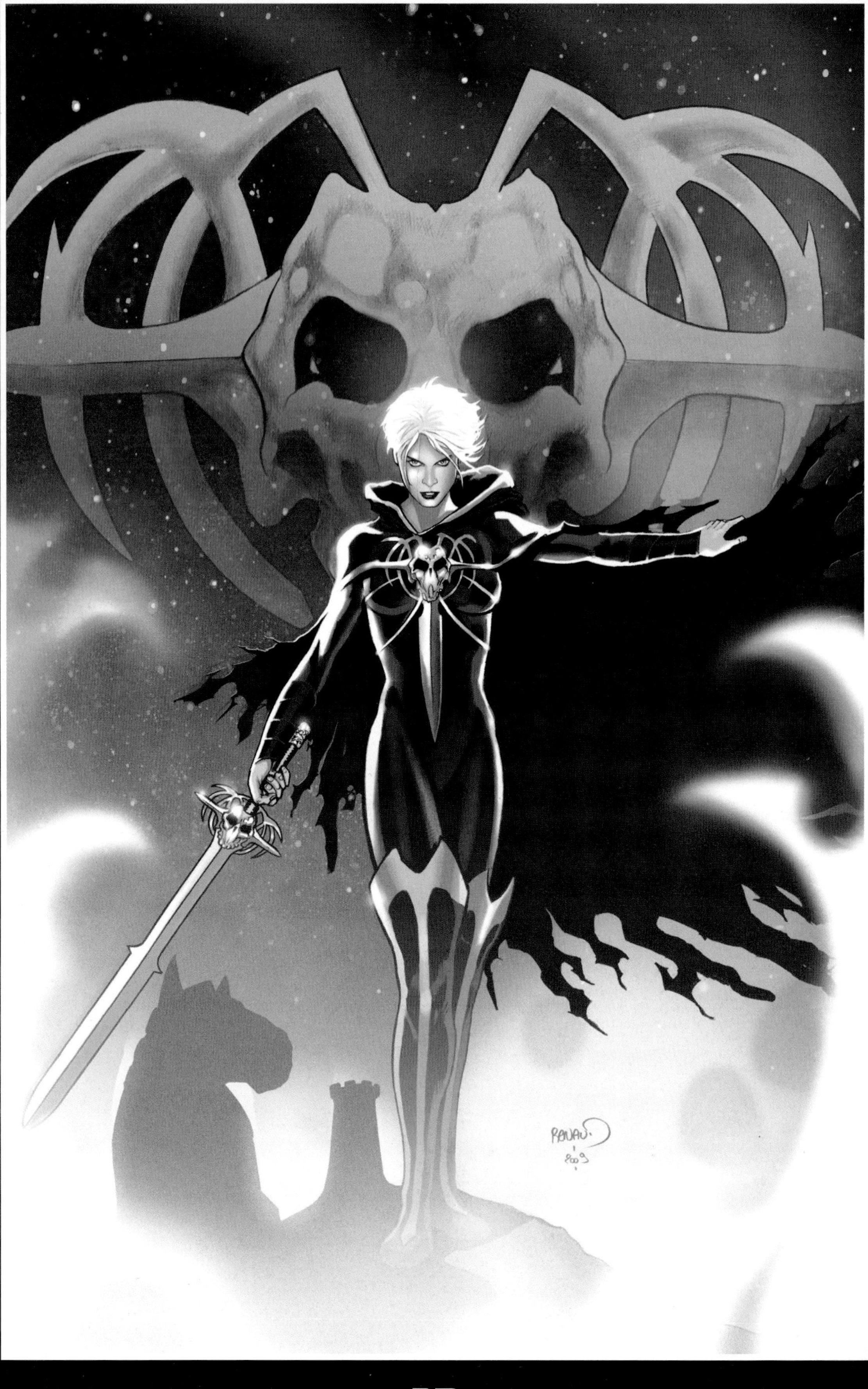

THE DRAGON OF THE MOON HAS ALWAYS BEEN THERE.

IT IS A CREATURE OF DEMONIC LUSTS AND APOCALYPTIC APPETITES.

I CAN HEAR IT, PHYLA. I CAN HEAR IT LAUGHING IN THE CORNERS OF MY MIND.

IT REALLY SCARES ME.

IT WANTS TO ESCAPE FROM OBLIVION. IT WANTS TO GET OUT.

I WAS ITS BRIDGE INTO THE REAL WORLD. IT COILED AROUND ME SO TIGHTLY, I BECAME ITS LIVING IMAGE.

BUT IT CAN'T USE ME ANY MORE.

SO IT NEEDS SOMEONE ELSE.

IT NEEDS TO FIND SOMEONE ELSE TO USE.

DON'T LET IT USE YOU, PHYLA.

DON'T LET IT USE YOU PHYLA.

HEATHER! HEATHER, DON'T GO!

DON'T GO...HEATHER... PLEASE...

WAKE UP! WAKE UP!

OH HOLY PAMA!

I CAN'T FEED YOU TO A GIANT DEMONIC DRAGON IF YOU'RE *ASLEEP!*

WHERE WOULD THE FUN BE IN *THAT?*

THE DRAGON'S WAKING *UP.* HE'S GOING TO BE *EVER* SO HUNGRY.

WHEN I FEED HIM, HE'S GOING TO BE *EVER* SO *GRATEFUL.*

AND WHEN I GET OUT OF THIS, MAELSTROM, I'M GOING TO *GUT* YOU LIKE A *DEER.*

BLAH BLAH *WHATEVER.*

POINT IS, DRAX, YOU *WON'T* GET OUT. I'VE GOT PHYLA'S QUANTUM BANDS. I'VE GOT THE POWER.

I GET TO MAKE THE DECISIONS.

LIKE... IT'S *SUPPER TIME!*

AAAHHH!

PHYLA!

SACRIFICE

DAN ABNETT and ANDY LANNING
WRITERS

WES CRAIG
ARTIST

WIL QUINTANA
COLORIST

VC'S JOE CARAMAGNA
LETTERER

PAUL RENAUD
COVER ARTIST

MICHAEL HORWITZ
ASST. EDITOR

BILL ROSEMANN
EDITOR

JOE QUESADA
EDITOR IN CHIEF

DAN BUCKLEY
PUBLISHER

ALAN FINE
EXEC. PRODUCER

IT SWALLOWED HER! IT JUST *SWALLOWED* HER!

MAELSTROM, YOU TWISTED--

YEAH, REALLY NOT INTERESTED IN *ANYTHING* YOU'VE GOT TO SAY, DRAX.

YOU'RE NOT A *SPARKLING* CONVERSATIONALIST.

WITH YOU IT'S ALL *THREATS* AND *SNARLS*.

ANYWAY, IT'S YOUR TURN. YOU'RE LIKE... *PUDDING.*

SO HOLD ONTO YOUR HAT AND KISS YOUR--

HEY. IS THAT A STAR? I NEVER NOTICED IT BEFORE.

OH ✖✖✖✖✖...

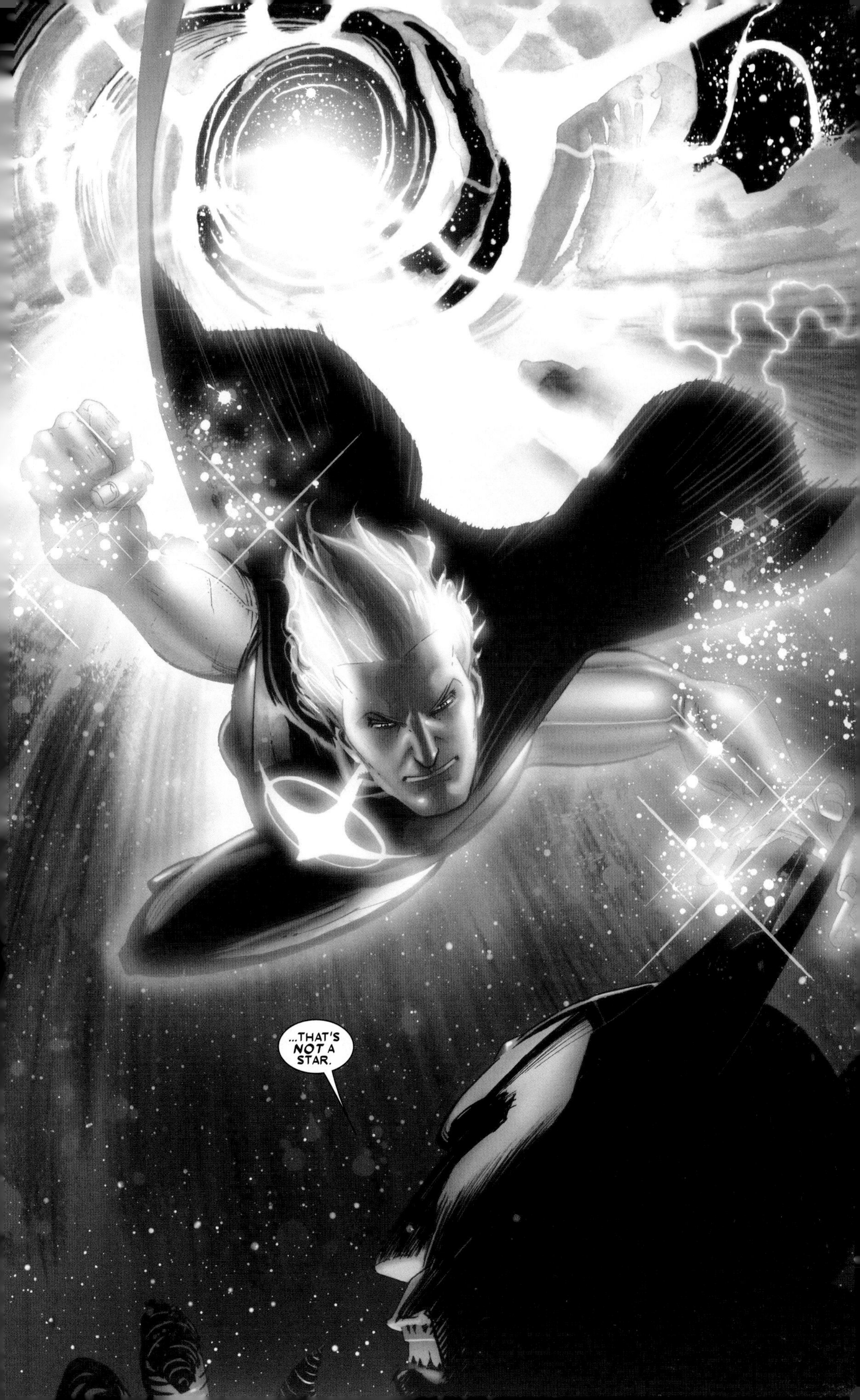
...THAT'S NOT A STAR.

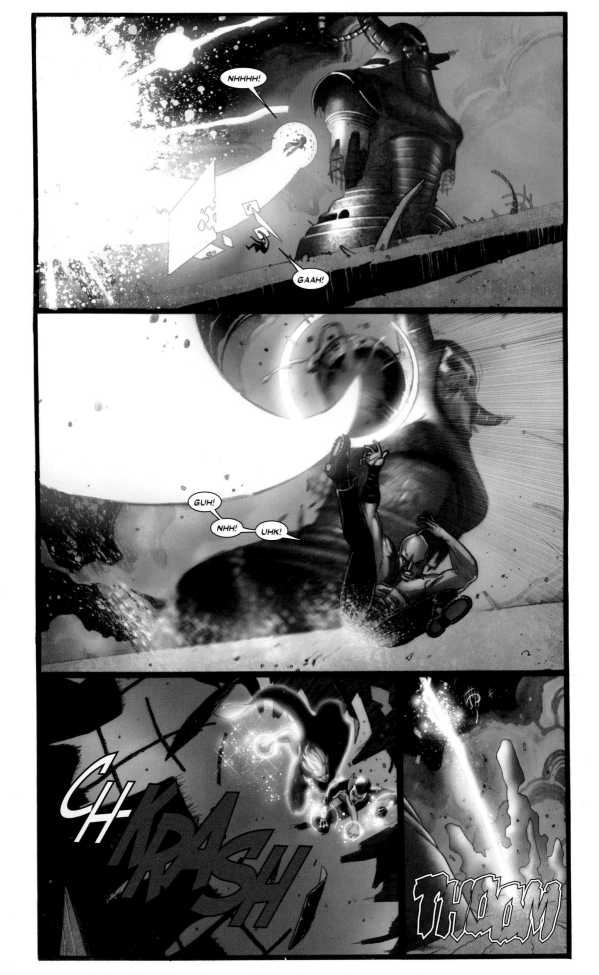

NHHHH!

GAAH!

GUH!

NHH! UHK!

CH- KRASH!

THOOM

WELL WHAT DO YOU KNOW... *WENDELL VAUGHN,* MY OLD DANCING PARTNER.

I HEARD THAT ANNIHILUS FRIED YOU LIKE AN EGG. I GUESS *EVERYONE'S* COMING BACK FROM THE DEAD THESE DAYS.

IT'S *SO* PASSÉ.

WHERE'S PHYLA, MAELSTROM? WHAT DID YOU DO TO HER?

SHE DISAGREED WITH SOMETHING THAT ATE HER.

WHAT DO *YOU* CARE?

BECAUSE I WORE THEM FOR SO LONG, MY SOUL IS *INEXTRICABLY* LINKED TO THE QUANTUM BANDS. I FELT THE USER OF THE BANDS *DIE.* HER DOOM BROUGHT ME HERE.

PHYLA-VELL IS DEAD, MAELSTROM. DID *YOU* KILL HER?

THE USER OF THE BANDS IS VERY MUCH *ALIVE.*

SEE?

THEY'RE *MINE,* VAUGHN. *MINE.*

NOW YOU SEEM TO HAVE COME BACK FROM THE DEAD IN A *QUANTUM LIGHT* FORM.

AND THE BANDS...WELL, I DON'T NEED TO TELL YOU THEY *CONTROL* QUANTUM LIGHT.

IN THE NEXT FIVE MINUTES IT'S GOING TO *SUCK* BEING YOU, WENDELL VAUGHN.

YOU WERE AN *IDIOT* TO FACE ME THIS WAY. I OWN YOU.

UGHHHN!

WHAM

I *TOTALLY* OWN YOU.

GAAAHH!

HANDS OFF.

OOH!

SHUNK

SHUNK

OH... GOD. THAT IS *SO* PAINFUL.

YEAH, THAT'S WHAT I THOUGHT WHEN YOU DID IT TO *ME*, YEARS AGO.

THANKS, DRAX.

YOU WANT ME TO *FINISH* THE JOB, VAUGHN?

NO, *I'LL* DEAL WITH MAELSTROM.

MHHMMM. OH, THAT FEELS GOOD. I'VE MISSED THE BANDS SO MUCH.

YEAH, OKAY, IT'S YOUR BIG MOMENT...

...VAUGHN GETS THE BANDS BACK. WOW. WE GET IT.

I JUST WANT TO SAY *ONE* THING.

WHAT?

BEHIND YOU.

※※※※.

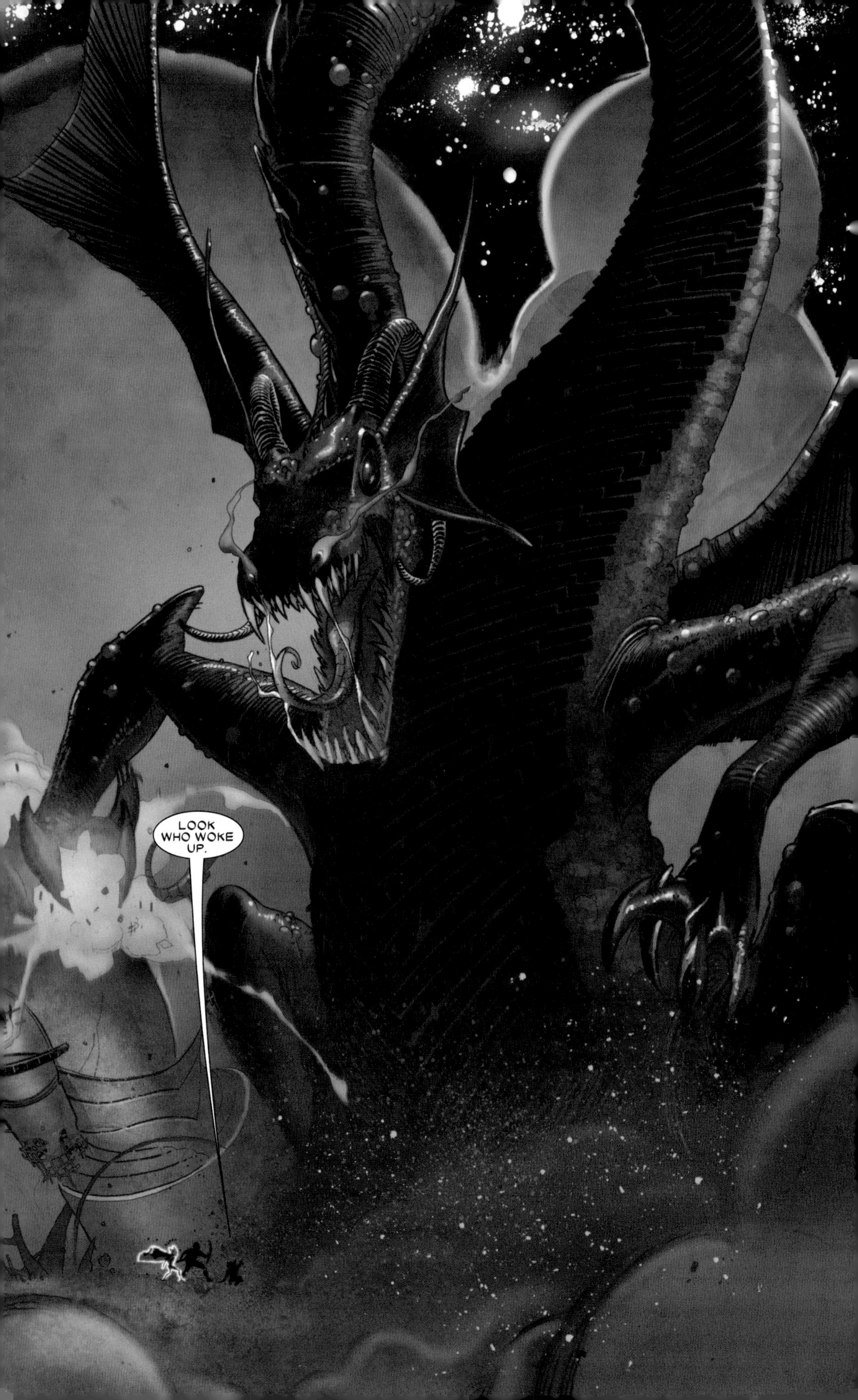
LOOK WHO WOKE UP.

THE DRAGON OF THE MOON. THAT'S PRETTY *MAJOR* LEAGUE.

DRAX, YOU KNOW ABOUT THIS STUFF. WHAT'S THE BEST THING TO USE AGAINST A DRAGON?

TRADITIONALLY?

Y-HUH.

I'D GO WITH A LANCE.

GOOD CALL.

ZHMMM ZHMMM

CH-ZZTTTT

OKAY, NOT EVEN *SLIGHTLY* WORKING.

OH, THIS IS PRICELESS! *PRICELESS!*

THE DRAGON'S NOT ONLY GOING TO GET THE LIFE FORCE OF PHYLA-VELL AND DRAX THE WHO'S-HIS-NAME DESTROYER, IT'S GOING TO GET VAUGHN'S ESSENCE *TOO!*

DELICIOUS!

IT'S GOING TO *LOVE* ME FOR THIS!

YOU PLANNED THIS ALL ALONG, YOU SON OF A *SHLAG!*

NO, NOT AT ALL! THIS IS JUST *SERENDIPITY!*

BUT I DO *LOVE* IT WHEN THINGS GET SERIOUSLY ✖✖✖✖ UP FOR THE SO-CALLED *GOOD* GUYS!

HRRAAHHH!

WHAT IS--?

SOMETHING WITH ITS GUT?

KR-TCSH

SPLORCH

IT STANK IN THERE.

I FOUND HEATHER, DRAX. I BROUGHT HER *BACK*.

OUT OF THE DRAGON'S *GULLET*.

HELL OF A THING, PHYLA.

HELL OF A THING.

TAKE HER.

PHYLA, I... THANK YOU.

THESE BELONG TO YOU.

THEY DO.

NO.

WENDELL, YOU'RE QUASAR. YOU'RE THE PROTECTOR OF THE UNIVERSE.

I TRIED MY BEST, BUT I NEVER CAME CLOSE TO FILLING YOUR SHOES.

AND I'M SO HAPPY TO SEE YOU ALIVE AGAIN.

I WAS JUST LOOKING AFTER THE BANDS UNTIL YOU CAME BACK.

I APPRECIATE THAT.

THEY'LL ALWAYS BE PART OF YOU, PHYLA-VELL. YOUR QUANTUM SWORD WILL STILL DRAW ITS POWER FROM THEM.

BUT I HAVE POWERS OF MY OWN.

SO IT WOULD APPEAR. WHAT HAPPENED TO YOU IN THERE?

STUFF.

I RESCUED HEATHER. THAT'S ALL THAT MATTERS.

NO. IT ISN'T.

WHAT DID YOU DO, PHYLA?

WHAT DID YOU PROMISE THE DRAGON? WHAT KIND OF PRICE DID YOU AGREE TO?

I WANTED YOU BACK. I GAVE IT *EVERYTHING* IT WANTED. YOU'D HAVE DONE *EXACTLY* THE SAME THING.

NOW SHUT UP AND KISS ME.

GOOD TO SEE YOU ALIVE AGAIN, WENDELL. LAST TIME WE MET, YOU WERE GETTING MURDERED ON NYCOS ARISTEDES.

THE GUARDIANS COULD USE SOME HEAVY MUSCLE LIKE YOU.

YOUR GUARDIANS WILL HAVE TO *WAIT*, DRAX.

I NEED TO GET BACK TO EARTH AND HELP *RICHARD RIDER.**

*SEE NOVA #23 --BAND-WEARING BILL

AND WE SHOULD--

DAMN! WHERE DID MAELSTROM GO?

HIS BIG PLANS ARE RUINED. AND WITHOUT THE BANDS HE'S HELPLESS.

MAYBE... BUT THERE'S ANOTHER THING THAT WORRIES ME...

I CAN FLY OUT OF THE REALM OF OBLIVION. I'M NOT SURE HOW *YOU* GUYS GET OUT.

WE'LL BE *FINE,* WENDELL VAUGHN...

...WE HAVE TO WAKE UP.

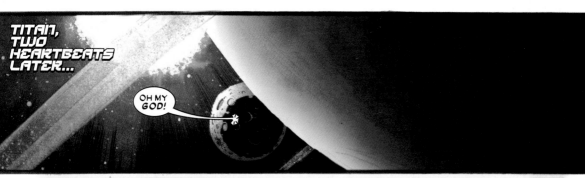

TITAN, TWO HEARTBEATS LATER...

OH MY GOD!

YOU'RE ALIVE! THANK GOODNESS!

YOU KILLED US. YOU KILLED US, YOU LUNATIC!

AAAHH!

YOU KILLED US! MENTOR, YOU KILLED US!

ONLY SO YOU COULD RESCUE HEATHER! I WAS TRYING TO HELP!

PHYLA! PLEASE!

WHAT HAPPENED TO YOU?

SOMETHING HAPPENED!

NOTHING. IT DOESN'T MATTER.

YOU GAVE TOO MUCH OF YOURSELF, PHYLA. TOO MUCH.

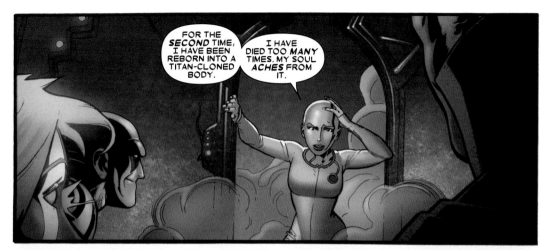

FOR THE *SECOND* TIME, I HAVE BEEN REBORN INTO A TITAN-CLONED BODY.

I HAVE DIED TOO *MANY* TIMES. MY SOUL *ACHES* FROM IT.

FATHER. YOU CAME FOR ME.

YOU'RE MY KID. WHAT *ELSE* WOULD I DO?

MENTOR.

I LOVE YOU, PHYLA-VELL.

AND I LOVE *YOU*, HEATHER DOUGLAS.

I'VE *MISSED* YOU.

I KNOW.

BUT WHAT DID YOU DO, PHYLA? WHAT DID YOU *DO?*

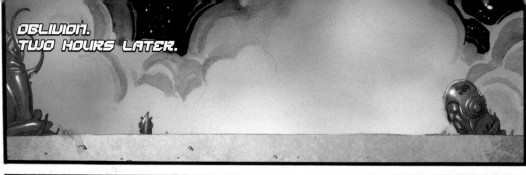

OBLIVION.
TWO HOURS LATER.

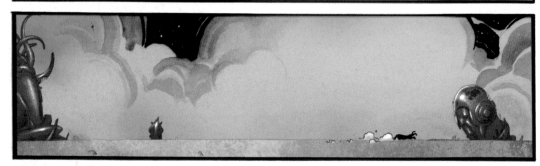

NNH

OH, HELLO.

TCH.

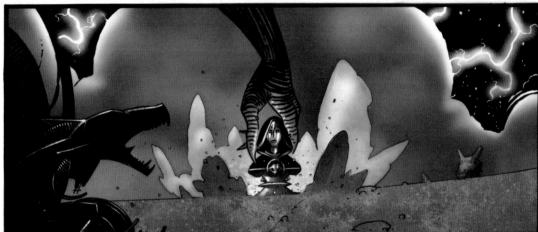

WELL...

...WE DID IT, MY LORD OBLIVION...

...DEATH HAS A *NEW* AVATAR.

AND THE *END WAR* IS ABOUT TO BEGIN.

NEXT: *WAR OF KINGS!*